The Poetics of Belief

Studies in
Coleridge,
Arnold,
Pater,
Santayana,
Stevens,
and
Heidegger

Studies in Religion

Charles H. Long, *Editor*
The University of North Carolina at Chapel Hill

Editorial Board

Giles B. Gunn
The University of North Carolina at Chapel Hill

Van A. Harvey
Stanford University

Wendy Doniger O'Flaherty
The University of Chicago

Ninian Smart
University of California at Santa Barbara
and the University of Lancaster

The Poetics of Belief

Nathan A. Scott, Jr.

Studies in
Coleridge,
Arnold,
Pater,
Santayana,
Stevens,
and Heidegger

The University of North Carolina Press, Chapel Hill and London

Library of Congress Cataloging in Publication Data

Scott, Nathan A.
   The poetics of belief

   (Studies in religion)
   Bibliography: p.
   Includes index.
   1. Philosophy, Modern. 2. Imagination—History.
3. Poetics—History. I. Title. II. Series: Studies in
religion (Chapel Hill, N.C.)
B791.S27   1985   121'.3   84-20801

ISBN 0-8078-1633-7

Designed by Patrick O'Sullivan.

To Six Friends in Charlottesville

Julian and Neva Hartt
J. C. ("Jack") and Charlotte
("Chots") Levenson
Kenneth and Beverly Thompson

Also by Nathan A. Scott, Jr.

Rehearsals of Discomposure: Alienation and Reconciliation in Modern Literature (1952)
Modern Literature and the Religious Frontier (1958)
Albert Camus (1962)
Reinhold Niebuhr (1963)
Samuel Beckett (1965)
The Broken Center: Studies in the Theological Horizon of Modern Literature (1966)
Ernest Hemingway (1966)
Craters of the Spirit: Studies in the Modern Novel (1968)
Negative Capability: Studies in the New Literature and the Religious Situation (1969)
The Unquiet Vision: Mirrors of Man in Existentialism (1969)
Nathanael West (1971)
The Wild Prayer of Longing: Poetry and the Sacred (1971)
Three American Moralists—Mailer, Bellow, Trilling (1973)
The Poetry of Civic Virtue—Eliot, Malraux, Auden (1976)
Mirrors of Man in Existentialism (1978)

Edited by Nathan A. Scott, Jr.

The Tragic Vision and the Christian Faith (1957)
The New Orpheus: Essays toward a Christian Poetic (1964)
The Climate of Faith in Modern Literature (1964)
Man in the Modern Theatre (1965)
Four Ways of Modern Poetry (1965)
Forms of Extremity in the Modern Novel (1965)
The Modern Vision of Death (1967)
Adversity and Grace: Studies in Recent American Literature (1968)
The Legacy of Reinhold Niebuhr (1975)

Contents

The
Poetics
of
Belief

1/ Introduction

The project to which this book is committed is one that undertakes to gather and review some of the focal testimony of the modern period regarding the role that may be played by the poetic imagination in the formation of *fundamental* belief. But it needs at once to be said that the concept of the poetic imagination does not require to be taken as connoting any sort of specialist élite, since, as that most fastidious of poets, Wallace Stevens, reminded us, by "poet" we ought to mean "any man of imagination."[1] So the decisive term, then, being really "imagination," the entire project will no doubt by many be felt immediately to be something questionable. For in our own late phase of modernity the concept of the imagination has suffered so great a decline in prestige as to have lost very nearly altogether its admissibility into the lexicon normally controlling intellectual exchange.

The idea of the imagination is, of course—discounting its various adumbrations in Plato and Longinus and Plotinus—most principally a modern conception descending from Tetens and Kant, the German Romantics (Herder, Schiller, the Schlegels, Novalis, Schelling), and Coleridge. And from those standing in this line (Ruskin, Nietzsche, Bergson, Croce, Santayana, Cassirer, Valéry) it received a powerful advertisement throughout the nineteenth century and the early years of the present century.[2] This was a tradition that took the imagination to be a sign of man's radical creativity and freedom, of his power to surpass the givens of experience in his search for patterns of order and coherence adequate to his total vision of himself in relation to the circumstances of nature and history. The imagination, said Wordsworth,

> Is but another name for absolute strength
> And clearest insight, amplitude of mind,
> And reason in her most exalted mood.[3]

And one whole stream of thought over a long period sponsored the conviction that it is indeed "that highest candle [which] lights the dark."[4]

Such a view of things, however, constantly faced a very fierce kind of opposition which was indeed already well launched in the morning-time of the modern age. For it was in the period spanned by the careers of such thinkers as Bacon, Hobbes, Locke, and Hume that that "dissociation of sensibility"[5] of which T. S. Eliot spoke long ago first set in. The central effort of the seventeenth and eighteenth centuries involved, of course, a resolute attempt at so reconceiving the fundamental norms of thought as to bring them into perfect conformity with the aims of the burgeoning scientific movement of the time. Fact and Judgment, as it was felt, needed to be shut off from Metaphor and Fancy, in order that men might achieve (as Thomas Sprat phrased it in his *History of the Royal Society* of 1667) "a close, naked, natural way of speaking" about the world, "bringing all things as near the Mathematical plainness as they can."[6] And thus Hobbes laid it down that "Judgment" alone gives us access to "truth" and that "Fancy"—the faculty of the mind operative in poetic apprehensions of reality—"without the help of Judgment, is not [to be] commended as a Vertue,"[7] since, given that principle of capricious frivolity which she supports, she stands always in need of correction by that sobriety which belongs to "Judgment, the severer Sister."[8] Indeed, so powerfully did he enforce this lesson upon the mind of his age that even Dryden is to be found submissively acceding that "imagination [or the Hobbesian "Fancy"] in a poet is a faculty so wild and lawless, that like a high-ranging spaniel, it must have clogs tied to it, lest it outrun the judgment."[9]

And the great campaign against the imagination launched by Bacon and Hobbes was vigorously continued in the closing years of the seventeenth century by Locke and by Hume and Hartley in the century that followed. Locke's distinction (in the *Essay Concerning Human Understanding*) between "Judgment" and "Wit" is in no essential way different from the Judgment-Fancy distinction of Hobbes, and he, too, regards the way of Judgment to be "a way of proceeding quite contrary to metaphor and allusion; wherein for the most part lies that entertainment and pleasantry of wit, which strikes so lively on the fancy, and therefore is so acceptable to all people, because its beauty appears at first sight, and there is required no labour of thought to examine what truth or reason there is in it."[10] In Locke's sense of things, Judgment supervises what he calls "the severe rules of truth and good reason," and he takes it for granted that Fancy, or the imagination, "consists in something that is not perfectly conformable"[11] to these rules. Nor is

Hume any less stringent; he conceives the imagination to be an affair of "whimsies and prejudice," and he tells us that it is not "amiss to remark, that . . . a lively imagination very often degenerates into madness or folly," since, when it acquires vivacity, it disorders all our faculties, prompting us to receive "every loose fiction or idea . . . on the same footing [with the conclusions of Judgment]."[12] Poets, he declares, are "liars by profession."[13] True, in his essay "Of the Delicacy of Taste and Passion" he says that "nothing is so improving to the temper as the study of the beauties . . . of poetry, eloquence, music or painting. . . . The emotions which they excite are soft and tender. They draw off the mind from the hurry of business and interest; cherish reflection; dispose to tranquillity; and produce an agreeable melancholy, which, of all dispositions of the mind, is the best suited to love and friendship."[14] But so to speak of the fruits of the imagination is very much like saying that they make an excellent surrogate for an aspirin tablet, and Hume is clearly far from being inclined to allow that they might possibly prove to be vehicles of any kind of truth or genuine insight into the meaning of human experience.

The mistrust of the imagination which is classically expressed in the modern tradition by Hobbes and Locke and Hume springs, of course, from a great fear of the threat which it is thought to present to the integrity of tough, hardheaded rational reflection on what is actually given in our world. And it is a concern to safeguard the autonomy and clarity of reason which has constantly prompted empiricist modes of thought to forswear the possibility of the imagination having even any adjunctive relation to cognition. Gilbert Ryle's famous book *The Concept of Mind* comes perhaps as close as any other to presenting the quintessentially characteristic version in contemporary (or post-Wittgensteinian) terms of an empiricist epistemology, and, eager though he is to correct Locke and Hume in certain particulars, his insistence on viewing imagination as an affair of "make-believe" or "pretending"[15] in no great way upsets the established grammar of philosophic empiricism in relation to this whole theme.

But, now, the traditional disapprobation of the imagination by empiricist philosophy has in recent years been paralleled by the even more radical disparagement that has come from that insurgency which, in the way of a kind of verbal shorthand, we refer to as structuralism. And its critique is more radical than that of philosophic empiricism, since it entails a sceptical view not merely of the veridicality of what the imagination may deliver but of the veritableness of subjectivity itself. The structuralists—such people, for example, as Michel Foucault, Jacques

Derrida, the late Roland Barthes, Gérard Genette, and Julia Kristeva—consider that "we are already, before the very least of our words, [so] governed and paralysed by language"[16] that the speaking "I" must be adjudged little more than a ghostly stereotype encoded by the particular *langue* to which it happens to be captive. In the terms of Saussure's duality,[17] we may say that *parole* is declared to be so inveterately subordinate to *langue* that the very idea of the mind as a center of any sort of creative power must be rejected out of hand. Man, we are told, far from being the impresario of his language is but a cypher at the behest of the norms and protocols governing his linguistic culture. Roland Barthes, for example, in his book *S/Z* instructs us with a dazzling virtuosity in the absurdity of taking Balzac's *Sarrasine* to be a reflection of what a particular writer has chosen to do with his medium, since all that we can behold and study in Balzac's story—or, for that matter, in *any* text—are the ways in which certain linguistic systems and codes dance out figurations. Moreover, even the notion of "reading" itself is thrown into question, since the person undertaking a transaction with the Balzacian text is himself nothing more than a function of the systems of signification by which he is constituted; and thus the interaction between "reader" and text is simply an affair of the *play* (*jeu*) of symbolic codes. The omniscient reader, in other words, is as much a delusion as is the omniscient author. In short, any kind of privileged subjectivity must be seen to have been displaced by the systems and codes and grids that rule us—and the notion of the self as an autonomous center of creativity being, therefore, only the sheerest fiction, the imagination must indeed be conceived to be something like a Ghost in the Machine.

Yet, however dogmatically the New Positivism may deny that man has any capacity for genuine transcendence, the fact of the matter remains that we (if an essentialist definition may be risked) are creatures who seem destined to be *liminars*. It is the anthropologist Victor Turner who in a series of notable books (*The Forest of Symbols* 1967, *The Ritual Process* 1969, and *Dramas, Fields, and Metaphors* 1974) has retrieved the concept of the "liminal phase" from the Belgian ethnographer Arnold van Gennep and his classic work of 1909, *Les Rites de passage*. Van Gennep, in working out the logic of "transition" rites, remarked three phases into which they invariably fall and which he identified as, first, separation, then margin (or *limen*, the Latin signifying "threshold"), and then reaggregation. That is to say, the neophyte first undergoes some detachment or dislocation from his established role in a social structure or cultural polity—whereupon he finds himself as novice in a "liminal" situation in which he is neither one thing nor another, neither here nor there, neither what he was nor yet what he will become. Then, in the third phase, the passage is completed by his reincorporation into a social or religious structure: no longer is he invisible by reason of his divestment of status and role, for, once again, he finds himself with acknowledged rights and obligations vis-à-vis those others who with him are members one of another in whatever body it is to which they jointly belong.

Now Victor Turner is careful to remark that "liminars" are, in most human communities, by no means the only déclassés, for always there are various "outsiders" (shamans, monks, priests, hippies, hoboes, and gypsies) who either by ascription or choice stand outside the established order, just as there are also various kinds of "marginals" (migrant foreigners, persons of mixed ethnic origin, and the upwardly and downwardly mobile) who may be "simultaneously members . . . of two or more groups whose social definitions and cultural norms are distinct from, and often even opposed to, one another."[18] But, though at many points he is strongly insistent on these distinctions, at many others he seems to be treating "outsiderhood" and "marginality" as merely special modes of "liminality," and it is the latter term which appears for him to be the decisive antipode to "aggregation."

What Professor Turner is most eager to remark, however, is the wrongheadedness of regarding liminality as a merely negative state of privation: on the contrary, as he argues, it can be and often is an enormously fruitful seedbed of spiritual creativity, for it is precisely amidst the troubling ambiguities of the liminar's *déclassement* that there is born in him a profound hunger for *communitas*. And Mr. Turner prefers the Latin term, since he feels "community" connotes an ordered, systemized society—whereas the liminar's yearning is not for any simple kind of social structure but rather, as he says, for that spontaneous, immediate flowing from *I* to *Thou* of which Martin Buber is our great modern rhapsode.[19] Which is to say that the liminar thirsts for *communitas*; this is what the naked neophyte in a seclusion lodge yearns for; this is what the dispossessed and the exiled dream of; this is what "dharma bums," millenarians, holy mendicants, and "rock" people are moved by—namely, the vision of an *open* society in which all the impulses and affections that are normally bound by social structure are liberated, so that every barrier between *I* and *Thou* is broken down and the wind of *communitas* may blow where it listeth.

Moreover, Victor Turner conceives it to be the distinctive mission of the liminar to lift *communitas* into the subjunctive mood: his special vocation, as a frontiersman dwelling on the edges of the established order, is to puncture "the clichés associated with status incumbency and role-playing"[20] and to fill for his contemporaries the open space of absolute futurity with a vision of what the theologians of Russian Orthodoxy call *sobornost*—which is nothing other than that catholicity, that harmony, that unanimity, that free unity-in-diversity, which graces the human order when we give our suffrage to the "open morality" (as Bergson would have called it) of agape.

But, though in Professor Turner's theory of culture (based in large part on his extensive field-researches amongst the Ndembu people of northwest Zambia) "liminar" is a technical term that speaks of a special type of social marginality, it ought surely not to be impermissible to broaden the concept out beyond its limited range in his schema, for liminality or "threshold" existence may, indeed, be thought of as defining the human condition as such. As the late Philip Wheelwright said in his fine book of 1954, *The Burning Fountain*: "Man lives always on the verge, always on the borderland of a something more."[21] And in no respect is this more obvious than in our experience of successiveness, of passage, of before-and-afterness: "we live from that which is no more toward what is not yet through a slender, fragile boundary line called 'now.' "[22] Which is why the Spanish philosopher Julián Marías insists that "the [human] situation is intrinsically historical"—because it consists of our being at once what we are "coming from" and what we are "going to."[23] And not only are we constantly in transit, but we are conscious of being so. Which is why the "I" of one moment can keep its identity with the "I" of the next: our being able to say on Wednesday morning that on the following Thursday morning Wednesday will be yesterday attests, in other words, to an integrity of selfhood that, in its capacity for transcendence of the moment, sustains us in our passage from one moment to another.

So the nature of the temporality in which we dwell commits us to a "threshold" existence. But, then, as Philip Wheelwright reminds us, our situation is also liminal with respect to the circumambient world, for, as he says, we find ourselves committed to "the threshold of otherness."[24] That is to say, no solipsistic account of things can have cogency, since I know the world with which I must reckon to be infinitely larger and more complex than my own brainpan; the self is always confronting the not-self. "No man is an island," for at every point the life of the individual is intersected and bisected by all the various things and persons forming the environment that sustains the human enterprise: "we stand, as it were, on the verge of the circumambient world."[25]

And, finally, "man's threshold situation . . . [has not only] a 'forward' dimension in time and an 'outward' dimension in its sense of otherness and in the development of that sense into a conception of 'the world'":[26] it also has a "vertical" or religious dimension, the dimension of depth. The proposition of Bishop Butler's which G. E. Moore took over as a kind of motto of his own philosophy says: "Everything is what it is and not another thing." But, of course, the world is not at all simply *what it is.* A modern philosopher may smugly declare this to be the case, but the more truly human attitude is surely that of astonishment that there is a world at all and that its processes and functioning are governed by the regularities which science studies. Moreover, scientific research itself, as the late Abraham Heschel once remarked, is only "an entry into the endless, not a blind alley. . . . One answer breeds a multitude of new questions. . . . Everything hints at something that transcends it. . . . What appears to be a center is but a point on the periphery of another center."[27] Which is perhaps in part why the distinguished French phenomenologist Maurice Merleau-Ponty refused the notion that "the thinking subject can absorb into its thinking or appropriate without remainder the object of its thought."[28] Indeed, again and again, we find ourselves brought up short before what can only be called Mystery—which is not the unknown but, rather, that surplusage of meaning in what is known, that inexhaustible Ground of reality by which we are moved whenever we perform an act of true attention before the things and creatures of the earth. Mystery is not, in other words, a name for a merely subjective reality. It is, rather, an ontological category, for it speaks not of anything foisted upon the world but of "a most powerful presence beyond the mind" which makes for "a fundamental norm of human consciousness."[29] It is not something which we infer from a psychological reaction but rather that to which the *sense* of Mystery, of wonder, of amazement, is a response. "We do not come upon it only at the climax of thinking or in observing strange, extraordinary facts, but in the startling fact that there are facts at all. . . . We may face it at every turn, in a grain of seed, in an atom, as well as in the stellar spaces."[30] And it is the encounter with the "verticality" of the world which has the effect of making "everything finite . . . [appear] to testify to its own finitude by half-revealing a transfinite dimension within itself,"[31] a taproot which connects it with a Something More.

So, as Abraham Heschel says, "We live on the fringe of reality."[32] And the term which Victor Turner has in recent years given currency, the term *liminality,* defines the situation not so much of a special type of man as it defines the human situation in the large, for we seem always to be at a *limen* or threshold, whether it be the threshold of time, or the threshold of the circumambient world, or the threshold of the Transcendent. Which is no doubt why a certain restlessness is one of the most conspicuous traits of the human spirit.

Man is, of course, in all sorts of ways bound by the necessities of nature. He needs air to breathe and space in which to abide; he cannot survive without the nourishment of food, and he must not be overly exposed to the summer's heat or the winter's cold. Yet, however adequate may be the provision he is able to make for food and shelter, his life is but of short duration, and "at the last a little earth is thrown upon our head, and that is the end for ever."[33] "But," as Pascal says, "if the universe were to crush him, man would still be more noble than that which killed him, because he knows that he dies and the advantage which the universe has over him; the universe knows nothing of this."[34] Which is to say that, though frail and at the mercy of all the vicissitudes and contingencies of nature and history, "the human spirit [has the power] on the other hand to lift itself above itself . . . and to make the whole temporal and spatial world, including itself, the object of its knowledge."[35] Man stands, as it were, above the structures and coherences of existence, being able to order them and reorder them toward ends of his own choosing. And not only can he make the structures of nature and history the object of his own thought and the instruments of his creativity; he can also make himself the object of his thought, and even the self which thus surmounts itself—and this on into indeterminate degrees of self-transcendence. Indeed, in every moment of his life he is restlessly and "intentively"[36] reaching beyond what is merely given in the here and the now, holding, as Philip Wheelwright says, "some particular patch of experience . . . up to contemplative attention, not for what it is but for what it indicates or suggests."[37]

Now when we speak of the imagination we mean, or ought to mean, nothing other than this pushing of the mind beyond what is merely given, as it reaches intentively after some fresh synthesis of experience. Imagination, in other words, is simply thinking in its primary, generative form whereby the things which are at hand are gratefully *gathered*[38] in a way that entails (to adopt a Kantian idiom) no fracture between sensibility and understanding. But it is not a univocal mode of thinking: indeed, as Philip Wheelwright very shrewdly suggests, it takes at least four forms. "There is," he says, "the Confrontative Imagination, which acts upon its object by particularizing and intensifying it. There is the Stylistic Imagination, which acts upon its object by distancing and stylizing it. There is the Compositive Imagination, which fuses heterogeneous elements into some kind of unity. And there is the Archetypal Imagination, which sees the particular object in the light of a larger conception or of a higher concern."[39]

In the first instance, we seek to discern "the character of particular things in the starkness and strangeness of their being what they are."[40] From the standpoint of scientific thought, of course, it is not the radical singularity of particular things and events that matters but rather the logical relations and the general laws that are instanced in particular cases. It is of the very essence of the peculiar asceticism represented by scientific mentality that it should assume that no significantly veridical information about the world can be derived from contemplation of the unrepeatable experience, the unique reality: so it is always withdrawing from particular realities in order to get to the universal rules which they may be taken to exhibit or confirm, and it is happy only when it reaches that region of unresisting generalities which can, completely and without remainder, be subdued by the abstractive intellect. But it belongs to our human nature to want to savor the full-fledged otherness, the radical "hecceity," of the immediate givens that comprise the environment of our lives: we want to perform an act of strict attention before *this* or *that*, in the dimension (as Gabriel Marcel would say) of its *presence*. And when a person or some nonhuman creature or natural object is approached as a *thou* and is thus enabled to "speak" to us, to penetrate that restless, diurnal world of familiarity in which we normally live, so that the soul is stirred to new apprehension and response—when this happens, it is indeed by dint of an achievement of imagination, of the Confrontative Imagination.

But, then, the world is a body wherein all things are members one of another, "interacting as in a story or fragment of a story."[41] Nothing that exists is an island unto itself. And thus the significance of one thing, when steadily contemplated, is seen to flow from the relations in which it stands to still other things consubstantial with itself. Which is in part why Coleridge in the *Biographia Literaria* insists that the things of earth are not "essentially fixed and dead": on the contrary, as he says, they are "essentially vital," for all the concrete singulars of the world are ignited by such a power of reciprocity as permits them so to trench upon one another as to make it inevitable that synecdoche and metaphor should be amongst the principal instruments of the imagination.

Here, for example, is the illustrative instance that Wordsworth offers in the Preface to the 1815 edition of his verse. He first quotes the following passage from his poem "Resolution and Independence":

As a huge stone sometimes is seen to lie
Couched on the bald top of an eminence,
Wonder to all who do the same espy

By what means it could thither come, and whence,
So that it seems a thing endued with sense,
Like a sea-beast crawled forth, which on a shelf
Of rock or sand reposeth, there to sun himself.
Such seemed this Man; not all alive or dead,
Nor all asleep, in his extreme old age.
. . . .
Motionless as a cloud the old Man stood,
That heareth not the loud winds when they call,
And moveth altogether if it move at all.

And then he goes on to say: "In these images, the conferring, the abstracting and the modifying powers of the imagination immediately and mediately acting are all brought into conjunction. The stone is endowed with something of the power of life to approximate it to the sea-beast; and the sea-beast stripped of some of its vital qualities to assimilate it to the stone; which intermediate image is thus treated for the purpose of bringing the original image, that of the stone, to a nearer resemblance to the figure and condition of the aged man; who is divested of so much of the indications of life and motion as to bring him to the point where the two objects unite and coalesce in just comparison."[42] And it is precisely such coalescences of heterogeneity within reality that solicit that integrative effort of the mind which Coleridge described as "esemplastic," when (as he said), by diffusing "a tone and spirit of unity, that blends, and (as it were) *fuses*, each into each," we seek "the balance or reconciliation of opposite or discordant qualities: of sameness, with difference; of the general, with the concrete; the idea, with the image; the individual, with the representative."[43] Such is the work of the Compositive Imagination.

There are, however, occasions when we neither want to synthesize or integrate heterogeneities nor simply to confront particulars but when we want to put a given "phenomenon, so to speak, out of gear with our practical, actual self, by allowing it to stand outside the context of our personal needs and ends,"[44] in order that we may win an objectivity which will enable us to see it freshly, unbedimmed by the film of familiarity and common association. "But . . . the relation between the self and the object is [not] broken to the extent of becoming 'impersonal.' . . . On the contrary, . . . [the] *personal* relation . . . [is] *of a peculiar character*. Its peculiarity lies in that the personal character of the relation has been, so to speak, filtered. It has been cleared of the practical, concrete nature of its appeal."[45] And when attention focuses itself on that which has been thus *distanced* but to which we are nevertheless *personally* related, the Stylistic Imagination begins to be at work, for, by "hushing . . . ordinary compulsions, . . . [and] veiling . . . ordinary associations,"[46] the mind is formalizing or stylizing a given reality in order that it may be more clearly perceived and appreciated.

Then, finally, the imagination presents itself in still another mode, for often it wants not to concentrate merely on "the very thing and nothing else,"[47] or to integrate multiplicities, or to distance and stylize, but to approach the particular as (to use Goethe's term) an *Urphä-nomen*, or as an Eminent Instance of something generic and universal. And, in this mode, it becomes the Archetypal Imagination. Certain things, of course, lend themselves more readily than others do to this kind of appropriation and even seem in some way primordially destined to impress themselves upon us as "concrete universals"—the sky, for example (as the residence of the gods), the sun, the moon and its phases, the tree (as image of the cosmos), water (as the *fons et origo* of life), the wheel, the harvest, fire, and stones.[48] But there is virtually nothing that may not be grasped as an archetype, as we search our experience for particular things and events that body forth felt meanings of fundamental import.

Now it is no doubt the case that many of those who give their allegiance to the decorums normally governing systematic thought are inclined to regard such modes of apprehension as have just been described—the confrontative, the compositive, the stylistic, and the archetypal—as issuing from (in Samuel Johnson's definition of the imagination) "a licentious and vagrant faculty . . . [which] has always endeavored to baffle the logician . . . and burst the inclosures of regularity."[49] Certainly Western philosophy, whether in its traditional or its contemporary phases, has only very rarely permitted itself to be fructified by the poetic imagination. And in this, surprising though it may be, not even does theology present any exception: amongst the major theologians of the modern period there is virtually none—excepting possibly Søren Kierkegaard and John Henry Newman—whose work would appear to have been influenced in any decisive way by poetic methods and modalities.[50] Both philosophers and theologians characteristically assume that the kinds of procedures and insights supervised by the poetic imagination represent "only a vague . . . and uncertain way of talking, more useful for expressing human feelings and aspirations than for . . . formulating coherent rational arguments."[51] And thus both give Dr. Johnson's "licentious . . . faculty" very short shrift indeed.

But the figures to whom this book is devoted—Coleridge, Arnold,

Pater, Santayana, Stevens, and Heidegger—are amongst those in the modern tradition who most powerfully remind us that, finally, there is no separating the poetic and the imaginative from the reflective and the metaphysical, since (as Elizabeth Sewell puts it) "the human organism, . . . which has the gift of thought, does not have the choice of two kinds of thinking. It has only one, in which the organism as a whole is engaged all along the line."[52] And, indeed, "the Reasoning Power in Man" becomes a fearfully enervated kind of "Spectre . . . when separated / From Imagination and closing itself as in steel in a Ratio,"[53] a Spectre "that Negatives every thing."[54]

Wisdom will doubtless, of course, avoid the exorbitance of the more incautious claims in behalf of the imagination that were occasionally made by the great Romantics. Blake, for example, says:

> This world of Imagination is the world of Eternity: it is the divine bosom into which we shall all go after the death of the Vegetated body. This World of Imagination is Infinite & Eternal, whereas the world of Generation, or Vegetation, is Finite & Temporal. There Exist in that Eternal World the Permanent Realities of Every Thing which we see reflected in this Vegetable Glass of Nature. All Things are comprehended in their Eternal Forms in the divine body of the Saviour, the True Vine of Eternity, The Human Imagination.[55]

Nor will it be forgotten that Shelley, in an equally extreme rhetoric, was proclaiming that the poetic imagination mirrors "the gigantic shadows which futurity casts upon the present" and—as "the influence which is moved not, but [which] moves"—is the great unacknowledged legislator of the world.[56] And there is much else in this manner to be cited in Wordsworth and Keats and Carlyle and numerous others—which makes, all of it, a grandiloquence representing the sheerest kind of fustian. But the partially extenuating circumstance was that these men found themselves to be facing a rampant and an overweening scientism which, through its major spokesmen (from Bacon to Locke, and from Hobbes to Hartley), said in effect that the things which the poetic imagination handles are merely "the mental rattle that awakened the attention of intellect in the infancy of civil society . . . [and that] for the maturity of mind to make a serious business of the playthings of its childhood, is as absurd as for a full-grown man to rub his gums with coral, and cry to be charmed to sleep by the jingle of silver bells."[57] So it was natural that the Romantics should feel the necessity of correcting a certain imbalance, and this was what they set out to do, albeit with some occasional excess.

Yet even in their error they were more right than were their opponents in theirs. For they were intending to preserve us (as Blake's great phrase says) "from Single vision & Newton's sleep."[58] And they knew that any kind of comprehensive and liberating vision of the world is far less dependent on *ratio* than on *intellectus*. With his characteristically elegant simplicity the Catholic philosopher Josef Pieper summarizes the distinction (as drawn by the medieval Scholastics) between *ratio* and *intellectus* in the following manner: "*Ratio* is the power of discursive, logical thought, of searching and of examination, of abstraction, of definition and drawing conclusions. *Intellectus*, on the other hand, is the name for the understanding in so far as it is the capacity of *simplex intuitus*, of that simple vision to which truth offers itself like a landscape to the eye."[59] *Ratio*, in other words, is an affair of "intellectual work": it is a term that speaks of attention all astrain, as it observes, scrutinizes, deduces, abstracts, categorizes, and legislates. And, in the gathering of *information* about things or of what may be called "discursive knowledge," *ratio* is, of course, indispensable. Nor is it wholly inoperative at the level of "primary knowledge" or metaphysical vision, where it may be an important condition if not the necessary cause of what is achieved. But, there, what is far more decisive is the contemplative gaze of *intellectus* whereby, through the analogical creativity of the imagination, the mind does not *assault* reality but simply spends its energies in, as Heraclitus says (in the *De anima*), "listening to the essence of things." Which is to say that the most *original* apprehensions of reality (not necessarily in the sense of temporal priority but of basic import) are those which are consequent upon an essentially poetic act of cognition. And it is a central body of modern testimony on this theme which is summarized in the chapters that follow—on Coleridge, Arnold, Pater, Santayana, Stevens, and Heidegger.[60] All these figures are in various ways declaring (Pater and Santayana somewhat less decisively perhaps than the others) that the necessary *praeparatio* for the constitution of *fundamental* belief is formed by a venturesome step forward by the imagination into that which is before us.

And such a testimony requires most especially to be heard in a time when we find ourselves to be "natives of poverty,"[61] in the sense of our no longer having at hand a scheme of ideas and a system of thought that enable us with clarity and assurance to give tongue to the deep things within us. "A tempest [has] cracked on the theatre,"[62] and, as a result, both the *philosophia perennis* and the *theologia perennis* have fallen away, so that we are now without any common grammar of thought wherewith we might give "a candid kind to everything."[63] Yet, difficult though this extremity may be, the experience of dispossession and dearth can offer a certain advantage, since the very collapse of so much that we have inherited from both Athens and Jerusalem, in releasing us from the ossified formulas of the past, grants new opportunities for humbly and obediently hearkening to that—anciently spoken of as the Logos—which assembles and sustains the things and creatures of earth. Once again we are given a chance, as it were, to accord the initiative not to the engines of our own speculation but to the mysterious fecundity of What Is. So, in a way, "the absence of God" helps—but only if our response to primal reality is of a kind that permits reflection to be truly "foundational." Which means that a kind of priority is to be given to *intellectus* as against *ratio*, and to the disciplines of imagination which it summons forth.

Acquiescence in this way of discovery and knowing is bound, of course, to be difficult in an age when the only glance regularly bestowed upon the world is that of "calculative thinking"[64] and when our normal concern is that of simply making things obedient to an enterprise of science or engineering. But, as the last great genius of modern philosophy, Martin Heidegger, was insisting throughout the last thirty years or so of his career, it is the poetic imagination that cultivates the art of "paying heed" to the quiddities and hecceities of the world; and, as he urged, to forswear this kind of heedfulness is to forfeit any chance of truly savoring the things which cannot possibly not be known—but which may be "forgotten." Indeed, mesmerized as we are by our eagerness to weigh, measure, manipulate, and exploit the materials of life, it is, in Heidegger's analysis of the *mal du siècle*, precisely our "forgetfulness" of the sheer ontological weight and depth of the world that has alienated us from that in relation to which alone human selfhood can be securely constituted. But, in pressing its relentless quest for intimacy of relationship with all the rich singularity that belongs to "things" in their intractable specificity, the poetic imagination, as Heidegger says, "deconceals" that wherewith they are inwardly sustained, that by which they are so assembled as to enable them to stand out before the gaze of the mind. It brings them "into the Open," and thus brings us into the neighborhood of Being: which is to say that the miracle it performs is "the letting happen of the advent of the truth of what is."[65] And, as Heidegger's great lesson argues, it is only when we give up the urge to exploit and master the things of earth and approach them in the marveling, reverential spirit of "paying heed" and "letting-be"[66] that we begin to move into the region of that-which-is and begin to have a "world." So, as he declares, it is "poetically [that] man dwells on this earth."[67] And it is something like this that is being said by the figures to whom this book is devoted.

2/ Coleridge on the Dignity of the Poetic Imagination

The image-forming or rather re-forming power, the imagination in its passive sense, which I would rather call Fancy = Phantasy, . . . this, the Fetisch & Talisman of all modern Philosophers (the Germans excepted) may not inaptly be compared to the Gorgon Head, which *looked* death into every thing—and this not by accident, but from the nature of the faculty itself, the province of which is to give consciousness to the Subject by presenting to it its conceptions *objectively* but the Soul differences itself from any other Soul for the purposes of symbolical knowledge by *form* or body only—but all form as body, i.e. as shape, & not as forma efformans, is dead—Life may be *inferred*, even as intelligence is from black marks on white paper— but the black marks themselves *are truly "the dead* letter." Here then is the error—not in the faculty itself, without which there would be no *fixation*, consequently, no distinct perception or conception, but in the gross idolatry of those who abuse it, & make that the goal & end which should be only a means of arriving at it. . . .

From the above deduce the worth & dignity of poetic Imagination, of the fusing power, that fixing unfixes & while it melts & bedims the Image, still leaves in the Soul its living meaning—[.]

—S. T. Coleridge[1]

Though Coleridge's achievement as poet and philosopher and theologian forms one of the enduring landmarks of the modern period, he has never been without intransigently hostile detractors. In the last century, from the 1830s on, a bilious estimate (particularly of his philosophical work) was rendered by De Quincey, Sir William Hamilton, Carlyle, J. H. Stirling, and numerous others, and, in the present century, T. S. Eliot's assertion that his career as a thinker represents the "stupefaction of his powers in transcendental metaphysics"[2] has been echoed again and again.

Much of this harshness has, of course, been focalized by the old charge (being made as early as De Quincey) that what is most remarkable about the author of the *Biographia Literaria*, of the *Philosophical Lectures*, of *Theory of Life* and *Aids to Reflection*, of *The Friend* and *On the Constitution of the Church and State*, is his adeptness in the art of plagiarism. René Wellek, for example, says: "At crucial points in his writings Coleridge used Kant, Schelling, and A. W. Schlegel, reproducing the very pattern of sentences and the exact vocabulary. Whatever the ethics or psychology of the situation, it seems impossible to give Coleridge credit for ideas simply quoted literally."[3] And Professor Wellek's allegation—which he supports with detailed notations over a half-dozen pages in the chapter on Coleridge in his *History of Modern Criticism*—is massively documented by Norman Fruman in his book of 1971, *Coleridge, the Damaged Archangel*,[4] where Wellek's list of Coleridge's indebtments is very greatly enlarged.

The issue here has by no one, however, been so sensibly adjudicated as by Thomas McFarland in his immensely impressive book *Coleridge and the Pantheist Tradition*. He does not, of course, want in any way at all to extenuate the fact of Coleridge's pilferings: indeed, as he says, his "borrowings are not only real, but so honeycomb his work as to form virtually a mode of composition."[5] But, though Mr. McFarland readily acknowledges, as one must, Coleridge's profound indebtedness to the Germans (to Kant, Fichte, Schelling, and Schlegel) as well as to Plato, he insists that the concept of "plagiarism," however pertinent it may be "to the stricken efforts of undergraduates to meet demands far beyond either their abilities or their interests," really "has no proper applicability to the activities . . . of a powerful, learned, and deeply committed mind."[6] Nor is he willing to grant that he is trying somehow to "open a special cultural category solely for the convenience of Coleridge." He very tellingly cites, for example, a passage in Ernst Cassirer's *The Philosophy of the Enlightenment* where Cassirer is himself acknowledging in the case of Lessing that "scarcely a single aesthetic concept and scarcely a single principle . . . did not have its exact parallel in contemporary literature . . . [and] could not have been documented in the writings of Baumgarten, the Swiss critics, Shaftesbury, Dubos, or Diderot." Yet this exacting and prodigiously learned philosopher and intellectual historian was wanting a generation ago, in the strongest possible way, to assert "the incomparable originality of Lessing's work," for, as he said,

> it is a complete mistake to seek to raise objections to the originality of Lessing's basic thoughts on the grounds of any such documentation of his sources. Lessing's originality does not manifest itself in the invention of new ideas, but in the order and connection, in the logical arrangement and selection, which he accomplished with the materials already available. . . . The decisive aspect of Lessing's achievement does not lie in the matter of his concepts themselves, but in their form, not in what they are in the sense of a logical definition, but in their . . . transformation. . . . Every concept that enters the magic circle of his thinking begins at once to undergo a transformation. Instead of remaining mere end products, they again become original creative forces and directly moving impulses.[7]

Now it is a similar judiciousness that Mr. McFarland eloquently urges with respect to Coleridge, since he rightly descries that in his critical and philosophical writing which asks for the invocation of such a principle as Cassirer applied to Lessing—"that it is possible for all a man's ideas to have an 'exact parallel in contemporary literature' and none the less to speak of his 'incomparable originality.' "[8] True, the Scots philosopher Sir William Hamilton in the Supplementary Dissertations that he provided in 1846 for his edition of *The Works of Thomas*

Reid laid it down that "Coleridge's systematic plagiarism is, perhaps, the most remarkable on record."[9] But Mr. McFarland reminds us of John Stuart Mill's severe estimate of Hamilton himself, that his own mindless plagiarisms (simply "strung together from German writers") reveal how much he was bound to be

> at a loss . . . [when] required to draw up a philosophical estimate of the mind of any great thinker. He never seems to look at any opinion of a philosopher in connection with the same philosopher's other opinions. Accordingly, he is weak as to the mutual relations of philosophical doctrines. He seldom knows any of the corollaries from a thinker's opinions, unless the thinker has himself drawn them; and even then he knows them, not as corollaries, but only as opinions.[10]

So, for all Hamilton's exertions in his quest of a large and formidable erudition, Mill conceives it to have been *mere* erudition, leaving, as he says, "only the remains of his mind for the real business of thinking":

> In the whole circle of psychological and logical speculation, it is astonishing how few are the topics into which he has thrown any of the powers of his own intellect; and on how small a proportion even of these he has pushed his investigations beyond what seemed necessary for the purposes of some particular controversy. In consequence, philosophical doctrines are taken up, and again laid down, with perfect unconsciousness, and his philosophy seems made up of scraps from several conflicting metaphysical systems.[11]

In other words, Mill's hermeneutical principle appears to be very much like Cassirer's, that "plagiarism is not the borrowing of material, but the borrowing of material without attendant thought,"[12] without any effort at genuine reticulation. And Mr. McFarland's whole point is that it is precisely the power of reticulation which is "so abundantly present in Coleridge as to become almost the hallmark of his intellectual activity."[13] The argument he presents in this connection over more than fifty pages of his extraordinarily distinguished book is undoubtedly the most cogent statement on this much vexed question to have been offered since the issue was first raised by De Quincey in the 1830s, and it ought to persuade serious students of Coleridge that they would be well advised to take him at his word when he says:

> In the Preface of my Metaphys. Works I should say—Once & all read Tetens, Kant, Fichte, &c—& there you will trace or if you are on the

hunt, track me. Why then not acknowledge your obligations step by step? Because, I could not do in a multitude of glaring resemblances without a lie / for they had been mine, formed, & full formed in my own mind, before I had ever heard of these Writers, because to have fixed on the partic. instances in which I have really been indebted to these Writers would have very hard, if possible, to me who read for truth & self-satisfaction, not to make a book, & who always rejoiced & was jubilant when I found my own ideas well expressed already by others, (& would have looked like a *trick*, to skulk there not quoted,) & lastly, let me say, because (I am proud perhaps but) I seem to know, that much of the matter remains my own, and that the Soul is *mine*. I fear not him for a Critic who can confound a Fellow-thinker with a Compiler.[14]

Indeed, John Stuart Mill, one of the most supremely intelligent men of the nineteenth century, gave it as his judgment shortly after the deaths of Bentham and Coleridge that they had been "the two great seminal minds of England in their age."[15] And though Mill himself, in his own basic commitments, stood firmly in the line of Bentham (notwithstanding the harshness of his critique of Bentham), he did nevertheless, with his characteristic perspicacity, define with absolute precision the nature of those currents of thought that Coleridge had released onto the English scene. The "Germano-Coleridgian doctrine," he said, "expresses the revolt of the human mind against the philosophy of the eighteenth century. It is ontological, because that was experimental; conservative, because that was innovative; religious, because so much of that was infidel; concrete and historical, because that was abstract and metaphysical; poetical, because that was matter-of-fact and prosaic."[16] And the approving manner in which he listed these particulars of the "Germano-Coleridgian doctrine" attests to the remarkable spaciousness of Mill's own vision, for, attached as he was to the experimental and the innovative and the matter-of-fact, he was yet generous enough to be prepared to acknowledge the partiality of those perspectives (descending from Locke, Hartley, Hume, Ricardo, and Bentham) by which he had himself been formed and the wholesomeness of their being weighed against by the kind of counterbalance that Coleridge had represented.

It will not, of course, be forgotten that in his young manhood Coleridge himself had ardently subscribed to the tradition of Locke and Hartley. Very shortly after he matriculated in the autumn of 1791 at Jesus College, Cambridge—which had been Hartley's own college—he was chiefly mingling with the left-wing radicals of the period and finding one of the principal inspirations of his thought in William Godwin's *Political Justice*. In his twenty-second year he said, for example, in a letter (11 December 1794) to his friend Robert Southey: "I am a compleat Necessitarian—and understand the subject almost as well as Hartley himself—but I go farther than Hartley and believe the corporeality of *thought*—namely, that it is motion—."[17] And in September of 1796 he named his first son David Hartley. But his second son who was born in May of 1798 he named Berkeley—which would seem to indicate a considerable shift in philosophic allegiance having occurred. And, indeed, three years later he was saying in a letter (16 March 1801) to his friend and patron Thomas Poole: "If I do not greatly delude myself, I . . . have overthrown the doctrine of Association, as taught by Hartley, and with it all the irreligious metaphysics of modern infidels—especially, the doctrine of Necessity."[18]

Now in the years immediately following his declaration to Southey of his "compleat Necessitarianism" not only had Coleridge been greatly affected by his reading of Berkeley and Spinoza, but the great decisive event of his life had also occurred—namely, his first encounter with Wordsworth's "Guilt and Sorrow" in the poet's own recitation of it and the meetings with Wordsworth that followed and that cemented their friendship in the spring and summer of 1797. In the *Biographia Literaria* he says:

> I was in my twenty-fourth year, when I had the happiness of knowing Mr. Wordsworth personally, and while memory lasts, I shall hardly forget the sudden effect produced on my mind, by his recitation of a manuscript poem. . . . There was here no mark of strained thought, or forced diction, no crowd or turbulence of imagery; and, as the poet hath himself well described in his lines "on revisiting the Wye," manly reflection, and human associations had given both variety, and an additional interest to natural objects, which in the passion and appetite of the first love they had seemed to him neither to need or permit. . . . It was not however the freedom from false taste . . . which made so unusual an impression on my feelings immediately, and subsequently on my judgment. It was the union of deep feeling with profound thought; the fine balance of truth in observing, with the imaginative faculty in modifying the objects observed; and above all the original gift of spreading the tone, the *atmosphere*, and with it the depth and height of the ideal world around forms, incidents, and situations, of which, for the common view, custom had bedimmed all the lustre, had dried up the sparkle and the dew drops.[19]

He goes on to tell us that "repeated meditations" on this peculiar excellence he "felt" in Wordsworth did eventually lead him to distinguish sharply between Fancy and Imagination as "two distinct and widely different faculties,"[20] since, clearly, such a poetry as Wordsworth was producing could not issue from any mere playing with "fixities and definites."[21] But he might also have said that, indeed, it was this early encounter with the poetry of Wordsworth that led him, even prior to any attempt at distinguishing Fancy from Imagination, to the very idea of "the powers and privileges of the imagination."[22] For it was undoubtedly his discovery of a poet who could *see* the things of earth with a freshness and penetration that had the effect of restoring to them all the lost sparkle and dewdrops, and who could then spread round them again the tone and atmosphere, "the depth and height of the ideal world"—it was undoubtedly his discovery of such a poet that prompted him radically to reassess his own allegiance to that whole mode of British rationalism which held the action of the mind to involve nothing more than a subconscious kind of mechanical association of the various elements of experience, without any measure (as Muirhead phrases it) of "selective attention or imaginative construction."[23] As Bertrand Russell once acutely remarked of the theory of mind descending from Hartley and Bentham, "In essence the doctrine is the same as the modern theory of the 'conditioned reflex,' based on Pavlov's experiments. The only important difference is that Pavlov's conditioned reflex is physiological, whereas the association of ideas was purely mental."[24] But Wordsworth's poetry, in disclosing the nature of poetic genius to be not only that of observing truthfully but also that of imaginatively *modifying* what is observed, had in effect borne in upon Coleridge the realization that the relation of the mind to the world is by no means at all anything like what the Associationists had declared it to be. So he resolved to overthrow "the doctrine of Association, as taught by Hartley, and with it all the irreligious metaphysics of modern Infidels—especially, the doctrine of Necessity."

It was, however, not Wordsworth's influence alone that had accounted for this conversion. For in September of 1798 Coleridge (using monies provided by Josiah and Thomas Wedgwood, sons of the famous potter) had gone to Germany with Wordsworth and his sister Dorothy. The Wordsworths spent only about six months in the country, but Coleridge remained until the following July, and his German experience was to prove to be the great watershed of his subsequent intellectual development. He took up residence in the town of Ratzeburg in the home of a learned and widowed pastor with eight children, where, as Coleridge said in a letter (20 October 1798) to his wife, "The German language is spoken . . . in the utmost purity—The Children often stand round my Sopha and chatter away—& the little one of all corrects my pronunciation with a pretty pert lip & self sufficient tone, while the others laugh with no little joyance."[25] Here he lived for four months, engaged principally in an intense study of the language, and, when he set out for Göttingen in February of 1799, he could, as he had recently said in a letter (4 January 1799) to Thomas Poole, "read German as English—that is, without any *mental* translation, as I read—I likewise understand all that is said to me, & a good deal of what they say to each other. On very trivial, and on metaphysical Subjects I can talk *tolerably*—so so!—but in that conversation, which is between both, I bungle most ridiculously.—I owe it to my industry that I can read old German, & even the old low-german, better than most of even the educated Natives."[26] "I have worked harder," he said, "than, I trust in God Almighty, I shall ever have occasion to work again."[27]

So, when he enrolled at the University of Göttingen in mid-February, he was well equipped to absorb German literary and philosophical culture, and this he proceeded to do with a prodigious energy. Indeed, one of the main fruits of his German sojourn was the large quantity of philosophical works that he purchased and sent back to England, and, judging from the classic passages in the first volume of the *Biographia Literaria* in which he speaks of his German indebtments, we may surmise that the writings of Kant and Fichte and Schelling were no doubt in the big bundle of books that he shipped home at the end of his stay—and Kant's most especially. For, as he said, "The writings of the illustrious sage of Königsberg, the founder of the Critical Philosophy, more than any other work, at once invigorated and disciplined my understanding." And, once Kant had taken hold of him, "as with a giant's hand,"[28] it was inevitable that the doctrine of Association should be overthrown.

Now the doctrine of Association—which had long been the reigning orthodoxy in the central tradition of British philosophy—said in effect that all of our ideas are empirically built up from sense experience, that the mind is merely a blank tablet on which the world imprints itself by way of a myriad of sensations. And to the question as to how a multitude of discrete sensations could give us the world *as world*, as a unified field of reality, the answer given was that our sensations get organized by means of association. Hartley laid the matter down in this way:

Sensations, by being often repeated, leave certain Vestiges, Types, or Images, of themselves, which may be called, *Simple Ideas of Sensation*.[29]

Sensory Vibrations, by being often repeated, beget, in the medulary substance of the Brain, a Disposition to diminutive Vibrations.[30] Any Sensations A, B, C, &c. by being associated with one another a sufficient Number of Times, get such a Power over the corresponding Ideas a, b, c, &c.
that any one of the Sensations A, when impressed alone, shall be able to
excite in the Mind b, c, &c. the ideas of the rest.[31] Simple Ideas will run
into complex ones, by Means of association.[32]

In other words, *mind* in this system, as Coleridge came to realize, "is
always *passive*,—a lazy *looker-on* on an external world."[33] Indeed, it is
wholly captive to a blindly mechanical kind of determinism, since all it
can do is to register reflexively whatever emerges from "association by
contiguity."

But it was precisely Kant's intention to overturn this whole scheme.
No, as he argued in the *Critique of Pure Reason*, the mind is not a
merely passive registrant of what the world imprints upon it but is
rather an essentially active and creative agent in the cognitive process.
For the world *as world* is not simply an affair of discrete "sensations"
that, like the pieces of a jigsaw puzzle, fit themselves together by a
process of association. On the contrary, it is the perceiving subject who,
by a labor of synthesis, unites the atomic data of sensory experience
into the various wholes—tables, trees, gazelles, mountains—that common sense assumes to be simply *there* but that, *as wholes*, are there
only as a result of a creative act of mind. This constructive effort
whereby the mind provides the *forms* in which experience appears and
grasps individuals as individuals—this is an effort which Kant declared
to be the work of the imagination. And he considered the work of the
imagination to be accompanied by the activities of sensibility and understanding, the former giving us awareness of spatial and temporal
order and the latter (involving the activity of mind in its discursive
mode) giving us those basic concepts—such as cause and effect, substance and attribute—wherewith experience may be analyzed and interpreted. But it is the productive imagination, as the essential wellhead of
both sensibility and understanding,[34] that he regarded as "the fundamental faculty of the human soul." For, in his account, the world, in so
far as it is *known*, is a construct of the imagination.

This, crudely summarized to be sure, is the argument that took
possession of Coleridge, "as with a giant's hand," in the months immediately following his return from the Continent in 1799, when, as he
turned to the recently acquired books he had purchased abroad, he
began intensely to work his way through the writings of "Kant, the

great german Metaphysician."[35] And it was as a result of Kant's impact upon him that he gradually reached the conclusion announced in a letter (23 March 1801) to Thomas Poole, that "If the mind be not *passive*, if it be indeed made in God's Image, & that too in the sublimest sense—the Image of the *Creator*—[then] there is ground for suspicion, that any system built on the passiveness of the mind must be false, as a system."[36] Indeed, as James Volant Baker rightly contends in his book on Coleridge,[37] it was his disenchantment with and increasing abhorrence of associationism that came to provide one of the unifying threads of all his most characteristic writings, of the poems and letters, *The Watchman*, *The Friend*, the *Biographia*, *The Statesman's Manual*, *Aids to Reflection*, the *Philosophical Lectures*, and much else. Of nothing was he so much convinced as he was that the whole tradition descending from Hobbes, Locke, Hartley, and Hume, in its tendency to represent the mind as largely an automaton at the behest of impressions and the law of association, was fallacious at the core. But he took the commitment of that tradition to a mechanistic psychology to be merely an expression of its deeper commitment to a vision of the universe in its entirety as an affair of nothing but mechanism. As he says at one point in chapter 8 of the *Biographia*, it is as if I, while in the very act of writing, am told that little more is involved than "the mere motion of my muscles and nerves; and [that] these again are set in motion from external causes equally passive, which external causes stand themselves in interdependent connection with every thing that exists or has existed. Thus, the whole universe . . . [is by way of being represented as cooperating] to produce the minutest stroke of every letter, save only that I myself, and I alone, have nothing to do with it, but merely the causeless and *effectless* beholding of it when it is done."[38] This he takes—the "mechanic" philosophy—to be a cheerless, dreary view of the world which "knows only . . . the relations of unproductive particles to each other; so that in every instance the result is the exact sum of the component quantities, as in arithmetical addition." So he does not hesitate to declare it to be "the philosophy of death," and he lays it down that "only of a dead nature can it hold good."[39]

But, if the account of the cognitive process offered by British tradition of the seventeenth and eighteenth centuries is to be jettisoned, how, then, are we to justify the possibility of the mind's making any real contact with its world-environment? Are we at last simply condemned to be desperately impaled on the horns of the Cartesian antinomy between the thinking subject and that which is "extended" in space, and is there no escaping the hopelessness of this kind of primitive dualism?

Of one thing at least Coleridge's studies in Schelling had made him certain, that propositions of the order of "I am" cannot be collapsed into propositions of the order of "it is" and that indeed the reverse is also the case, that propositions of the order of "it is" cannot be collapsed into propositions of the order of "I am": whistling one's way, in other words, into some monistic idealism or into some monistic materialism offers no real escape from the presumed disjunction between the knowing subject on the one hand and the object which is known on the other. There is, in short, no erasing the difference between the knower and the known, between the Subject and the Object. Yet the fact remains that the knower is what he is by virtue of that which he knows. For the self to be conscious is for it to be conscious of the not-self. Which is to say that the most immediate datum of experience involves a certain coadunation of the perceiver and the perceived, of the self and the not-self: the "I," in so far as it is conscious, is always conscious *of*, so that, at least from the standpoint of the human order, reality itself is the point of meeting between Subject and Object. Moreover, this meeting is not merely an affair of the mind's passively and mechanically registering that which is imprinted upon it by the "inanimate cold world"[40] without: on the contrary, "we receive but what we give,"[41] and this "ennobling interchange / Of action from without and from within"[42] is on *our* side facilitated by what Coleridge denominates as the Imagination—"that reconciling and mediatory power, which . . . [in] organizing (as it were) the flux of the Senses by the permanence and self-circling energies of the Reason, gives birth to a system of symbols, harmonious in themselves, and consubstantial with the truths, of which they are the conductors."[43]

No sooner, of course, do we ask what the things are which the Imagination reconciles and between which it mediates than we begin to realize how much Coleridge's doctrine of the Imagination is but one ingredient of his general theory of the mind. This is a theory very largely founded on his distinction between "reason" and "understanding"—to establish which, as he says in the *Biographia*, "was one main object of *The Friend*."[44] And, indeed, though he returns to the issue again and again in the *Aids to Reflection* and *The Statesman's Manual*, his clearest statement of the distinction is to be found in the first volume of *The Friend*, at the point where he says:

> I should have no objection to define Reason with Jacobi, and with his friend Hemsterhuis, as an organ bearing the same relation to spiritual objects, the Universal, the Eternal, and the Necessary, as the eye bears to

material and contingent phaenomena. But then it must be added, that it is an organ identical with its appropriate objects. Thus, God, the Soul, eternal Truth, &c. are the objects of Reason; but they are themselves *reason*. . . . Whatever is conscious *Self*-knowledge is Reason; and in this sense it may be safely defined the organ of the Super-sensuous; even as the Understanding wherever it does not possess or use the Reason, as another and inward eye, may be defined the conception of the Sensuous, or the faculty by which we generalize and arrange the phaenomena of perception: that faculty, the functions of which contain the rules and constitute the possibility of outward Experience.[45]

Now students of Coleridge do not win much profit by fidgeting over the question as to how deeply he was indebted to Kant's *Vernunft* and *Verstand* for his "Reason" and "Understanding": the latter may in some degree represent a special adaptation of the former, but what is basically at issue is a distinction between reason in its intuitive and in its discursive mode, a distinction which had entered the philosophic tradition long before Kant and which Coleridge might indeed be presumed to have had more immediately at hand by way of the Cambridge Platonists, for whom he kept a constant affection. In any event, to whatever degree the distinction itself may have been derived from other thinkers, his own motive for invoking it was his desire to account for the mind's ability to grasp at once particulars and universals. "Every man," he says, "must feel, that though he may not be exerting different faculties, he is exerting his faculties in a different way, when in one instance he begins with some one self-evident truth . . . and in consequence of this being true sees at once, without any actual experience, that some other thing must be true likewise . . . or when, in the second instance, he brings together the facts of experience, each of which has its own separate value, . . . and making these several facts bear upon some particular project, and finding some in favour of it, and some against it, determines for or against the project, according as one or the other class of facts preponderate."[46] And his point is that Understanding, being "the science of phaenomena," is operative in the latter case, whereas Reason, being "the organ of the supersensuous," is operative in the former. "The ground-work, therefore, of all true philosophy is the full apprehension of the difference between the contemplation of reason, namely, that intuition of things which arises when we possess ourselves, as one with the whole . . . and that which presents itself when . . . we think of ourselves as separated beings, and place nature in antithesis to the mind, as object to subject, thing to thought, death to life. This is abstract knowledge, or the science of the mere understanding."[47]

But, now, as Walter Jackson Bate has shrewdly remarked, given Coleridge's thoroughgoing organicism, his conviction that the world requires to be understood as a living whole, he was bound to feel some embarrassment at having himself construed the mind as a duality between two separate faculties. Just as the locus of the real in the natural world is neither the particular nor the universal but rather those actualities in which universals and particulars are to be found reciprocally bearing witness to each other, so, too, the mind itself must surely be capable of conjoining and fusing the insights that are delivered by the Reason and the Understanding.[48] And Coleridge conceived the bridge between the two to be the Imagination: this is the "synthetic and magical power" that "blends, and (as it were) *fuses*, each into each."[49]

The famous passage on the Imagination in the *Biographia* indicates, of course, that he considers it to present itself in two modes:

> The IMAGINATION . . . I consider either as primary, or secondary. The primary IMAGINATION I hold to be the living Power and prime Agent of all human Perception, and as a repetition in the finite mind of the eternal act of creation in the infinite I AM. The secondary Imagination I consider as an echo of the former, co-existing with the conscious will, yet still as identical with the primary in the *kind* of its agency, and differing only in *degree*, and in the *mode* of its operation. It dissolves, diffuses, dissipates, in order to recreate; or where this process is rendered impossible, yet still at all events it struggles to idealize and to unify. It is essentially *vital*, even as all objects (*as* objects) are essentially fixed and dead.[50]

And I. A. Richards, who seems occasionally to have had a genius for trivializing Coleridge's thought, was clearly intending to debilitate "the oracular sublimity of . . . [his] definition of [the Primary Imagination]"[51] when he rendered its import as involving nothing other than that "normal perception that produces the usual world of the senses, . . . the world of motor-buses, beef-steaks, and acquaintances."[52] But, as Basil Willey more properly says, "Coleridge is here summarizing the great struggle and victory of his life—his triumph over the old tradition of Locke and Hartley, which had assumed that the mind in perception was wholly passive."[53] True, the world which the Primary Imagination gives us may, at this point or at that, be an affair of motor buses and beefsteaks, but what Coleridge wants to emphasize is the essentially creative act being performed by the mind in the most ordinary acts of perception: he wants to say that it knows what it knows not by dint of any merely passive reception of the great world without but as a result of that labor of coordination, composition, and construction which it performs upon those manifolds of raw sense data that are presented by the natural order.

But, then, if we are to find ours to be a world so invested with *value* as to be a satisfactory dwelling place for the human spirit, it is not enough to make do merely with the quotidian reality provided by the Primary Imagination. Through that energy with which it orders the myriad influxions of Nature that crowd in upon us, the mind gives us a *world*, but it must undertake a still further exertion if we are to apprehend "the *Natur-geist*, or spirit of nature" which indwells all things and which "puts the form together"[54]—otherwise, we shall face an "inanimate cold world" and shall find ourselves dealing with nothing more than "fixities and definites" which *as objects* "are essentially . . . dead." And it is this further labor of the mind which is the province of the poetic imagination, or of what Coleridge calls the Secondary Imagination. Unlike the faculty he calls Fancy—which, to be sure, "has no other counters to play with, but fixities and definites"[55]—the Secondary Imagination "dissolves, diffuses, dissipates, in order to recreate . . . [and] to idealize and . . . unify." And what it dissolves and dissipates is the cold, inanimate, routinized, banal world of the daily round—(in William James's phrase) that "big blooming buzzing confusion" through which *l'homme moyen* somnambulates his way from Monday to Tuesday to Wednesday. As the late Irwin Edman said many years ago in his fine little book *Arts and the Man* (unfortunately, now well-nigh forgotten),

> Just as meat to the dog is something to be eaten, and the cat simply something to be chased, so the chair to a tired man or an executive is simply something to be sat on; and to the thirsty man water, however lovely its flow or sparkle, simply something to be drunk. The man of affairs intent upon future issues or the next step, the scientist interested in some special consequence of the combination of two elements, the hungry or the lustful intent upon the fulfillment of one absorbing and immediate desire—all these hasten from moment to moment, from object to object, from event to event. Experience is a minimum and that minimum is bare. Only one aspect of its momentary practical or impulsive urgency is remembered; all else is forgotten or more precisely ignored.[56]

And the world described in this passage is, of course, the world of the

Primary Imagination; it is, as Edman would say, a world full of "dead spots," everywhere crusted over with stereotypes, with the commonplace, with staleness and vapidity; it is a world robbed by common usage of any loftiness or glory. But, then, Coleridge invites us to think of how a Shakespeare deals with experience. He cites the passage from *Venus and Adonis* in which Shakespeare speaks of a lark at daybreak: "the gentle lark"

> From his moist cabinet mounts up on high,
> And wakes the morning, from whose silver breast
> The sun ariseth in his majesty;
> > Who doth the world so gloriously behold,
> > That cedar-tops and hills seem burnish'd gold.

Here, as Coleridge wants to say, is an example of how the poetic imagination renovates and reinvests with life the spiritless, prosaic world of everyday, "so carrying on the eye of the reader as to make him almost lose the consciousness of words—to make him *see* everything—and this without exciting any painful or laborious attention, without any *anatomy* of description . . . but with the sweetness and easy movement of nature."[57] Indeed, to handle the materials of experience in this way is, he declares, "to give the charm of novelty to things of every day . . . by awakening the mind's attention from the lethargy of custom, and directing it to the loveliness and the wonders of the world before us; an inexhaustible treasure, but for which, in consequence of the film of familiarity and selfish solicitude we have eyes, yet see not, ears that hear not, and hearts that neither feel nor understand."[58]

This work of renovation which the poetic imagination performs is not, however, a matter of any kind of mere embroidery: its struggle "to idealize and to unify" does not come down simply to smartening things up by ornamentalizing them, by decking them out in ornate and showy trappings. This may be the intention of Fancy, which tends to be something indolent and frivolous, but the poetic imagination is aiming at something much more serious. For since it "is essentially *vital*, even as all objects (*as* objects) are essentially fixed and dead," it wants, as we may say, to unfix and then to refix that which the Primary Imagination has already fixed—in cliché.

In that passage in *The Notebooks* which forms the epigraph of this chapter Coleridge suggests that the products of the Primary Imagination are an affair of "*fixation*," and he proposes that it is the business of the poetic imagination to *un*fix and to melt and bedim that which is fixed.* He knew, of course, that it is in the very nature of the kind of cognitive act performed by the Primary Imagination to "fix" this and to "fix" that *as an object of reflection*, but, in his sense of reality, in point of fact, the things and creatures making up the actual world are not at all "fixed" (and dead). True, their being "fixed" is a necessity of discursive thought apart from which (at the level of the Primary Imagination) human experience would never be organized in the way in which it must be if we are to take dominion of the world and have at our disposal the order of "facts." But, finally, the world is something more than a myriad of isolated, determinate "facts": it is, as Coleridge conceived it, a seamless garment in which the "facts," though preserving their identity, yet melt into one another to form the living whole that proceeds from "the infinite I AM." And, in his view, it is this to which the enabling impulse of the poetic imagination makes it eager to bear testimony.

His map of the mind—as it involves Reason, Understanding, Fancy, the Primary Imagination, and the Secondary Imagination—may not, of course, strike his readers today as particularly attractive. But there is at least one passage in the *Biographia* that needs to be pondered by those who are inclined to respond impatiently to what may at first appear to be his large reliance on a cumbrous Faculty Psychology, and it ought to suggest that Coleridge was far from being anybody's fool. It is the passage in which he says:

---

*In the passage referred to (Entry No. 4066 of *The Notebooks*) Coleridge, to be sure, is actually speaking not of the Primary Imagination but of Fancy—which, as he suggests, *fixes* that which the poetic imagination "unfixes." But this same figure of "fixing" would seem equally applicable also to the work of the Primary Imagination. True, the Primary Imagination, unlike Fancy, is essentially creative, for it dissolves the chaos of raw sensory experience in such a way as to give us all the myriad *Gestalten* apart from which the daily conduct of practical life would be impossible. And thus, given this creativeness, the Secondary Imagination (or the poetic imagination) may be said to be identical with the Primary "in the kind of its agency." But the world of the Primary Imagination is a world of "familiarity and selfish solicitude" that requires itself in turn to be "*un*fixed." And, indeed, Entry No. 4066 of *The Notebooks* indicates that, finally, Coleridge himself is by way of conflating the Primary Imagination and Fancy. Here he speaks of Fancy as "the imagination in its passive sense"—which would seem, of course, to mark its difference from the Primary Imagination, which, in the labor of synthesis it performs on sense-data, represents an *active* principle. Fancy, we are told, gives us merely "fixations" of our experience which must be "unfixed" by the poetic imagination: yet, as he says, apart from these "fixations," "there would be . . . no distinct perception or conception." And, since it is the Primary Imagination which makes perception possible, Coleridge appears, then, clearly in effect to be setting aside any sharp distinction between it and Fancy.

The office of philosophical *disquisition* consists in just *distinction*; while it is the privilege of the philosopher to preserve himself constantly aware, that distinction is not division. In order to obtain adequate notions of any truth, we must intellectually separate its distinguishable parts; and this is the technical *process* of philosophy. But having so done, we must then restore them in our conceptions to the unity, in which they actually co-exist; and this is the *result* of philosophy.[59]

In other words, though the mind performs various operations which require to be distinguished from one another, it is in its own fundamental nature essentially one. And, indeed, when it is at full stretch, when it is, as Wordsworth would say, seeing "into the [very] life of things" (*Tintern Abbey*), the word Coleridge wants always to use is "imagination." His distinction between the Primary and the Secondary Imagination must perhaps stand, though one may yet wonder about the appropriateness of the latter, the poetic imagination, being declared to be "an echo" of the former, since its task is not at all that of "fixing" objects *as objects* but of unfixing—and thus of "idealizing" and "unifying"—that which, *as fixed*, exudes something like a kind of death.

But, however it may be necessary to understand the relation between what Coleridge laid down as the two modes of imagination, it is at least clear, as Walter Jackson Bate rightly says, that it is the poetic imagination which represents "the highest exertion . . . that the 'finite mind' has to offer,"[60] and this effort moves, ultimately, toward a joyous discovery of that "interpenetration of man and nature" which at last permits the distinction between Subject and Object to be quite overcome. What is here at issue is the distinction than which there is none dearer to Coleridge, the distinction between *natura naturata* and *natura naturans*. *Natura naturata*—"nature natured"—is the stale, fixed, empty, dead world that is established by the Primary Imagination. And, when the poet undertakes to do nothing more than slavishly to copy or reproduce in some way this world, Coleridge can only sigh, "what an emptiness, what an unreality there . . . is in his productions . . . !"[61] But *natura naturans*—"nature naturing"—is something altogether different, and when the poet undertakes, as he ought, "to make the external internal, the internal external,"[62] this is what he apprehends and discloses in turn to us, *natura naturans*, a world striving to fulfill itself, a world instinct with energy and life, between which and ourselves a strange and marvelous bond is discovered. "Believe me," he says, "you must master the essence, the *natura naturans*, which presupposes a bond between nature in the higher sense and the soul of man."[63]

Now it is at this point that we begin, indeed, to approach the real heart of Coleridge's understanding of the work and mission of the poetic imagination. For he conceives its principal task to be that of breaking down all the barriers between "the Percipient & the Perceived," in order that we may "see into the *Life* of Things."[64] And he takes it for granted that we all need to be brought to something like that crucial moment of grace at which the Ancient Mariner finally arrives. This skinny little vagrant, after embarking as a member of the crew on a ship heading toward the equator, finds his vessel being driven by storms into that frigid region in the vicinity of the South Pole. For days it drifts through the treacherous waters in mist and snow, the sailors being transfixed with terror by the fearful sounds of the cracking and growling ice. Then at last there comes through the fog an albatross—which the sailors hail "As if it had been a Christian soul." "It ate the food it ne'er had eat, / And round and round it flew," proving indeed to be a bird of good omen, for, gradually, the helmsman is able to steer the ship through the fog, as favorable south winds spring up behind. But the albatross does not desert the ship: it continues to follow and comes "every day, for food or play, . . . to the mariners' hollo." There comes a day, however, when, strangely and suddenly, the Mariner commits an act of motiveless malignity: he takes up his crossbow and fatally wounds this kindly and beneficent bird that had "made the breeze to blow." At first his mates are severe in their condemnation, but, after a time, as their voyage appears to be prospering, they change their minds: "'Twas right, said they, such birds to slay, / That bring the fog and mist"—and thus they themselves become accessories to the crime. But their good fortune lasts not long, for the breezes abate after a time: the sails drop down, and, under "a hot and copper sky," the ship idly rests upon the "painted ocean" day after day. Its water supplies now exhausted, the men's tongues wither at the root, and they turn their "evil looks" upon the Mariner: "Instead of the cross, the Albatross / About my neck was hung." At last, their "throats unslaked" and their "black lips baked," they begin to collapse. "With heavy thump, a lifeless lump, / They dropp'd down one by one." And the Mariner, now "all alone . . . on a wide, wide sea" with his remorse and shame, looks up to heaven and tries vainly to pray and looks down upon the sea where he descries only "a thousand slimy things." But, then, there comes a moment when, as he looks down at water snakes frolicking in the ship's shadow, he finds himself blessing them:

Beyond the shadow of the ship,
I watched the water-snakes:

They moved in tracks of shining white,
And when they reared, the elfish light
Fell off in hoary flakes.

Within the shadow of the ship
I watched their rich attire:
Blue, glossy green, and velvet black,
They coiled and swam; and every track
Was a flash of golden fire.

O happy living things! no tongue
Their beauty might declare:
A spring of love gushed from my heart,
And I blessed them unaware:
Sure my kind saint took pity on me,
And I blessed them unaware.

The self-same moment I could pray;
And from my neck so free
The Albatross fell off, and sank
Like lead into the sea.[65]

Here is, of course, the great moment of the poem, the moment in which the Mariner cries out, "O happy living things!"—and, in doing so, not only finds that he can bless but also finds himself blessed as well. And it is precisely such a discovery as his of "the chain of love which binds human society and the universe,"[66] it is precisely this that Coleridge considers it to be peculiarly within the province of the poetic imagination to induce. The Primary Imagination, which "fixes" things *as things*, is surely not at work, as Coleridge would say, in the transformation which the Mariner's sensibility undergoes. For the Mariner is at last looking at the water snakes not merely *as snakes*, as so many slimy things of the deep; on the contrary, he is seeing them "with the sweetness and easy movement of nature"; he is seeing them with "the deep power of Joy"[67]—which is for him to see them not with the eyes of the Primary Imagination but with the eyes of the poetic imagination. And the special kind of receptivity which Coleridge calls "Joy" is, as he says in the Ode on "Dejection,"

    the spirit and the power,
Which wedding Nature to us gives in dower
    A new Earth and new Heaven,
Undreamt of by the sensual and the proud.[68]

Joy—which is (in Dorothy Emmet's happy formulation) that "state in which the imagination can wait, and watch for its chance"[69]—is that, in other words, which engenders the kind of profound rapport with the world that is of the very essence of poetic apprehension. In short, Joy *is* liberation from those "fixities and definites" that exude nothing but death.

Now to see, as the poetic imagination does, with "more than an act of mere sight," to see in such a way as to "be possessed . . . by . . . [the] sole self"[70] of what one faces, is to be brought into view of our weddedness to Nature and of what Coleridge considers to be the really great thing—namely, that all the creatures of earth are caught up within *One Life*,

> the one Life within us and abroad,
> Which meets all motion and becomes its soul,
> A light in sound, a sound-like power in light,
> Rhythm in all thought, and joyance every where.[71]

An entry of 1799 in *The Notebooks* records his readiness to "make a pilgrimage to the burning sands of Arabia, or &c &c to find the Man who could explain to me that there can be oneness."[72] In a letter to his friend William Sotheby in 1802 (10 September) he says: "Nature has her proper interest; & he will know what it is, who believes & feels, that every Thing has a Life of its own, & that we are all *one Life*."[73] And this emphasis on the One Life, as it is sounded over and again, strikes one of the great ground notes of his thought.

But in what does this One Life consist? What is the character of this oneness? It is the answer to this crucial question that is given, perhaps more clearly than at any other point, in a fascinating passage in one of the essays in *The Friend*. He says:

> Hast thou ever raised thy mind to the consideration of existence, in and by itself, as the mere act of existing? Hast thou ever said to thyself thoughtfully, It is! heedless in that moment, whether it were a man before thee, or a flower, or a grain of sand? Without reference, in short, to this or that particular mode or form of existence? If thou hast indeed attained to this, thou wilt have felt the presence of a mystery, which must have fixed thy spirit in awe and wonder. The very words, There is nothing! or, There was a time, when there was nothing! are self-contradictory. There is that within us which repels the proposition with as full and instantaneous light, as if it bore evidence against the fact in the right of its own eternity. Not TO BE, then, is impossible: TO BE, incomprehensible. If thou hast

mastered this intuition of absolute existence, thou wilt have learnt likewise, that it was this, and no other, which in the earlier ages seized the
nobler minds, the elect among men, with a sort of sacred horror. . . . It
was this which, raising them aloft, and projecting them to an ideal distance from themselves, prepared them to become the lights and awakening voices of other men, the founders of law and religion, the educators
and foster-gods of mankind.[74]

Coleridge is here probing the experience of what the distinguished
theologian of our own period, the late Paul Tillich, called "ontological
shock."[75] It is the experience one has when, for whatever reason, one
finds oneself asking the question, "Why is there something; why not
nothing?" And, as Tillich reminded us—as, indeed, Coleridge is also
reminding us—to ask the question is to be shocked into the realization
that one cannot go back *behind* Being. "If one asks why there *is* not
nothing, one attributes being even to nothing. Thought is based on
being, and it cannot leave this basis."[76] Or, as Coleridge says, "The
very words, There is nothing! or, There was a time, when there was
nothing! are self-contradictory." But, then, given "this intuition of absolute existence" or of the supremacy of Being, Coleridge goes on to
ask how we shall name the power which gives rise to "this idea of
Being, Being in its essence, *Being* limitless. . . . Whence did it come?"[77]
Well, he says:

To no class of phenomena or particulars can it be referred, itself being
none: therefore, to no faculty by which these alone are apprehended. As
little dare we refer it to any form of abstraction or generalization: for it
has neither co-ordinate or analogon! It is absolutely one, and that it *is*,
and affirms itself *to be*, is its only predicate. And yet this power, nevertheless, is! In eminence of Being it IS! And he for whom it manifests itself in
its adequate idea, dare as little arrogate it to himself as his own, can as little appropriate it either totally or by partition, as he can claim ownership
in the breathing air, or make an enclosure in the cope of heaven. He bears
witness of it to his own mind, even as he describes life and light: and,
with the silence of light, it describes itself and dwells in *us* only as far as
we dwell in *it*. The truths, which it manifests are such as it alone can
manifest, and in all truth it manifests itself. By what name then canst thou
call a truth so manifested? Is it not *revelation*? Ask thyself whether thou
canst attach to that latter word any consistent meaning not included in
the idea of the former. And the manifesting power, the source and the cor-
relative of the idea thus manifested—is it not GOD? Either thou knowest it
to be GOD, or thou hast called an idol by that awful name![78]

So, then, the "bond between nature in the higher sense and the soul of man," "the one Life within us and abroad," the chain that binds the human spirit to all the things and creatures of earth, even to a flower or a grain of sand, is nothing less than Being itself. And the poet, in "imitating" not the thing *as thing* but the *Geist* within the thing, gives us (in Wordsworth's phrase) a "sentiment of Being," of that which by its indwelling of all things makes them, for all their infinite multitudinousness, finally One. Indeed, it is on this, as Coleridge would say, that the "dignity of poetic Imagination" ultimately rests, on its conveyance to us of presentiments of the immanence within the natural order of an infinitude beyond "the light of sense" whose fullest manifestations can only be called *revelation*—and "the manifesting power, . . . is it not GOD?"

It would seem, indeed, that the doctrine of the poetic imagination (or of the Secondary Imagination) is in Coleridge far more crucially the linchpin of his philosophy of religion than of his literary aesthetics. Certainly it is from his writings that there emerges one of the great statements of the modern period regarding the formative role played by the imagination in the establishment of a religious perspective on the world. But, within the terms of his vision of the One Life and of the pervasive presence of Being in all things, is not the poetic imagination by way of being made the handmaiden of that which causes *every*body, it seems, the orthodox and the heterodox alike, alarm—namely, pantheism? H. D. Traill in the 1880s descried a pantheistic tendency in Coleridge's thought,[79] and during the past hundred years such an estimate has been rendered by many others—a recent judgment being that of the distinguished British philosopher and theologian D. M. MacKinnon, to the effect that his version of the "ontological argument" entails "metaphysical implications of a deeply pantheistic kind."[80] The whole question has, of course, been studied more exhaustively by Thomas McFarland than by anyone else, and he thoroughly documents how much Coleridge's struggles with Spinoza, Leibniz, Jacobi, and Schelling paradoxically reflect at once his attraction to and his immense detestation of any sort of pantheistic monism.[81] Nor should it go unremarked that at least Coleridge himself conceived it to be the great purpose of his theological work "to overthrow Pantheism . . . [and] to establish the diversity of the Creator from the sum whole of his Creatures."[82] Moreover, he was convinced that pantheism could be overthrown only from the standpoint of a Trinitarian doctrine of God: "We must go," he said, "either to the Trinity or to Pantheism."[83] But, then, as it may be objected, that unity (or "consubstantiality") of Being which it is the unique office of the poetic imagination to discern and the manifesting power behind which requires to be called God—this, as it may be argued, would appear in the Coleridgean account to be something more aboriginal than the distinctions within the Godhead itself of Father, Son, and Holy Spirit: it would seem to be (if, indeed, the Godhead is triune in character) something like the *"ground* for the Trinity, or, in Coleridge's phrase, a *prothesis,* which is not in its own nature either triune or personal, but is merely the impersonal base from which the Trinity proper is evolved."[84] And thus, despite Coleridge's frequently expressed intention to be true to the witness of Scripture and the Oecumenical Councils, it may be also charged that his orthodoxy was by no means impeccable, given the degree to which he was by way implicitly of introducing into the Godhead "a process of development . . . which is incompatible with its immutable perfection, and with that golden position of the schoolmen that God is *actus purissimus sine ulla potentialitate.*"[85] This was the objection expressed by W. G. T. Shedd more than a century ago, and his contention then was that, no, "there is no latency in the Divine Being. He is the same yesterday, to-day, and forever."[86]

Now Shedd's estimate does no doubt fairly reflect that which the typical exponent of an *un*reconstructed Christian theism might still be expected to render. But the "neo-classical" theism of recent Christian theology is by no means so certain that immutability and impassivity are the attributes that an authentic Christian faith may be expected to impute to the Deity.

John Macquarrie, for example, reminds us that the very name of God, as disclosed to Moses in the great theophany at Mount Horeb—I AM THAT I AM—suggests how remote any notion of impassivity was at least from the ancient Israelites' understanding of Yahweh. For, though very early on, the name of Yahweh came to be associated with the Hebrew verb *hyh* or *hwh* (meaning "to be"), this verb meant for the Hebraic mind at once not only "to be" but also "to become," so that the name of God given unto Moses refers not to any principle of immutability but, rather, to "the ongoing process of being."[87] And Professor Macquarrie insists that this Hebraic understanding of Being as dynamic entails no contradiction or inconsistency. "Whatever becomes," he says, "must, in some sense, *already be*; yet the fact that it is becoming implies that it *is not yet* what it is on the way to becoming." And thus he reasons that, since that which *becomes* already in some sense *is*, Being must itself include an element of becoming and requires to be thought of not as "a static, changeless, undifferentiated ultimate"[88] but as dynamic and as containing within itself a principle of potentiality. He suggests also that, deeply rooted though the conception of God as Being is in the history of Christian reflection, it is precisely the doctrine of the Trinity which has safeguarded "a dynamic as opposed to a static understanding of God,"[89] since it represents (as, for example, in the whole idea of Perichoresis or "circumincession") the symbolic way in which the theological tradition has tried "to elucidate the picture of God as he appears in the biblical narrative and in the history of the Christian community"—as "a God who embraces diversity in unity; who is both transcendent and immanent; who is dynamic and yet has stability."[90] So the kind of objection to Coleridge that Shedd was raising more than a century ago may need itself to be regarded as something more than a little questionable.

But, tension though there may be perhaps between Coleridge's organicist-"dynamic" philosophy and the sort of theology he was developing in *The Friend, Aids to Reflection, Confessions of an Inquiring Spirit*, the *Opus Maximum*,[91] and *The Notebooks*, it is beyond the scope of our present purpose to assess the degree to which he did in fact succeed in reconciling these two phases of his total effort. For what wants most immediately to be pondered when his doctrine of the imagination is in view is the brilliant boldness with which he declared that "uncommitted energy" that Yeats was later to think of as defining the imagination[92] to be not so uncommitted after all. Freedom from all mechanism, from all necessitarianism, Coleridge did, to be sure, consider the imagination to represent, when it is healthy and vigorous. But it was a part of his genius to discern that, indeed, the surest sign of its health and vigor is the relentlessness with which it drives on toward a vision of the world as One and toward that which is the Ground of the unity of life. And thus it is his lengthened shadow that falls across all subsequent projects—Arnold's, Pater's, Santayana's, Stevens's, and Heidegger's—that seek to define the dependence of *fundamental* belief upon something like poetic vision.

3/ Arnold's Version of Transcendence— The *Via Poetica*

By the England over which Victoria presided we are bequeathed but three religious thinkers—John Henry Newman, Frederick Denison Maurice, and Matthew Arnold—who, by reason of the relevance of their legacies to contemporary discussions, appear to be genuinely living guides; and it is a considerable oddity of modern intellectual life that Arnold who is, of this great trio, the most truly prophetic figure should, from his own time unto ours, have been regularly responded to in a hostile and dismissive way.

Paul Ricoeur suggests that the hermeneutics of culture in the modern period may be thought of as having had two great styles, the one being determined by an intention to demystify received traditions and the other being distinguished by an intention to rehabilitate and salvage a heritage of proclamation and kerygma: he speaks of the former as "the school of suspicion" and of the latter as "the school of restoration."[1] And we will have no difficulty in assigning Marx and Nietzsche and Freud on the one hand or Newman and Karl Barth and Reinhold Niebuhr on the other to their proper spheres. But Arnold's career, like that of Rudolf Bultmann or Paul Tillich, resists being situated wholly on either side of the divide between a hermeneutic of suspicion and a hermeneutic of restoration, since it was committed at once to a project of iconoclasm and a project of retrieval. On the one hand, as he considered the condition of the Christian faith in the nineteenth century, he found himself confronting a religion which had "materialized itself in the fact, in the supposed fact," which had "attached its emotion to the fact, and now," as he said, "the fact is failing it"[2]—which meant, he felt, that candor required the exposure of how vaporous and illusory indeed was the "fact" on which orthodoxy had for so long been wont to rest its case. But, then, he was equally convinced that the real genius of the witness made by the Christian faith is in no wise consubstantial with the mythological accretions it has gathered in the course of its history, and thus he conceived it to be a part of his duty to try to rescue the heart and substance of the Gospel from its unthinking dogmaticians, for, otherwise, he knew that it was bound to be "touched with the finger of death." So, for all his concern to explode the old notions of literal inspiration in Scripture and to fashion a new version of the *theologia perennis*, it was with good reason that Arnold declared his to be "an attempt conservative, and an attempt religious."[3]

Indeed, it is just his way of uniting "suspicion" and "restoration" that nettled his contemporaries and that, as it would seem, is still felt to be his great offense. His radical friends on the Continent regarded his "attempt conservative . . . and . . . religious" as a timorous evasion of what was exigent in the religious situation of the time. And the champions of conventional orthodoxy were prepared to ask of Matthew Arnold as Newman had asked of Thomas Arnold, his father—"but is *he* a Christian?" In short, as he himself might have said (with one of his favorite Germanisms), the *Zeitgeist* was against him. And so, in some ways, it has remained ever since. The religious despisers of culture, of course, occupy pretty much the same ground today that they occupied a hundred years ago—though, to be sure, amongst the cultured despisers of religion a certain shift of position is sometimes observable, for, now, their preference seems often to be for a religion which, in resting on some form of the *credo quia absurdum*, invites dismayed bemusement over its immolation of intelligence: whereas (as I have elsewhere remarked) "when they confront a religion which is affirmative of the vitalities of culture and which looks toward some reciprocity between itself and those vitalities, they indignantly declare it to be a fraud,"[4] and there is much condescending talk about what a pity it is that the authentic substance of religion is by way of being scuttled.

So it is not altogether strange that, falling between these lines of force, the author of *St. Paul and Protestantism* (1870), *Literature and Dogma* (1873), and *God and the Bible* (1875) should be in some degree a casualty of a climate which during the past hundred years, in matters related to the religious enterprise, has tended (in both its secular and traditionalist quarters) to be intolerant of the particular platform Arnold elected—namely, that of conservative reform. And the animus of F. H. Bradley and T. S. Eliot—that he was merely engaged in "phrase-making" and "literary clap-trap,"[5] and that the phrasemaking involved a deplorable confusion of "poetry and morals in the attempt to find a substitute for religious faith"[6]—has become the controlling sentiment that informs what is now the well-nigh canonical verdict. Indeed, so much is this the case that one might be fairly confident in placing a large bet on his work having never been seriously consulted by that avant-garde within contemporary theology whose program, more than forty years after Rudolf Bultmann's launching of his *Entmythologisierung*, is perforce, however much Bultmann's scheme may be deemed requiring of modification, essentially his: which is to say that it is also that of Matthew Arnold, who may rightly be claimed to be the first major specialist of the modern period in "demythologization."

There were, of course, others before Arnold—most notably perhaps, the "left-wing" Hegelians David Friedrich Strauss and Ludwig Feuerbach, and those who followed in their line—who had undertaken in various ways to "naturalize" the Christian mythos, but it is Arnold's distinction to have attempted a reinterpretation of the Christian faith that aspired after a systematic consistency with those texts in which that faith finds its classical expression. True, his account of the animating intentionality of the biblical witness will now seem egregiously mistaken, but he did, nevertheless—unlike so many of the new radicals of his period—take it for granted that theological reconstruction, audacious as it needed to be, must be able to claim an essential continuity between its own forms and those of the original Christian witness, if, Christianly speaking, it is to carry any force. And it is his steadfast adherence to this fundamental assumption that, given the whole drift and aim of his theological program, makes him Bultmann's great progenitor in the nineteenth century.

In, as he called it, an "iron time / Of doubts, disputes, distractions, fears,"[7] Arnold found himself compelled to acknowledge that "There is not a creed which is not shaken, not an accredited dogma which is not shown to be questionable, not a received tradition which does not threaten to dissolve."[8] Yet, though pilgriming "between two worlds, one dead, / The other powerless to be born,"[9] this "foil'd circuitous wanderer" was keen enough to know that, nigh unto the end of the modern age, "two things about the Christian religion must surely be clear to anybody with eyes in his head"—the one being "that men cannot do without it; the other, that they cannot do with it as it is."[10]

But, as he listened to the buzz and hum of all the new gospels and postulations that were rushing into the public forums of his time, he also knew that what imperiled theistic religion far more than its own incoherences was the ever-increasing decline in the status of the imagination as an instrument of cognition. The extraordinary advances being realized by the new science and technology were—with the help of an H. T. Buckle, a T. H. Huxley, and a Herbert Spencer—fast intimidating the people of the age into identifying "reality" with the public operables comprising the physical world and "truth" with those verifiable assertions purporting to describe that reality. In short, given the collapse of traditional systems of belief, his contemporaries were, he felt, at the point of finding in science itself a beeline to a new metaphysical orientation, being prepared to regard the "certified" procedures of empirical inquiry as the one really valid way of escaping from the illusionism of outworn creeds. And Arnold knew that, were such a positivism to become triumphant in that part of our culture where assumption rules, it would have a blighting effect not only on religion but on that whole field of valuation which is in fact beyond the range of scientific judgment. So nothing more quickly stirred up his asperities than some precipitous and self-assured apologetic for modern scientism. In this regard, his witness was so frequently made from the standpoint of his concern for the conservation of literary values that we are often by way of assuming that his literary essays carry the main current of his work and that his theological authorship represents merely the musings of "a man of letters who occasionally forgot himself to the extent of writing books about religion."[11] But, as Basil Willey reminds us, this is quite seriously "to misconceive the true proportions of his work . . . [and] to miss his centre of gravity,"[12] for in point of fact he was most centrally concerned to defend the life of the imagination, whether in its aesthetic or its religious phases, against the imperialistic claims of modern positivistic science. And thus his theological work is deeply of a piece with his entire critical effort.

As one committed, however, to conservative reform, Arnold wanted in the 1870s to submit the received theological tradition to a very drastic surgery. He was convinced that, on the cardinal point, the conception of deity projected by traditional theistic supernaturalism—of "a great Personal First Cause," a "moral and intelligent Governor of the Universe,"[13] "a sort of magnified and non-natural man"[14]—was like a currency which, though once negotiable, has lost its cash value. Even, in the term that Arnold thrusts into anguished italics—even *"the *masses*,"[15] he felt, are fast approaching such a position as the French astronomer Laplace enunciated in his famous words to Napoleon: *Je n'ai pas besoin de cette hypothèse.* "The masses, with their rude practical instinct, go straight to the heart of the matter. They are told there is a great Personal First Cause, who thinks and loves, the moral and intelligent Author and Governor of the universe; and that the Bible and Bible-righteousness come to us from him. Now . . . they begin by asking what proof we have of him at all," for "they require to be able to ascertain that there *is* this Governor."[16] And, at least in this particular, Arnold was inclined to feel that the masses were far more clearheaded than a Wilberforce or a Pusey or even a Martineau would have allowed, since with him it was axiomatic that any theological account of the meaning of human existence must, if it is to have cogency, find its primal ground in the actualities of man's experience. Religion begins, as he insists over and over again, "with experience," with experience of "the Eternal not ourselves"; and whatever offers itself in the way of a theological proposition, if lacking any experiential basis, will manifestly fail to prove itself. When the Psalmist, in dwelling on the joy and peace that come from righteousness, says: "Thou art my hiding-place, thou shalt preserve me from trouble; if my delight had not been in thy law, I should have perished in my trouble"—he is speaking not as a mystagogue, for his declarations spring "from experience." Or when St. Paul meditates on the mystery of *necrosis*, on how "to die with Christ to the law of the flesh . . . [is] to live with Christ to the law of the mind," again, he is not spouting "mere theurgy,"[17] since the renewing power of identification with Christ has, as Arnold sees it (and as Ignatius of Loyola had seen it long before), proved itself in the rhythms of Christian experience. But Arnold's estimate of modern sensibility told him that, increasingly, all the metaphysical pontifications of "learned religion" about the "great Personal First Cause" were, indeed—for Mr. Higginbottom and Mrs. Stiggins and Mr. Bugg—but so much "theurgy." The doctors of theological science, he says,

> employ the word *God* with such extraordinary confidence! as if "a Great Personal First Cause, who thinks and loves, the moral and intelligent Governor of the Universe," were a verifiable fact beyond all question; and we had now only to discuss what such a Being would naturally think about Church vestments and the use of the Athanasian Creed. But everything people say, under these conditions, is in truth quite in the air.[18]

In short, the first principle governing Arnold's reflections on religion—and in this he is happily joined by virtually every major theologian of our own period—is that it is utterly futile for a system of faith to employ modes of thought that contradict the fundamental experience of the people of our age. And since he knew that his contemporaries—living in the world of Charles Darwin, James Clerk Maxwell, Michael Faraday, and Samuel Morse—were increasingly baffled by the notion of some sort of immutable, self-subsistent Being who, as the divine *Pantokrator*, controls the universe from "up there," he felt certain that this was a piece of metaphysical lumber (or, as he called it, a "piece of science,"[19] meaning pseudoscience) that must simply be relegated to the discard.

Though he is frequently taxed with having done so, Arnold was by no means, however, proposing, in the manner of Feuerbach, to convert "theology" without remainder into "anthropology." Indeed, the most basic reason for his impatience with traditional theism was that its doctrine of the *ens realissimum*, of the *deus faber*, did, as he felt, inevitably promote a kind of anthropomorphism that, at the level of *theos*, has the effect of nullifying what is radically transcendent in the ultimate otherness we descry (in Gerard Manley Hopkins's phrase) "deep down things"—so that we end up talking about "the Eternal not ourselves" as if it were "a man in the next street"[20] or "a sort of elder Lord Shaftesbury . . . infinitely magnified."[21] And *thus* to trust the anthropomorphic image for the handling of the question of transcendence is, as Arnold believed, very radically to misconceive that inexhaustible depth and ground of reality with which the religious imagination is actually engaged. For God—and "God," as he reminds us, is but a name[22]—is not "an infinite and eternal substance" or "the great first cause"[23] but "the Eternal not ourselves that makes for righteousness." Which is to say that, for Arnold, the referent of the monosyllable "God" is that prevenient reality (*what*ever it may be)—transcendentally other than ourselves—which faith discerns as assembling and holding together our world in such a way as permits us to feel that it is basically *for* us rather than *against* us. And he wants very much to insist on the "not ourselves," for, with him, again, it is a first principle that, ultimately, the religious enterprise concerns nothing that is a part of our own human equipment but has to do, rather, with something that is *totaliter aliter*—and which is to be spoken about (as it would be put in the ugly jargon of our own period) in a "nonobjectifying" way.

But the surgery to which Arnold was proposing to submit the *theologia perennis* was by no means limited to the cardinal premise of traditional theism. For his project also involved, in one of its most essential elements, a liberation of the Christian message from the mythological forms in which the biblical testimony embeds it. Given his dedication to "an attempt conservative and an attempt religious," he did not, of course, suppose that reconstruction could simply dispense with the biblical witness, for, in his own peculiar way, he wanted to give his suffrage to something like the traditional view of theology as *ministerium verbi divini*. He seems always to have felt, in other words, that any theological program claiming to set forth an authentic account of the Christian faith must seek not to cast aside the mythological forms of the biblical kerygma but, rather, to reinterpret them. And, indeed, his impatience with critical work in the mode of Bishop John Colenso[24] was, at bottom, due to his sense of its being *merely* negative and of its being calculated therefore to do little more, finally, than raise "a titter from educated Europe."[25] Yet, though he could not find in Colenso's *The Pentateuch and Book of Joshua Critically Examined* the requisite "tact" and "delicacy of perception," he was in no doubt at all about the necessity of a radical critique, for he was convinced that, unless the Christian Scriptures could be rescued from the clutches of Protestant bibliolatry, "a spirit of sober piety" stood no chance of surviving the corrosions of a secular age.

And, here, we are brought back to Arnold's word about the spiritual crisis of the age being consequent upon religion having "materialized itself in the fact, in the supposed fact," which "is [now] failing it." For this is the crucial formula on which he grounds his diagnosis of what is problematic in the modern situation. He is saying that the great mistake made by nineteenth-century Christianity, and indeed by the whole precedent tradition, has been that of taking the Christian message to be a system of objective truths about the universe, and this a system being supposed to have the status of fact as "fact" is conceived by empirical science. But now, says Arnold, this system is "failing," as modern scientific inquiry increasingly exposes the speciousness of its "factuality"—and the result is that "there is not a creed which is not shaken, not an accredited dogma which is not shown to be questionable, not a received tradition which does not threaten to dissolve." So, as he concluded, since something in us still vibrates to the essential story that Christianity tells about humankind, what is required is a bold new hermeneutical stratagem that, by cutting beneath the rigidified integuments of archaic myth, will reach the irrefragable truth in the Christian vision and render it invulnerable before any further meddling of scientific criticism.

Though Arnold in none of his writings is to be found to be a genuinely systematic thinker, it is in *Literature and Dogma* that he gives us the largest account of his program. Yet already, three years earlier, in his book of 1870, *St. Paul and Protestantism*, he is disclosing the kind of tack that he was consistently to take. For, here, it becomes apparent that he considers a hermeneutic of religion relevant to the modern scene necessarily to be one centrally focused on the problem of language. Which is not to say that Arnold is to be found advancing anything that, in these post-Wittgensteinian days of our misery, stands a chance of being regarded as a genuinely rigorous theory of language. But at least he saw with great clarity what must surely be the starting point of any such theory: namely, the recognition that, in its most fundamental semantic aspect, language has two main uses—which are (in the formulation of the late Philip Wheelwright) "to designate clearly as a means to efficient communication, and to express with maximum fullness."[26] Or, as Arnold would phrase it more simply, language may be used in a "scientific" way and in a "literary" way, and, as he began to argue in *St. Paul and Protestantism*, what has chiefly bedeviled Christian theological discourse in the modern period has been its persistence in attributing a "scientific" character to the "literary" language of religion.

The distinguished French Orientalist Ernest Renan was contending in his book of 1869 on St. Paul that, though, thanks to the efforts of Protestantism, he had long reigned as "the Christian doctor *par excellence*," his reign was at last coming to an end. But, no, says Arnold: though the Protestantism which has advanced its own interests by exploiting Paul may be coming to an end, "the reign of the real St. Paul is only beginning; his fundamental ideas, disengaged from the elaborate misconceptions with which Protestantism has overlaid them, will have an influence in the future greater than any which they have yet had,—an influence proportioned to their correspondence with a number of the deepest and most permanent facts of human nature itself."[27] And thus "the needful thing is . . . to rescue St. Paul" from Protestantism, or, as Arnold normally prefers to say, from "Puritanism," since he takes Puritanism, particularly in its Calvinist and Arminian forms, to be in the English-speaking world "the strong and special representative of Protestantism."[28]

The Puritan scheme—with its covenants of works and redemption, and its elaborate protocols of original sin and justification through imputed righteousness and predestination—is, as Arnold views it, distinguished above all else by the assurance with which it sets forth the many complicated arrangements contrived by God for the settlement of human destiny. Indeed, its way of rendering *Heilsgeschichte* in terms of an exceedingly intricate "machinery of covenants, conditions, bargains, and parties-contractors . . . could have proceeded from no one but the born Anglo-Saxon man of business, British or American."[29] Nor is it content with its own doctrinal ingeniousness: on the contrary, it wants very much to insist that its protocols are supported by the authority of St. Paul. And it is just here that a certain mischief is made, for what in St. Paul is trope and dramatic gesture the doctors of Protestantism convert into "scientific" propositions. The ancient Hebraic community, Arnold suggests, had "a much juster sense of the true scope and limits of diction in religious deliverances than we have,"[30] had indeed in its religious statements a veritable genius for a powerfully evocative poetic language: "so, to describe the vivid and figured way in which St. Paul . . . uses words," he speaks of him as "Orientalising."[31] When the biblical people, for example, say, "God is jealous, and the Lord revengeth" (Nahum 1:2), they are not aiming at a "scientific theology," no more than is Aeschylus in one of his great choric passages on guilt and destiny: no, they are "Orientalising." Or, similarly, when St. Paul tells us that "as by the offense of one judgment came upon all . . . even so by the righteousness of one the free gift came upon all men unto justification of life" (Romans 5:18), he, too, is "Orientalising," using as a vivid figure of rhetoric what the authors of the Westminster Confession use as a formal scientific proposition.

And so it is, Arnold contends, with the language of the Bible in general, as it also is with the entire range of what is today spoken of as the "first order" discourse of the religious imagination: it is a mythopoeic language characteristically lyrical and dramatic, and thus (in a word of Wilbur Marshall Urban's of which Arnold would have approved) "to lose the *vis poetica* is at the same time to lose the *vis religiosa*."[32]

"The language of the Bible, then," says Arnold, "is literary, not scientific language"—and so it is generally, as he would lay it down, with the "first order" language minted by the religious imagination: it is "language *thrown out* at an object of consciousness not fully grasped, which inspired emotion."[33] Indeed, as he urges, "the [very] word 'God' is used in most cases as by no means a term of science or exact knowledge, but a term of poetry and eloquence, a term *thrown out*, so to speak, at a not fully grasped object of the speaker's consciousness, a *literary* term, in short; and mankind mean different things by it as their consciousness differs."[34] True, the metaphysicians and theologians convert the literary term into a scientific term, when they begin to speak of God as "an infinite and eternal substance, and [as] at the same time a person, the great first cause, the moral and intelligent governor of the universe,"[35] but what Arnold calls "religion given"—

that is, religion in its "first order" mode—finds its most essential medium, he insists, not in the constructions of metaphysics and "scientific theology" but in the vaulting movement of the poetic imagination toward what Rudolf Otto was later to speak of as the *mysterium tremendum et fascinans*[36] (and what Arnold himself speaks of as "the Eternal not ourselves").

Indeed, man's tendency is "always to represent everything under his own figure,"[37] and thus the biblical people, as they meditated on that "dearest freshness deep down things," spoke of the Eternal as a Father, as the high and holy One who formed the earth and the world, as the Rock of our salvation who hears our cries and attends unto our prayers and whose mercy is from everlasting to everlasting. The Psalmist, for example, says: "The Lord is my light and my salvation; whom shall I fear? the Lord is the strength of my life; of whom shall I be afraid? . . . The Lord is my strength and my shield; my heart trusted in him, and I am helped." And all this, says Arnold (in the term he appropriates from Goethe), is *Aberglaube*, or "extra-belief." The immediate fact of experience is "the Eternal not ourselves," the *mysterium tremendum et fascinans*—or, as he likes to put it, "*the stream of tendency by which all things fulfill the law of their being.*"[38] But this *not ourselves*, this *stream of tendency*—which, as conceived by Arnold, may not be too far distant from the neoclassical theism of such thinkers as Alfred North Whitehead and Charles Hartshorne—does not become what Coleridge called a "living *educt* of the Imagination"[39] until it takes on that special kind of translucence which is bestowed upon it in some great *Aberglaube* through the agency of *theo-poiesis*.[40]

"*Extra-belief*, that which we hope, augur, imagine, is the poetry of life, and has the rights of poetry. But it is not science; and yet it tends always to imagine itself science, to substitute itself for science,"[41] and thus it requires always to be deciphered and interpreted—without any timidity or reserve. Most especially does Arnold consider it to be necessary to submit the Christian Scriptures to interpretation, since he takes it for granted that the primitive apostolic testimony is but a witness to the true Word—which is none other than the event of Jesus Christ. Protestant bibliolatry, to be sure, absolutizes the original preaching of this Word which is recorded in the New Testament canon, but the real object of this preaching, as Arnold supposes, was not its own exaltation but rather the unveiling of the Word that was incarnate in Jesus of Nazareth. So he assumes that cutting to the bone of *Aberglaube*, of the "extra-belief" in which the apostolic testimony is embedded, is something that is implicitly warranted by the very logic of the Christian kerygma itself.

Now it is just on this point that Arnold is very severely reprehended by one of his recent interpreters, Stephen Prickett, who argues that his basic hermeneutical position is riddled with incoherence and self-contradiction. For, says Mr. Prickett, Arnold's accordance of priority in the religious enterprise to the poetic imagination must necessarily commit him to a view of the poetic process as yielding insights that can be come by in no other way and that are indeed inseparable from their poetic form: "poetry" and the "truth" it apprehends must be held to be indivisible. But Arnold is in fact, as he insists, finally to be found electing quite a different view of the matter, since he is in effect by way of supposing that that which "lies behind poetry . . . can be distilled from it; the kernel can be broken from out of the shell."[42] And thus, as Mr. Prickett contends, "What Arnold calls the 'concrete' world of poetry and of religious language finally becomes a mere visible manifestation of an abstract 'reality' encompassed by scientific laws and non-figurative philosophic language."[43]

Such an objection to Arnold's procedure does itself, however, surely rest on a profound misconstruction of how it is that the "primal thinking" of the poetic imagination is properly to be appropriated in an age (as Arnold would have said) of "criticism." Mr. Prickett's assumption seems to be that it is rightly esteemed only when it is left uninterpreted and, as it were, unbroken. And, in this, he is no doubt joined by what occasionally appears in our own period to be a very considerable adversary movement harboring a great animus toward the whole enterprise of "interpretation." Interpretation, as Susan Sontag was saying some years ago (in a book significantly entitled *Against Interpretation*), tends inevitably to "deplete" the poetic universe and to set up what is merely "a shadow world of 'meanings.' "[44] It is, she contended, "the revenge of the intellect" on the world of the imagination; so her whole testimony lined itself up behind a manifesto which said, "In place of a hermeneutics we need an erotics of art."[45] And, weary as we may often now feel in this "postcritical" time of all the philology and exegesis that are a part of the weight of our modern inheritance, Susan Sontag's animadversions doubtless touch with some poignance one fiber of contemporary sensibility.

Yet, finally, there is no escaping the fact that the deliverances of the poetic imagination do give rise to thought.[46] Language—itself already drenched, by reason of its own nature, in the Idea—is, after all, the agency whereby they are set forth, and their most essential *matière* is nothing other than the stuff of human experience: so they "push toward speculative expression."[47] And most especially is this so with respect to the kind of material Arnold is handling in his theological essays—namely, those poetic representations that constitute a "language of avowal"[48] consequent upon an immediate encounter of a "precritical" people with the Sacred. For it is a part of "the distress of modernity,"[49] a part of its deep pathos, that we, having lived through the adventure of the Enlightenment and all that has followed in its wake, cannot stand (if unendowed with what is a most rare genius now for the naked encounter with religious reality) where the ancient doxologist who stuttered forth the Ninetieth Psalm stood—

> Lord, thou hast been our dwelling
> place in all generations.
> Before the mountains were brought
> forth, or ever thou hadst formed the
> earth and the world, even from ever-
> lasting to everlasting, thou art God.

This primitive naiveté of the religious imagination is simply not any longer available to those whose consciousness has been scored by the legacies of Descartes, Hume, Kant, Nietzsche, Freud, and Wittgenstein. Which is not, though, to say anything like what the young Dionysiacs of American "radical theology" in the 1960s were saying, that we live in a "secular city" that belongs to a time *post mortem dei*: it is, rather, to say, as Paul Ricoeur has so constantly insisted in these past years, that we are in a situation that requires us to aim not (by dint of some *sacrificium intellectus*) at the primitive naiveté of archaic man but at the "second naiveté . . . [which is] the postcritical equivalent of the precritical hierophany,"[50] and this of course being an achievement of interpretation, of "restoration," of hermeneutics—since "we are in every way children of criticism, and . . . [must, therefore,] seek to go beyond criticism by means of criticism, by a criticism that is no longer reductive but restorative."[51]

Now it is this "distress of modernity" that Arnold deeply understood. But, good hermeneut that he was, he never supposed that the *interpreter* posits the really decisive meanings and that the "language of avowal" is at last simply to be eliminated. On the contrary: he expects "the total man" never to allow his "Hellenism" to overmaster his "Hebraism," since, in our own late time, *Glaube* must necessarily be a refinement of *Aberglaube*. The reconstruction of the Christian message, for all the pertinence we may desire it to have to modern experience, must, in other words, begin with the testimony of the biblical people: as he says in a significant passage in *Literature and Dogma*, we must "take their fact of experience, . . . keep it steadily for our basis in using their language, and . . . see whether from using their language with the ground of this real and firm sense to it, as they themselves did, somewhat of their feeling, too, may not grow upon us."[52] In short, Arnold takes it for granted (*pace* Mr. Prickett) that the *Aberglaube* of the mythopoeic imagination constitutes "the unsubstitutable language of . . . [that] domain of experience that we . . . call the experience of 'avowal.' "[53] True, he refused to accord it any sort of talismanic status, for, as he protested, "after all, the Bible is *not* a talisman, to be taken and used literally."[54] But, nevertheless, he wanted to live within the aura of the biblical witness, steeped in *Aberglaube* as it may be, and his whole effort as an interpreter was calculated (whether successfully so or not being another question) to keep a strict continuity between his own reformulations and the original testimony, for, as he felt, the great thing which is never to be forgotten is that "poetry gives the idea, and it gives it touched with beauty, heightened by emotion."[55]

It is, then, by no means quite the case, as Stephen Prickett argues, that Arnold "constantly finds himself in the position of . . . attributing to poetry an importance . . . that his theory demands should be attached to the abstract concepts"[56] that may be extrapolated from poetry. Far from it: on the contrary, so paramount is the role that he accords the poetic imagination in the religious enterprise that it may, indeed, be said to be for him the very means of transcendence, the vital agent whereby we first "hail" the numinous, the *mysterium tremendum*, the *not ourselves*. And he is thus a major figure in that modern tradition reaching from Vico to Heidegger which says in effect that it is the office of the poet to name the Holy—though Arnold, like many of his confreres in this tradition (and, even perhaps strangely enough, Croce would need to be included amongst them), by "poet" would not mean the professional versifier but anybody who, finding himself required to express an *o altitudo!* before the surplusages of meaning thronged within the familiar realities of nature and history, undertakes to use a richly figurative language or "depth language"[57] by way of reckoning with that mysterious fecundity and plenitude of the world which appears to have a transcendent source.

Moreover, it is just in that aspect of his thought being reviewed here that we are to locate Arnold's immense relevance to the theological ferment of our own period. For ours is, of course, a time in which much of the most creative intelligence is, in one way or another, seeking to take what the avant-garde in German theology calls *ein Schritt zürück* (a step backward) behind the hardened protocols of theological tradition, in order newly to experience that primitive enthrallment by "the Eternal not ourselves" which originally gave birth to theological reflection. And, in its effort once again to become a truly "foundational" discipline, it is not surprising that recent theology should be rediscovering, as it frequently is, the peculiar talent of the poetic imagination for being an agency of primary truth. In this, it is doubtless the late Martin Heidegger who has been the most influential guide, but, long before this great sage began to issue such texts as *Erläuterungen zu Hölderlins Dichtung* and *Über den Humanismus* and *Holzwege* from the fastnesses of his little mountain village of Todtnauberg in West Germany's Black Forest, Matthew Arnold in the 1870s was undertaking—with, as it would seem when he is thought of in the context of his own period, even greater audacity—to suggest how inevitably and inseverably religion is grounded in the poetic imagination; and his theological essays surely deserve a far more sympathetic reading than they have generally received.

Nor will a really close reading of Arnold sustain the frequently iterated charge that his is a poetic that, in its tendency to promote a *religio poetae*, looks toward the fin-de-siècle aestheticism of the 1890s. Among recent commentators, it is William Madden who perhaps most forcefully brings forward this stricture, though he is but one of many others who have voiced a similar judgment.[58] And, admittedly, many of Arnold's aperçus lend themselves to such an interpretation—as, for example, the famous opening line of the essay on "The Study of Poetry" which says: "The future of poetry is immense, because in poetry, where it is worthy of its high destinies, our race, as time goes on, will find an ever surer and surer stay."[59] Or, again, in the late book that he entitled *Discourses in America* (1885), he tells us that poetry has "not only the power of refreshing and delighting us" but has "also the power . . . [of] fortifying, and elevating, and quickening"[60] us. But, though one may assemble a sizable number of passages in this mode, his intention surely is never to endorse such a religion *of* poetry as was later to be promoted by such a figure, say, as Oscar Wilde or by the young Yeats. The Wordsworthian strain in Arnold's thought is, of course, one of its most persistent elements, and he keeps always a strong sense of the healing and consolatory power of poetry. But, finally, he is not proposing to sponsor a *new* religion—of "the best that has been thought and said in the world" by its great poets; nor is he intending to offer poetry as a *surrogate* for the old religion of the prophets and the apostles. He wants rather to assign the poetic imagination merely a Virgilian function, as that which brings us into the precincts of the *not ourselves*—by (if the neologism may be permitted) *deconcealing* it, in the way that anything is made manifest when it is addressed by a language appropriate to its nature; and he assumes—as in varying ways Coleridge and Keble and Newman had done before him—that it is, indeed, in the language of the poetic imagination that the religious consciousness finds its primary vehicle.

But, then, beyond their various other strictures, Arnold's numerous hostile critics add the charge that, yes, with him religion is an affair of *mere* poeticizing and that he disallows any genuinely veridical claim in behalf of what it *says*. T. S. Eliot, for example, who was incorrigibly resistant to his testimony, laid it down that his books about Christianity "aim . . . to affirm that the emotions of Christianity can and must be preserved without the belief"; that he wants "to get all the emotional kick out of Christianity one can, without the bother of believing it"; and that "the effect of Arnold's religious campaign is to divorce Religion from thought."[61] Or, again, the late Lionel Trilling, in his handsomely designed book on Arnold, having convinced himself that the author of *Literature and Dogma* is by way of regarding religious discourse as a matter of *mere* poeticizing, says, in a particularly stringent passage: "That Christianity is true: that is, after all, the one thing that Arnold cannot really say. That Christianity contains the highest moral law, that Christianity is natural, that Christianity is lovely, that Christianity provides a poetry serving the highest good, that Christianity *contains* the truth—anything but that *Christianity is true*."[62] So Trilling suggests in effect that we think of Arnold as a type of that modernist whom Santayana (thinking particularly of the Catholic modernist, such as Loisy or Tyrrell) declared to be one who "has ceased to be a Christian to become an amateur, or if you will a connoisseur of Christianity."[63] And even Basil Willey, who is one of the most sympathetic interpreters of Arnold's religious thought,[64] is to be found suggesting in a recent essay[65] that his conception of poetic and religious language is convertible into that notion of "emotive" language as "pseudo-statement" which I. A. Richards was advancing in his famous early book, *Science and Poetry*.[66]

Now in Richards's scheme—which was, of course, an arrantly positivist scheme—the "pseudo-statement" is one for which, in contrast to the "certified statements" of scientific discourse, no veridical claim can be made, since (in his definition of it) it is "a form of words which is justified entirely by its effect in releasing or organizing our impulses and attitudes."[67] But nothing could be further from Arnold's understanding of religious discourse (or, more particularly, of Christian theological discourse) than Richards's notion of the pseudo-statement. "That Christianity is true: that is, after all, the one thing," Trilling maintains, "that Arnold cannot really say." Yet this, as one needs to insist, is precisely what he wants most to assert—namely, what he speaks of over and again in the *Last Essays on Church and Religion* as "the natural truth of Christianity." Liberalism was, he felt, increasingly tending to think of Christianity as untenable. "And therefore it is so all-important," he says, "to insist on what I call the *natural truth* of Christianity, and to bring this out all we can."[68] "I believe," he asserts in a characteristic sentence, "that Christianity will survive because of its natural truth."[69] And, in this, he was greatly enheartened by the tradition reaching from Hooker and the Cambridge Platonists through Bishop Butler to Coleridge.[70] For it was in this line of thought that he found support for his own view, that the truth of Christianity proves itself in experience, by the way it comports with " 'our natural sense of things.' "[71]

When Arnold spoke of "the natural truth of Christianity," he did not, in other words, have in mind the "natural religion" of any sort of deism, for, as Professor Robbins reminds us, "he was too much a child of Goethe and the scientific *Zeitgeist* ever to find in external Nature teleological evidence for the existence of a moral and beneficent Governor of the universe."[72] His insistence that "Christianity has natural truth" was, rather, prompted by his conviction that its account of the human situation finds its main confirmation in "the facts of experience," and it is in relation to these, he felt, that the Christian witness is to be "verified." When "they ask: 'How are we to *verify* that there rules an enduring Power, not ourselves, which makes for righteousness?'—we may answer at once: 'How? why as you verify that fire burns,—*by experience! It is* so; try it! you *can* try it.' "[73] "We hear the word 'verifiable' from Mr. Arnold pretty often," said F. H. Bradley with much disdain; but, as he declared, "such a tyro's question" as to what verification really entails it never occurred to him to raise.[74] Yet Arnold's position is by no means so naive as Bradley (and Trilling after him) would make it out to be, and, as Professor Robbins rightly suggests, it may in fact, for all the informality of its exposition, be seen as anticipating the "radical empiricism" of William James,[75] as it may also be felt to look toward the kind of empirical theology which on the American scene is associated with such thinkers as Henry Nelson Wieman and Bernard Meland, Charles Hartshorne and Schubert Ogden.

But, certain though he was of the "natural truth" of Christianity, Arnold was never for a moment by way of confusing this "natural truth" with scientific truth. Always, his contention is in effect that the mythopoeic language of religion is to be taken, as Reinhold Niebuhr was proposing in his Gifford Lectures, "seriously but not literally."[76] It is language "thrown out" at a vast object not fully grasped, at the Eternal not ourselves—and, as such, it wants (as he might have said had he been a contemporary of Kenneth Burke) to "dance out" our sense of the transcendent Mystery that lowers upon us.

So the fashionable line amongst commentators on Arnold during the past generation, that, in reducing religious discourse to an affair of *mere* poeticizing, he strips it of any ontological claim—this is, as any thorough and unbiased reading of his work ought to indicate, quite without substantial warrant. And it is equally mistaken, as Professor Livingston properly insists, to try in the manner of certain recent inter- preters to assimilate Arnold to the views of a post-Wittgensteinian thinker like R. B. Braithwaite.[77] True, Professor Braithwaite himself records his sympathy for Arnold's general outlook in his Eddington Lecture, *An Empiricist's View of the Nature of Religious Belief*, but his own position—that religious assertions are merely assertions of "an intention to carry out a certain behaviour policy"[78]—would seem to stand at a very great distance indeed from that of the author of *Litera- ture and Dogma* for whom the language of the religious imagination, poetic though it must necessarily be, carries genuine truth-claims, and claims that are experientially verifiable.

The total theory of interpretation, then, which emerges from Arnold's writings of the 1870s—from *St. Paul and Protestantism*, *Lit- erature and Dogma*, *God and the Bible*, and the *Last Essays on Church and Religion*—represents a structure of thought which, once it is res- cued from the scholiasts, may be seen to be a very considerable achieve- ment, and one that touches with great suggestiveness much that is currently at issue in the intellectual forums of our own period. Yet there is a striking pathos that appears in Arnold's career as a religious thinker, when one remarks, on the one hand, the extraordinary subtlety of his hermeneutical program and, on the other, the thinness of what it actually yielded in the way of restatement of the Christian faith.

His concern to set forth "the natural truth of Christianity" prompts him to embrace the view that "the object of religion is *conduct*,"[79] and he considers the difference between morality and religion to be but "a difference of degree." As he says, in one of his most frequently quoted passages, "Religion . . . is ethics heightened, enkindled, lit up by feeling; the passage from morality to religion is made when to morality is applied emotion. And the true meaning of religion is thus, not simply *morality*, but *morality touched by emotion.*"[80] So it is not surprising that he conceives " 'righteousness' . . . [to have been] in a special manner the object of Bible-religion,"[81] one of the great "master-words" indeed of both Testaments: for "the Hebrew people," he declares, "conduct . . . [was] three-fourths of our life and its largest concern,"[82] and the *not ourselves* which weighed so heavily upon them was "the Eternal not ourselves which makes for righteousness." Israel's most fundamental conviction was that "righteousness tendeth to life" (Proverbs 11:19), that "the righteous shall be recompensed in the earth" (Proverbs 11:31), and that "he that pursueth evil pursueth it to his own death" (Proverbs 11:19). But, to Israel's chagrined astonishment, it discovered, as the generations followed one another, that the strange cunning of history appeared to ordain that the *un*godly should prosper and that the earth should be "given unto the hand of the wicked" (Job 9:24). So, most especially as a result of all the humiliation brought by the Babylonic exile, Israel began to look toward the coming of a redeemer—the Son of Man, the Messiah—who would at last usher in "the kingdom of righteousness."

"Now," says Arnold, "it is clear that righteousness, the central object of Israel's concern, was the central object of Jesus Christ's concern also."[83] But, whereas "the kingdom of righteousness" had been for Israel a preeminently social-political reality which she herself was to administer, Jesus interiorized and spiritualized this whole conception. "Self-examination, self-renouncement, and mildness . . . were . . . the great means by which Jesus Christ renewed righteousness and religion,"[84] and, in his dispensation, finding one's own soul became the paramount issue. Moreover, whereas the Messiah had traditionally been expected to be a political strategist and a social revolutionist, he took "the humble, inward, and suffering 'servant of God' of the prophets . . . and . . . [elevated] *this* as the Messiah."[85] He "found Israel all astray, with an endless talk about God, the law, righteousness, the kingdom, everlasting life,—and no real hold upon any one of them."[86] So he "set going a great process of searching and sifting; but this process had for its direct object the idea of *righteousness*"[87]—most especially in regard to "faults of self-assertion, graspingness, and violence . . . which we may call faults of *temper* . . . and . . . [in regard to] faults of *sensuality*."[88] "To have the *heart* and *thoughts* in order as to certain matters, was conduct"—and "faults of *conduct* were what Jesus said the real commandments of God are concerned with."[89] This, says Arnold, was "the 'method' of Jesus": it was a method adjusted to the fact that man is defiled by the things that come from *within* his heart. So *metanoia* was his watchword, for he was aiming at a change of the *inner* man.

Then, as Arnold suggests, in addition to his *method* Jesus had also "a rule of action" which was his *secret*, and it was simply this: "He that loveth his life shall lose it; and he that hateth his life in this world shall keep it unto life eternal" (John 12:25). In other words, his "method" directed the disciple's eye inward, and "after putting him by his method in the way to find *what* doing righteousness was, by his secret Jesus put the disciple in the way of *doing* it."[90] And Arnold insists that this "method of inwardness" and this "secret of self-renouncement" find their verification in the universal experience of the race, since in no other way can we come by grace and truth and peace and all the felicities which the New Testament speaks of as "fruits of the Spirit."

Now "Jesus could not but use the dominant phrases of the Jewish religion, if he was to talk to the Jewish people about religion at all."[91] So he subsumed the old conception of "the Anointed Prince conquering the earth in the cause of righteousness" under his own preferred conception of "the mild and suffering servant of God"[92]—and then said: "He that believeth on me, believeth not on me, but on him that sent me" (John 12:44). True, his word that "I came forth from the Father" (John 16:28) has been pounced on, says Arnold, by the doctors of theological science and made the basis for elaborate Trinitarian schemes that speak of *persons* being *co-equal* and *co-eternal*, the Son being of one *substance* with the Father and the Spirit *proceeding* from the Father and the Son. But all this is *Aberglaube*, for the only "Paraclete that Jesus promised . . . was the Muse of *righteousness*; the Muse of the work-day, care-crossed, toil-stained millions of men,—the Muse of humanity."[93]

Or, again, says Arnold,

> the whole centre of gravity of the Christian religion, in the popular as well as in the so-called orthodox notion of it, is placed in Christ's having, by his death in satisfaction for man's sins, performed the contract originally passed in the Council of the Trinity, and having thus enabled the magnified and non-natural Man in heaven, who is the God of theology and of the multitude alike, to consider his justice satisfied, and to allow his mercy to go forth on all who heartily believe that Jesus Christ has paid their debt for them.[94]

But, as he urges, the *real* "centre of gravity of the Christian religion is in the *method* and the *secret* of Jesus."[95] His method did, to be sure, lead up to his secret, and his secret was dying to "the life in this world" and living to "the eternal life." And, since he was constantly "above the heads of his reporters," it is not surprising that their minds came to be ruled by "the miracle of the corporeal resurrection" which they declared him to have foretold. Yet, in Arnold's formulation, the simple truth of the matter is that, long before his crucifixion atop Mount Calvary, "Jesus had died, by taking up daily that cross which his disciples, after his daily example, were to take up also"—just as he "had risen to life long before his crowning Resurrection, risen to life in what he calls '*my joy*,' which he desired to see fulfilled in his disciples also."[96]

So Arnold finds the master-idea of the Gospels, the Pauline Epistles, the Epistle attributed to St. James, and the Epistle to the Hebrews—indeed, he finds the real "ground-thought" of the entire New Testament to be nothing other than *righteousness*, and this seen in the perspective of the *method* and the *secret* that form the center of Jesus' testimony.

"As time went on, and Christianity spread wider and wider among the multitudes, and with less and less of control from the personal influence of Jesus, Christianity developed more and more its side of miracle and legend; until to believe Jesus to be the Son of God meant to believe the points of the legend,—his preternatural conception and birth, his miracles, his descent into hell, his bodily resurrection, his ascent into heaven, and his future triumphant return to judgment."[97] All this, of course, is *Aberglaube*, "the *popular science* of Christianity," with which, however, Arnold wants not at all to be sharp, since, as he tells us, "for the popular science of religion one . . . ought to have . . . an infinite tenderness. It is the spontaneous work of nature, . . . the travail of the human mind to adapt to its grasp"[98] vast realities which are beyond its grasp. But, then, for all his impatience with bibliolatry, Arnold in his theological thinking was at least something of a biblicist: which is to say that, being unprepared to embrace anything comparable to Newman's doctrine of "development," he was eager to be sharp with "the *learned science* of Christianity,"[99] and all the incrustations that (by way of the Fathers and the Schoolmen and the doctors of the Reformation) this had added unto the *Aberglaube* of the apostolic people he conceived to be an unmitigated disaster. For the final effect of the *learned science* of the tradition is simply that of obscuring "the real 'essence of Holy Scripture' "—which, for the Old Testament, is "*To him that ordereth his conversation right shall be shown the salvation of God!*" and, for the New Testament, is "*Follow Jesus!*"[100]

In short, what he calls "the true greatness of Christianity" is for him wholly resident in the *method* and the *secret* of Jesus. And all else is "extra-belief."

Now this, as one is bound to conclude, is an account of the Chris- ✓
tian witness that skips with a vengeance. In Arnold's handling of biblical thought, his "demythologizing" intentions are, of course, admira-
ble. But, for all his desire to produce a true rendering of the essential
spirit and tenor of the Old Testament, so intent is he on finding it to be
nothing more than a manual of "righteousness" that he manages to
gloss it in such a way as completely to extrude its central and overriding
conception—namely, that Yahweh is a God of the Covenant, that the
People of God are a People of the Covenant, and that their relationship
with him is covenantally grounded. Nor, in sweeping aside Old Testament messianism as a bit of *Aberglaube* inessential to the basic structure of Hebraic thought, does he even begin to reckon with what is
interesting and genuinely profound in the interpretation of history
projected by biblical prophetism. And nowhere in his account of the
Hebraic sources of Christian theology does he attempt any serious estimate of how the Old Testament envisages what Walther Eichrodt
speaks of as "the cosmic powers of God."[101]

Similarly, in his version of the New Testament, of "religion new-
given," one marvels at what he contrives to elide. In this connection,
given his concern that everything, as it were, be hung on the teaching of
Jesus, it is quite extraordinary, for example, that his account of it
should, again, completely pass over its most vital and primary theme—
the Kingdom of God (which "is not a place or community ruled by
God" but "the power of God [which is] expressed in [his] deeds").[102]
And this fatal remissness is not unrelated to his failure in any way to
address himself to the eschatological dimension of the Gospels and of
the other pivotal texts in the New Testament canon. Nor can his rendering of Pauline thought (in *St. Paul and Protestantism*), for all its
occasional brilliance, be considered even minimally adequate, given its
well-nigh total neglect of what is so much of the essence of Paul's
theology—as it involves his analysis of sin, his very high Christology,
his doctrine of grace, and his doctrine of the Church.

Moreover, the offhandedness with which Arnold was inclined to
approach the great masters of Christian theology made it perhaps inevitable that his own theological work should prove to be something that,
as we feel, Irenaeus, Augustine, Anselm, Aquinas, Luther, Calvin, Pascal, and Schleiermacher would not even have barely recognized as belonging to the universe of Christian valuation. The Catholic modernist
George Tyrrell, looking back on Arnold's legacy from a remove of
scarcely a generation, found something repugnantly frigid in "Matthew
Arnold's 'righteousness' as the characteristic of the Divinity," a "sort
of university God, a personification of the Nicomachaean ethics,"[103]

which struck him as being of a piece with a whole theological style uncalculated to render an adequate justice to the distinctive genius of Christian theology. And one knows full well that, had they ever troubled to notice his theological writings, the judgments of Arnold that would have come, after Tyrrell, from Jacques Maritain, Karl Barth, Reinhold Niebuhr, and Paul Tillich would doubtless have been even more severe.

The English philosopher Renford Bambrough, in his interesting book *Reason, Truth and God*, suggests that Arnold ought to have said, " 'I do not and cannot accept *Christianity*, but I offer you what remains when its essential falsehood has been exposed and excised.' "[104] And the snappishness of tone in this dictum expresses the kind of condescension that nearly everybody permits himself when Arnold's religious thought is in view; but it hardly represents, as any close and sympathetic reading of his work should indicate, the appropriate attitude toward his whole undertaking. True, he kept a great concern to appease what he called "the hard-headed modern multitudes," but he did not count himself amongst those who supposed that by "public meetings, Church-disestablishment, marrying one's deceased wife's sister, secular schools, industrial development, man can very well live; and that if he studies the writings, say of Mr. Herbert Spencer into the bargain, he will be perfect, [and that] . . . the Bible is become quite old-fashioned and superfluous."[105] Indeed, his was an altogether different spiritual universe from that of such conventional Victorian agnostics as George Henry Lewes, John Morley, Henry Sidgwick, and Leslie Stephen. For him Christianity and its Bible were, as Basil Willey rightly says, "the pre-eminent sources of regeneration, the supreme inspiration to live the life of the spirit."[106] And his deep attachment to the English church would have made him feel it inconceivable that its services should be replaced "by ethical lectures and readings from Confucius or the Upanishads or J. S. Mill"[107] or Auguste Comte. But, profound as his devotion to the Christian faith was and for all the sincerity of his desire to produce a restatement of it for "the hard-headed modern multitudes" that would be a true rendering of its essential message, his theological effort did suffer a sad miscarriage—through what was finally, one feels, some failure of patience that kept him from *listening* to the tradition with the requisite tenacity and intentness.

Yet, unsatisfactory as his constructive efforts may be, they were consequent upon the definition of a hermeneutical program which itself represents one of the truly brilliant feats of the intellectual imagination in the nineteenth century; and it is that program, however miscarried it may have been in its execution, that certifies Arnold's high claim as a systematic thinker (to say nothing of the poet of "Empedocles on Etna," "Stanzas from the Grande Chartreuse," "The Scholar Gypsy," "Dover Beach," and "Thyrsis") to be regarded as one of the most creative strategists of religious reflection in the modern period. And most especially should this be thought to be so in the context of the present time, when, experiencing "the crisis of secularization" even more acutely than did the major Victorians (whose distinction it is in the English-speaking world to have been the first to have been traumatized by its impact), we feel with a special poignance the need to renovate the religious imagination by making it step once again (in Stevens's phrase) "barefoot into reality,"[108] but doing so in a manner plotted (at least in part) by the *via poetica*—which is precisely the project of which Matthew Arnold is one of our great modern masters.

4/ Pater's Imperative– To Dwell Poetically

I require of you only to look.
                    —St. Teresa of Avila

and yet poetically, dwells
Man on this earth.
                    —Friedrich Hölderlin

Though during the past twenty years Pater's writings have occasionally been discussed in thoughtful ways by academic specialists in Victorian studies, none of these reassessments has been quite radical and eloquent enough to win any fundamental reinstatement of his legacy for the educated public at large. Hillis Miller is no doubt right in regarding the richness of his work as entitling him to be accounted the peer of Cole-ridge and Arnold and Ruskin in the English nineteenth century.[1] And that the line descending in various ways from him should include such figures as Yeats and Proust, Santayana and Bernard Berenson, Roger Fry and Virginia Woolf, and Joyce and Wallace Stevens ought surely to suggest that he is one of the central strategists of modern intelligence. Yet it remains generally the case in the intellectual community of our period that the name Walter Pater tends only to awaken some impatient recollection of that dim episode of the Aesthetic Movement and the fin-de-siècle decadence of Swinburne and Wilde and the *poètes maudits* of the 1890s: a faint memory will be summoned up of an Oxford don who talked about our needing to burn with a hard, gemlike flame, but he and his message will seem very distant indeed from these late days of our own superiority.

As in the settling for our time of so many other reputations, T. S. Eliot played a decisive role in establishing such an image of Pater as has permitted countless people infinitely less distinguished than Pater himself to feel comfortable in their condescension toward him. In his famous essay of 1930, "Arnold and Pater," Eliot, quite drunk with his recently embraced Anglo-Catholicism, was eager to deal very severely with those who had sponsored one or another kind of "appropriation of religion into culture"—and the measure of his eagerness in this regard is the insult and denunciation which he intemperately directs upon both Arnold and Pater. Arnold, he tells us, had not "the power of connected reasoning at any length: his flights are either short flights or circular flights," so that nothing is to be found "in his prose work . . . [that] will stand very close analysis." Moreover, for all his concern to rehabilitate the Christian witness in an age of radical secularity, he aims merely "to affirm that the emotions of Christianity can and must be preserved without the belief"—which is to say that he wants only to get "all the emotional kick out of Christianity . . . without the bother of believing it." And the coarseness of such a judgment[2] is splendidly matched by Eliot's verdict on Pater, who represents, as he declares, but "a new variation" on "the vague religious vapourings" of Arnold. He, too, was one "incapable of sustained reasoning," who "could not take philosophy or theology seriously." True, he had a certain natural bent toward "all that was liturgical and ceremonious," but his "High Churchmanship," unlike that of Newman and Pusey and the Tractarians, was responsive only to "the sensuous expressions of orthodoxy," and thus he presents an " 'aesthetic religion' " which is merely "a matter of feeling" and whose principal consequence was little more than the "untidy lives" it engendered amongst "a number of writers in the 'nineties." No, as this arbiter wanted to have it, Pater is nothing but a second-rate Victorian whose influence upon any "first-rate mind of a later generation" is indeterminable.[3] Which is a verdict that offers an occasion for a small bit of amusement, when one notices how a line in Pater's essay on "Shakespeare's English Kings" ("No! Shakespeare's kings are not, nor are meant to be, great men")[4] is echoed in J. Alfred

Prufrock's confession, "No! I am not Prince Hamlet, nor was meant to be"—or how the great coda of *East Coker* echoes *Marius the Epicurean* and the Conclusion of *The Renaissance*:[5]

> Home is where one starts from. As we grow older
> The world becomes stranger, the pattern more complicated
> Of dead and living. Not the intense moment
> Isolated, with no before and after,
> But a lifetime burning in every moment
> And not the lifetime of one man only
> But of old stones that cannot be deciphered.

Now Eliot's argument ("Arnold and Pater") is, of course, utter nonsense, but, given the suasiveness lent his opinions by the immense prestige he commanded, his contempt for Pater proved over the span of a generation to be something like a benchmark for contemporary assessment, so much so that even one so admiring of Pater as Lord David Cecil could find no impropriety in speaking of him as a "low-spirited hedonist."[6] But even in his own period Pater, as Henry James might have said, was one whose "really beautiful time" lay always ahead, for, unlike a Carlyle or an Arnold or a Ruskin, he had no great talent for thrusting himself forward in Victorian forums, for bullying the public into acknowledgment of his authority, and for winning a large discipleship. This shy Fellow of Brasenose College, Oxford, somewhat bald in middle age and a little portly, whose dark broadcloth and heavy, clipped moustache gave him the appearance of "a retired major in the Rifle brigade,"[7] had so little taste for public disputation that when, to his astonishment, the Conclusion of *The Renaissance* (with its enjoining the reader to get "as many pulsations as possible into the given time") was vigorously objected to by conservative Oxonians as scandalously sanctioning a dangerous sort of antinomianism, he simply suppressed it in the second edition of 1877 rather than defend it (quietly restoring it, however, in the third edition of 1888). And though in his last years a certain fame had come his way, his general reticence still made it possible for Henry James, in writing to Edmund Gosse in December of 1894, a few months after Pater's death, to speak of this "faint, pale, embarrassed, exquisite" man as "the mask without the face."[8]

It was no doubt Pater's great reserve and reticence that kept him ever from expressing his own experience of Victorian religious anguish in terms of such naked poignancy as those of the essayist and mathematician at University College, London, W. K. Clifford, when he spoke of his being a generation that had been fated to see "the spring sun shine out of an empty heaven, to light up a soulless earth," a generation that had felt indeed "with utter loneliness that the Great Companion is dead."[9] The sort of travail expressed by Clifford—and by James Anthony Froude, Matthew Arnold, John Addington Symonds, John Ruskin, and so many others—was not, of course, unknown by Pater. For, when he went up to Oxford in 1858, he was intending to take orders in the Church of England and soon fell much under the influence of the kind of theological liberalism represented by Arthur Penrhyn Stanley and Frederick Denison Maurice and Benjamin Jowett. But by 1866 he was finding it necessary to remark in his essay on Coleridge (the anonymous appearance of which in *The Westminster Review* in January of that year marked his first publication) that "modern thought is distinguished from ancient by its cultivation of the 'relative' spirit in place of the 'absolute.' " And, very clearly, he had traveled a great distance indeed since his matriculation at Queen's College eight years earlier, for his intention in the essay on Coleridge to speak as a champion of "the 'relative' spirit" cannot be mistaken. His great charge is that Coleridge, in his role as metaphysician and theologian, had had too great a lust for the Absolute: his "chief offense" lay in "an excess of seriousness . . . arising . . . from a misconception of the perfect manner." One does not " 'weep' " or " 'shriek' " over the collapse of a received tradition: what is requisite is "a kind of humour"[10] that permits one urbanely to remark the passing of what must pass—and this Coleridge did not have. So the pathos of a Clifford regarding the erosion of the religious terrain Pater would not, on principle, permit himself: since he conceived "metaphysical questions . . . [to be] unprofitable,"[11] he chose rather to embrace "the wholesome scepticism of Hume and Mill."[12]

Yet, though Pater himself was prepared to speak of the wholesomeness of that scepticism which he found in Hume and Mill, he was in so doing surely by way of misrepresenting himself in no small measure. For the essential tonality of his mind bears hardly any resemblance at all to that of so thoroughly secular a man as Stuart Mill. True, by the time he had reached his full maturity he appears to have become persuaded that that whole structure of thought denominated in our own period by Martin Heidegger as "onto-theo-logy" was just so much metaphysical lumber that one could quite easily do without. And the more purely theoretical passages in *The Renaissance* make clear, as do many of his other writings, a deep temperamental attachment to English empiricism, for he remained always convinced that the noumenality of the world—what things are *in themselves*—must forever surpass the reach of the human mind. But he despised as heartily as did the Arnold of *Culture and Anarchy* the new secular ethos of his time that seemed everywhere to be in the ascendancy and to be promoting the superstition that human welfare lay in some new arrangement of "the mere machinery of life," in some new mode of *doing* rather than *being*.[13] And he had no sympathy at all for the Mr. Gradgrinds of the world—those who (in Dickens's account in *Hard Times*) proceed "upon the principle that two and two are four, and nothing over," who keep always the multiplication table in their pockets, "ready to weigh and measure any parcel of human nature, and tell you exactly what it comes to," supposing that it is all "a mere question of figures, a case of simple arithmetic." For in such an apprehension of the world, so lacking in "breadth" and "centrality" and "repose,"[14] there was for such a man as Pater a fearsome kind of godlessness, and against this *trahison* of the age he (as he said in a letter to Vernon Lee [Violet Paget]) saw it as a matter of "duty" to chart "a . . . sort of religious phase possible for the modern mind . . . the conditions of which phase it is the main object of my design to convey."[15]

Now, in taking the measure of this design, one needs to begin at the very beginning, with an essay entitled "Diaphanéité"[16] which Pater wrote, when he was not yet quite twenty-five, in the early summer of 1864 and which he is thought to have read that July before a little Oxford literary society called "Old Mortality." "There are some unworldly types of character," he suggests, "which the world is able to estimate. It recognises certain moral types, or categories, and regards whatever falls within them as having a right to exist. The saint, the artist, even the speculative thinker, out of the world's order as they are, yet work, so far as they work at all, in and by means of the main current of the world's energy," and the world can manage, therefore, to find "room for them in its scheme of life." But there is another type of character for which it has "no place ready in its affections" and with which it does not easily reckon. This is the Diaphanous Personality, which is distinguished by its concern "to value everything at its eternal worth" and to see "external circumstances as they are." It approaches the world with an utter "simplicity in purpose and act" and is untainted by any kind of predatoriness or desire to master and control and manipulate: it is an adept in the discipline of what the late Martin Heidegger called "letting-be,"[17] and it does not value "things and persons as marks or counters of something to be gained, or achieved, beyond them." The "guilelessness" of this "clear crystal nature" is sometimes mistakenly thought to be merely a sort of "indifferentism," but its guiding motive is *disponibilité*, or what Pater terms "receptivity": it wants to be *open* and intransitively attentive to all the things and creatures of earth, not just as so many appurtenances of the human enterprise but as having, each in its own way, such an inherent dignity as results from each having (as Pater's friend Gerard Manley Hopkins phrased it) its own "pitch of self," its own "instress" and "inscape." "All things," says Hopkins, "are upheld by instress and are meaningless without it."[18] And by "instress" he means that *élan* or ontological energy wherewith a bird or a flower or a cloud in the sky is assembled into the given Gestalt which it constitutes and made to be what it is—rather than another thing. Whereas "inscape" simply *is* the pattern or the form which a thing's instress makes. And it is this dimension of the natural and the human order—the dimension of instresses and inscapes, of quiddities and hecceities—that fascinates the Diaphanous Man. Moreover, though Pater never quite gets round clearly to saying so, one finds it difficult to resist the surmise that what is presupposed by the ethic of *diaphanéité* (of openness, of transparency, of what Heidegger calls *Gelassenheit*)[19] is a kind of sacramentalism, a sense of a "dearest freshness deep down things"[20] that charges the world with a grandeur we ignore at a very great cost to ourselves. "He who is ever looking for the breaking of a light he knows not whence about him, notes with a strange heedfulness the faintest paleness in the sky."[21] And it is the *pietas* that may be called forth by this "dearest freshness," this breaking of light, that forms perhaps the essential element in what Pater conceived to be the "religious phase possible for the modern mind."

He never published this "Old Mortality" paper, however, and, apparently, the only remaining copy at the time of his death was that in the possession of Charles Lancelot Shadwell (his former pupil and, later, Provost of Oriel College, Oxford), who, as his literary executor, issued it in the posthumous collection, *Miscellaneous Studies*, which first appeared in 1895. But, though Pater himself never sought an audience for it, it yet provides the essential preparation for a reading of the first masterpiece of his career, the book that Macmillan published in March of 1873 under the title *Studies in the History of the Renaissance*.[22]

Indeed, it is the Crystal Man[23] who is really the central focus of *The Renaissance*. By reason of its splendidly cadenced and remarkably eloquent prose the book, of course, remains one of the great modern classics. Yet, with all its misattributions of art works, its misrenderings of historical fact, and its derivativeness from such historians as Giorgio

Vasari, Jules Michelet, Giovanni Battista Cavalcaselle, Cesare Guasti, Carlo Amoretti, and Otto Jahn, we do not go to *The Renaissance* for instruction about Pico della Mirandola, Botticelli, Luca della Robbia, Michelangelo, Leonardo da Vinci, the school of Giorgione, Joachim du Bellay, and the eighteenth-century German Hellenist Johann Joachim Winckelmann (these figures being Pater's main subjects). True, the book is filled with brilliant aperçus and carries many occasional insights into particular works of art that are astonishing in their cogency and penetration. But what is bound to be most captivating for a contemporary reader is the ethic, the discipline, of diaphaneity that is being adumbrated at the beginning of the volume in its Preface, at the end in its Conclusion, and at numerous other points in the main body of the text.

Pater's commitment to the phenomenalist interpretation of experience advanced by the classic English empiricists is, of course, made evident again and again throughout the book. "At first sight experience," he says, "seems to bury us under a flood of external objects, pressing upon us with a sharp and importunate reality, calling us out of ourselves in a thousand forms of action. But when reflexion begins to play upon those objects they are dissipated under its influence; the cohesive force seems suspended like some trick of magic; each object is loosed into a group of impressions—colour, odour, texture—in the mind of the observer."[24] So, though he is quite as eager as Arnold that we should "see the object as in itself it really is," he wants to lay it down that "the first step towards seeing one's object as it really is, is to know one's own impression as it really is,"[25] for this is the one residue that our contact with the world deposits in the mind. In short, to know one's impressions and to discriminate and realize them as distinctly as one possibly can is to *see*—and *seeing* (in the sense not primarily of riveting the eye but of *paying heed*) is our only way of *receiving* the manifold richness of Creation.

But each impression or intuition is an affair of a single moment—and, of course, it is of the nature of each moment to be in perpetual flight. Early and late, indeed, Pater follows one of his great masters, Heraclitus, in viewing the world as everywhere pervaded by ceaseless flux. In, for example, his book of 1893, *Plato and Platonism*, he tells us that "the most modern metaphysical, and the most modern empirical philosophies alike have illustrated emphatically, justified, expanded, the divination . . . of the ancient theorist of Ephesus [Heraclitus]."[26] Yet he felt very strongly that Heraclitus's teaching is misconstrued when it is identified wholly with an emphasis on the transiency and inconstancy of things. In *Marius the Epicurean* (1885) he suggests that Heraclitus's doctrine about perpetual change was "but the preliminary step towards a large positive system of almost religious philosophy," since he conceived continual change to be an "indicator of a subtler but all-pervading motion—the sleepless, ever-sustained, inexhaustible energy of the divine reason itself, proceeding always by its own rhythmical logic, and lending to all mind and matter, in turn, what life they had."[27] And he makes a similar point in *Plato and Platonism*, where, again, he insists that Heraclitus wanted, finally, to identify a principle of order amidst this "world of chaotic mutation" and that, above all else, he was searching for "an antiphonal rhythm, or logic, which, proceeding uniformly from movement to movement, as in some intricate musical theme, might link together in one those contending, infinitely diverse impulses." He believed, in other words, that, even amidst all the flux of universal change, there is a "Wisdom . . . [that] 'reacheth from end to end, sweetly and strongly ordering all things.' "[28]

Now, even if Pater himself is not to be found invoking such "an antiphonal rhythm" as he descried in the Heraclitean scheme, he was, nevertheless, most certainly wanting to propose the possibility of a kind of transcendence of sheer motion and flux—and this, in his view, lay in such a strict attentiveness to each moment as will redeem it from all extraneousness and irrelevancy and permit it to be ignited with a "hard, gem-like flame."[29] We are situated in the immense theatre of the world—as the Psalmist says, of the sun and moon, of fire and hail, of mountains and hills, of beasts and flying fowl, of young men and maidens, and old men and children[30]—and only a certain number of experiences (or impressions) are given to us. Which means that, if we are in any deep way to be leavened by the rich bounteousness represented by all the marvelous variety of existence, we must, as Pater urges, by way of a most stringent discipline or *ascêsis* cultivate a very careful kind of attentiveness to the "virtue"[31] (i.e., the radically distinctive property) of each passing moment and to what it brings—of a sort of family relationship with the things and creatures of earth. "To burn always with this hard, gem-like flame . . . is success in life. . . . Not to discriminate every moment . . . is, on this short day of frost and sun, to sleep before evening."[32]

Indeed, the chief reason why the Crystal Man is prepared to make large room in his life for art is because "the picture, the landscape, the engaging personality . . . in a book, *La Gioconda*, . . . are valuable for their virtues, as we say, in speaking of a herb, a wine, a gem. . . . Our education becomes complete in proportion as our susceptibility to these impressions increases in depth and variety."[33] Which is to say that, his misgivings about what he calls "heavy realism"[34] notwithstanding, Pater takes it as axiomatic that authentic art bears a referential relationship to the actual world. True, the artist transcribes not "mere fact, but ... his sense of it."[35] Yet, finally, he does not create ex nihilo, if he wants to exert a serious claim upon us. For we have only "an interval, and then our place knows us no more," so that "our one chance lies in expanding that interval, in getting as many pulsations as possible into the given time"[36]—and this, in turn, means that any art, literary or visual,[37] which is to engage us deeply must make our attentiveness to *actual* things more wakeful. And, in this connection, it is significant that the major heroes of *The Renaissance*—Botticelli, Michelangelo, Leonardo, Giorgione, and, most especially, Winckelmann—are all presented as exemplars of Pater's special sort of *ascêsis* by reason of the extraordinary *receptivity* they represent toward the manifold influxions of reality; and this is to say that they are conceived to be examples of the Crystal Man, of him who embodies in a singular way *diaphanéité*, an openness and a transparency vis-à-vis the world something like Heidegger's *Gelassenheit*.

The essential logic, then, of the book of 1873 would hardly seem to be of the kind suggested by the traditional view of Pater as an effete connoisseur of the rare and the strange, as a mandarin self-indulgently specializing in a hedonistic sensualism. For his refusal of that myth of the world as merely a huge *res extensa*, silent and lifeless; his conviction of its bidding us indeed at every point to join it in a relationship of reciprocity that requires us to cultivate the virtue of *diaphanéité*, of "constant and eager observation";[38] his vision of "the splendour of our experience"[39] within our inherited universe—all this belongs to a basic pattern of ideas which, in its tendency to invest the things of earth with a radical kind of holiness, appears to reflect an *anima naturaliter religiosa* (and one for whom religious value is not subsumed under but does itself subsume aesthetic experience).

But, already in the weeks immediately following the first appearance of *The Renaissance*, the misreading of Pater's intentions began. For the word carried by the Conclusion about "getting as many pulsations as possible into the given time" strangely gave the entire book "the insidious appeal of some prose *Fleurs du Mal*,"[40] and, difficult as it may now be to imagine, in conservative Oxford it quickly made an occasion of scandal. The Chaplain of Brasenose College, John Wordsworth, who as a colleague had been on friendly terms with Pater, sent him a brusque letter warning that "it may be my duty to oppose you":

after a perusal of the book I cannot disguise from myself that the concluding pages adequately sum up the philosophy of the whole; and that that philosophy is an assertion, that no fixed principles either of religion or morality can be regarded as certain, that the only thing worth living for is momentary enjoyment and that probably or certainly the soul dissolves at death into elements which are destined never to reunite. . . . My object in writing is not to attempt argument on these conclusions, nor simply to let you know the pain they have caused me and I know also many others. Could you indeed have known the dangers into which you were likely to lead minds weaker than your own, you would, I believe, have paused. Could you have known the grief your words would be to many of your Oxford contemporaries you might even have found no ignoble pleasure in refraining from uttering them.[41]

And the letter ends by begging Pater not henceforth to participate as an examiner in the College's divinity examinations. But, within Oxford, Wordsworth's renunciation was only one of many rebuffs that came Pater's way. In, for example, 1874, the year as it so happened when it was the prerogative of Brasenose to name a Proctor for the University, Pater, who had been assured of the nomination, was in the event turned aside, this resulting at least in part (as Thomas Wright suggests)[42] from the opposition of Benjamin Jowett, the distinguished Master of Balliol, in whom *The Renaissance* had excited a considerable repugnance. Or, again, in the following year John Fielder Mackarness, the Bishop of Oxford, denounced Pater's book in a pastoral letter to his clergy.[43] And, outside Oxford, Mrs. (Margaret Wilson) Oliphant spoke for many when, in her review of the book in *Blackwood's Magazine* (November 1873), she declared that

Mr. Pater's volume, though there are bits of very pretty writing in it, and here and there a saying which is worth quoting, is full of so much "windy suspiration of forced breath," and solemn assumption of an oracular importance, that the critic scarcely knows whether to laugh or frown at the loftiness of the intention. . . . The book is *rococo* from beginning to end,—in its new version of that coarse, old refrain of the Epicureans' gay despair, "Let us eat and drink, for tomorrow we die"—as well as in its prettiness of phrase and graceful but far-fetched fancies.[44]

And this philippic prompted George Eliot, a few days after its appearance, to send a letter to the Editor of *Blackwood's* informing him that she "agreed very warmly with the remarks made by your contributor this month on Mr. Pater's book, which seems to me quite poisonous in its false principles of criticism and false conceptions of life."[45]

Now the responses of the mid-1870s to *The Renaissance*, in all their wrongheadedness and miscomprehension, did indeed, in projecting an image of Pater as a mannered proficient in *sensualité*, have a decisive effect on the shaping of the canonical verdict, not only about the book of 1873 but about the drift of his work as a whole. And this represents one of the more unfortunate miscarriages of modern literary and intellectual life, since the canonical verdict does so egregiously distort his real message. For what he most wanted to enunciate was his conviction that, if we are to come into our full human stature, we must (in Hölderlin's phrase) dwell "poetically . . . on this earth."[46]

This phrase of Hölderlin's fascinated Martin Heidegger, the last great genius of modern philosophy, and one of his more remarkable essays of the early 1950s—which is entitled ". . . dichterisch wohnet der Mensch . . ."[47]—is devoted to a lengthy meditation on what he took to be implied by Hölderlin's notion of "poetic dwelling." But this essay is only one of many he produced in the 1940s and 1950s on similar themes.[48] For, in his later years, he became convinced that "the poet" (*der Dichter*) presents us with the purest and most instructive example of "the thinker" (*der Denker*), since he, in so far as he truly keeps faith with his primary vocation, is an unexampled adept at "paying heed" to the sheer specificity of all the various things with which the world is furnished. For Heidegger, in other words, the true poet is preoccupied never with the light that never was on land or sea but always with the light of ordinary day, and he solicits our attention to the concrete particularity of lived experience. And thus, as Heidegger says in one of the *Holzwege* essays, poetry brings "beings as such for the first time into the Open."

Normally, of course, we move through the world from day to day, paying only so much attention to this or that as the necessities of one or another occasion allow, and the things and persons making up our environment are no more than cues for action or signals of desire, offering not even the merest approximation of what would be there, were we to take the trouble of paying heed. So everything is gross and banal and full of dead spots. Which is why we do not have a "world" in which to "dwell," for to have a world is to have a unified matrix of meanings and relations—and this one does not have until "beings as such . . . [are brought] into the Open." Which is in turn to say, for Heidegger, that one can have a world only in so far as one manages to be a "poet" (the chief differentia of the poet being not so much his versifying as his performing a certain kind of attentive act before the things of earth).

So, on Heidegger's reckoning, really to inhabit this earth is to *dwell poetically*, for it is only in this way that we can be rescued—as *Pater* puts it—from "the fatal, irresistible, mechanic play of circumstance."[49] And this is why the author of *Erläuterungen zu Hölderlins Dichtung* says that it is the poet who *names* "the gods" (meaning by "gods" whatever it is that "assembles" things into the aspect of stability and trustworthiness) and thus mediates "the Holy."

Now it is, of course, a hazardous thing to do to speak of this German master of our own century in relation to the Victorian don who produced *The Renaissance*, since one is bound to invite the demurrer, so distant do they at first seem from each other, that a very strange brew is being arranged. But the lesson that long ago Eliot was laying down in his famous essay of 1917 on "Tradition and the Individual Talent" deserves still to be remembered, that intellectual and literary history presents us not with just so many silent monuments but with something like a forum that is very much astir, a forum in which no single figure "has his complete meaning alone," since that meaning stands constantly to be modified or illumined not only by those who have gone before but also by those who come after.[50] Which means that Emerson may be found to comment on Nietzsche, and Proust on Augustine, and Sterne on Joyce, and so on ad infinitum. So, for all their difference of lineage and idiom, there is no impropriety at all in juxtaposing (as I have done) Pater and Heidegger, most especially since Heidegger's whole concept of *der Dichter* and "poetic dwelling" does so closely parallel and clarify Pater's vision of the Crystal Man and *diaphanéité*, these latter being the conceptions that are at bottom regulating the structure of thought which we confront in *The Renaissance*.

The pattern of ideas that was most truly essential to this book went by and large, however, unrecognized, and not only did Pater have to endure a critical response that was absurdly wide of the mark: he even found himself in 1877 being held up as a figure for ridicule by a young man only recently down from Oxford, W. H. Mallock, who, in a book entitled *The New Republic*, presented a series of imaginary dialogues satirizing (under pseudonyms), among others, Arnold and Jowett and Ruskin, as well as Pater himself, who appears as a Mr. Rose. Mallock's parody was something cruel indeed, representing Mr. Rose as a languid and vaguely homosexual aesthete who dedicates himself to the savoring of exotic perfumes and *objets d'art* and whose extravagant conversational eccentricities prompt a certain Lady Ambrose to remark that he " 'always seems to talk of everybody as if they had no clothes on.' "[51] Thomas Wright—whose early biography of Pater has aptly been called by Iain Fletcher "one of the (unintentionally) comic masterpieces of our literature"[52]—with his characteristic impercipience, declares that "*The New Republic* is simply capital fun, of a kind that no sensible man would mind."[53] But, coming after the profound disappointment Pater must have suffered as a result of all the distortions his critics had practiced on "the sober and strenuous ideal"[54] he had put forward in the book of 1873, it is difficult to imagine his having been undistressed by Mallock's humorous deprecations.

Indeed, it is very probably the bruising effect of the general reception of *The Renaissance* that explains the halting tentativeness of Pater's literary efforts over the next several years. In April of 1874 he published in *The Fortnightly Review* a fine essay on Wordsworth which, in its account of how the poet of *The Prelude* could be lifted from the natural order to a sense of "the brooding power of one universal spirit," presents an exact estimate of Wordsworth's genius and which at the same time, in its defense of that "impassioned contemplation" whereby life may be approached "in the spirit of art," continues his meditation on the ethic of *diaphanéité*.[55] Then, again, in November of 1874 *The Fortnightly Review* published his essay on Shakespeare's *Measure for Measure*. And in the following years in *The Fortnightly* and *Macmillan's Magazine* he issued a few things—the first of his "imaginary portraits" ("The Child in the House"), the first of his Greek studies ("The Myth of Demeter and Persephone"), and various other pieces—but none of this was major work. In 1878 the Macmillan firm warmly endorsed his proposal to bring out a new collection of his essays, but no sooner was he faced with his proofs than he lost heart altogether, and he wrote to Alexander Macmillan to say (30 November 1878): "I hope you will forgive me all the trouble I have given you. But, sincerely, I think it would be a mistake to publish the essays in their present form; some day they may take a better and more complete form. Please send me a line of assent at once."[56] And a few days later he sent Macmillan "a cheque" for thirty-five pounds to cover the costs of typesetting, requesting in the note that accompanied it that the type be broken up.

Pater's habits of restraint and reticence never, of course, allowed him to express any sort of regret or complaint about the reception of his work: only "those nearest to him," says A. C. Benson (meaning no doubt his sisters Hester and Clara), knew his "dark moods of discouragement."[57] Yet the record of his literary life surely suggests that in the years immediately after the first edition of *The Renaissance* he was a deeply wounded man.

Gradually, however, as it would seem, he recovered some firmness of spirit, for by the spring of 1881 he had a new project well in hand, and one that was to prove so exacting that in 1883 he felt obliged, though retaining his fellowship, to resign his Brasenose tutorship, despite the considerable inconvenience entailed by the consequent loss of a sizable portion of his income. Pater's own sense of the significance of this project—a novel, with its setting in the Roman Italy of the Antonines in the second century A.D., which was to be called *Marius the Epicurean*—is perhaps most clearly indicated by the footnote he prepared for the Conclusion of *The Renaissance*, when, after having suppressed it in the second edition of 1877, he restored it in the third edition of 1888. The footnote says: "This brief 'Conclusion' was omitted in the second edition of this book, as I conceived it might possibly mislead some of those young men into whose hands it might fall. On the whole, I have thought it best to reprint it here, with some slight changes which bring it closer to my original meaning. I have dealt more fully in *Marius the Epicurean* with the thoughts suggested by it."[58]

Now, more clearly perhaps than anything else that may be cited, the final sentence of this note suggests something of what it was that prompted Pater to undertake the writing of the book that did at last appear in 1885 and that requires to be thought of as the central statement of his career. Though deeply responsive to Catholic Christianity in its Anglican expressions,[59] "the wholesome scepticism" he had learned from Hume and Mill made it impossible, as his essay on Coleridge indicates, for him to accept "vague scholastic abstractions" or any sort of "absolute." Like an American theologian of our own period, he felt that "if we are to have any transcendence . . . it must be in and through the secular," that "if we are to find grace it is to be found in the world and not overhead."[60] Which meant, for him, that, if whatever it is that gives ultimate meaning and dignity to the human order is to be found (as a later writer was to phrase it) in "The actual landscape with its actual horns / Of baker and butcher blowing,"[61] the highest discipline to be cultivated is that of keeping oneself *receptive* and *open* and *attentive* to the things of this world. "I require of you only to look," says St. Teresa of Avila, and it is a similar exaction that is being held up by the Conclusion of *The Renaissance* as having a primary claim upon us. And, since in Pater's view the principal office of art is to cleanse and stimulate and refine our vision, it was natural that he should accord it the kind of propaedeutic role that he conceived it to have in that whole process whereby transcendence is relocated in the dimension of immanence and we learn to "dwell poetically" on this earth. But by many of his contemporaries all this was impatiently dis-

missed as "art for art's sake" and "Neo-paganism" and hedonistic sensualism. And thus, as it seems, there came a time, most especially after
the whole affair of *The New Republic*, when (like Newman, after the
gratuitous attack upon him by Charles Kingsley) he felt obliged to
produce an *Apologia* that might have the effect of finally clarifying his
real motives. As his letter of 22 July 1883 to Violet Paget about this
crucial project said (see note 15), "I regard this present matter as a sort
of duty. For . . . there is a . . . sort of religious phase possible for the
modern mind . . . the conditions of which phase it is the main object of
my design to convey." His great hope, in other words, was that, by
casting his position in the form of prose fiction, he might more fully
disclose the emphatically religious intention controlling his fundamental endeavor and thereby put to rest the charges that taxed him with a
frivolous aestheticism.

The novel that Pater had completed by the end of the summer of
1884 and that Macmillan published in the following year is, of course,
a book so much straining against the limits of its genre that many
readers are doubtless inclined to wonder if in any sense it can be called
a novel at all, and it may well be that we ought indeed to think of
Marius the Epicurean as the first "antinovel" in English literature of
the modern period. As Percy Lubbock long ago remarked, "In *Marius*
probably, if it is to be called a novel, the art of drama is renounced as
thoroughly as it has ever occurred to a novelist to dispense with it." So
little is brought into the foreground. Virtually nothing is dramatized in
action. "The scenes of the story reach the reader by refraction, as it
were, through the medium of Pater's harmonious murmur."[62] And that
murmur is very nearly all that we *hear*, for the personages of the novel
seem never to be engaged in the kind of talk that enlivens *Mansfield
Park*, *Middlemarch*, *Bleak House*, and *Women in Love*: Marius seems
never to be spoken to or himself to engage another in genuine conversation. Everything is oblique, is presented retrospectively, and the remarkable paucity of character, incident, and dialogue is bound to try
the patience of those who come to the book with the kinds of expecta-
tions that are conventionally satisfied by realistic prose narrative.

Yet, demanding of his reader as Pater is, *Marius* reflects at every
point a "meticulous discipline of thought and expression,"[63] and nothing could be further from the truth than T. S. Eliot's exasperated complaint that it is simply "incoherent."[64] On the contrary: as Harold
Bloom rightly says, it "is a surprisingly unified narrative"—or, as he
more precisely puts it, it is "a unified reverie"[65] whose "four parts are
four stages on the life's way"[66] of its protagonist. And Marius—more

centrally than the figures at the fore in the other "imaginary portraits" (Florian Deleal of "The Child in the House," Sebastian van Storck, the Watteau of "A Prince of Court Painters," Gaston de Latour)[67]—is Pater's type and example of the Diaphanous Personality, of the Crystal Man, of openness and *disponibilité* and "poetic dwelling." For he is one whose "whole nature . . . [is] one complex medium of reception, towards the vision . . . of our actual experience in the world."[68] And thus he represents the "sort of entire transparency of nature that lets through unconsciously all that is really lifegiving in the established order of things."[69] Which is to say that Marius, as Diaphanous Man, is dedicated to *seeing*. And, of course, what he comes ultimately to *see* is the *promise* of "a perfect humanity, in a perfect world,"[70] this leading him, in turn, given the circumstances in which it is beheld, to embrace the Christian faith.* But, as Auden says in *For the Time Being*, though "the garden is the only place there is, . . . you will not find it / Until you have looked for it everywhere and found nowhere that is not a desert."[71] So Marius has to go the long way round—which involves for him a pilgrimage that will lead from his inherited pagan religion ("the religion of Numa") to, first, Cyrenaicism and then to Stoicism and ultimately to the new Christian movement that is sweeping across the Graeco-Roman world.

The opening chapters beautifully describe the atmosphere enveloping the remote country estate and its fine old villa called *White-nights* where Marius grows up, under the careful guardianship of his adored mother. And, here, the decisive influence is the simple patriarchal religion of ancient Rome—the religion of the field and the hearth and the household gods—which it is the tradition of the place scrupulously to observe. Even as a boy, Marius, since his father is dead, is obliged, as the last male of his line, to be the president of the various liturgies followed by all the servants and retainers on the family estate, and to this priestly office in all its aspects he brings a gravely punctilious devotion, for he conceives the world to be " 'touched of heaven' " and has a great sense of "the sacredness of time, of life and its events, and the circumstances of family fellowship; of such gifts to men as fire, water, the earth" (1:6). So the prayers and ceremonies that belong to the daily round and the urns of the dead in the family chapel all receive from him a quiet, reverent service, this being of a piece with "many another homely and old-fashioned trait" (1:15) in his nature. The "*conscience,*

---

*Henceforth all references to *Marius* will be enclosed within parentheses in the main body of the text, identified by volume number and page.

of which the old Roman religion was a formal, habitual recognition, [has] . . . become in him a powerful current of feeling and observance" (1:5), and he wants not to "fall short at any point of the demand upon him of anything in which deity . . . [is] concerned" (1:17–18).

But, then, with his mother's death, the time comes when this young Tuscan must leave his estate, to complete his education in a distinguished rhetorician's school in Pisa modeled on Plato's Academy. And this juncture marks an important turning point, for not only is he a nestling leaving the house of his forebears but the shock of his mother's death has "turned seriousness of feeling into a matter of the intelligence," has "made him a questioner" (1:43), and has somehow led him to think of the "much cherished religion of the villa . . . as but one voice, in a world where there [are] . . . many voices it would be a moral weakness not to listen to" (1:44). So he takes off to Pisa a great new susceptibility—and, there, he falls under the influence of a prodigiously brilliant and charming schoolmate, a young man named Flavian, who quickly gains an easy dominion over him.

Pisa, which is a fashionable bathing center, is, with its gay and bustling streets, marked by all the "urbanities . . . [and] graceful follies" that one might expect to find in such a town, and Marius is greatly stirred by its promise of freedom and adventure. The excitement and glamor of this urban world present a scene quite different from that of the "gray monastic tranquillity" (1:47) of *White-nights*, and the capricious waywardness of Marius's new friend, Flavian, makes him a fine exemplar of the moral climate of the place. Three years older than Marius, Flavian is a young dandy who loves "dress, and dainty food, and flowers" and who cultivates "that foppery of words . . . which was common among the *élite* spirits of that day" (1:51). There will come a time, indeed, when, for Marius, "evil things present themselves in malign association with the memory of that beautiful head" and when he will consider Flavian to be "an epitome of the whole pagan world, the depth of its corruption, and its perfection of form" (1:53).

Meanwhile, Flavian having been appointed to help Marius in his studies, the two are constantly together, and Flavian's intellectual sophistications enable him to introduce Marius to a range of literature and ideas that he has had no previous chance to encounter. It is Flavian who introduces him to Lucian and to Apuleius, and it makes a small irony that one afternoon he should be reading with Marius the tale of Cupid and Psyche in Apuleius's *Metamorphoses*, for (as Gerald Monsman has rightly remarked)[72] the story of Psyche's "love of Love" presents, within the design of the novel, a kind of parable of a similar yearning in Marius that will ultimately lead him to embrace that *Urbs Beata* whose founder is none other than Christ himself.

Flavian, however, locked up as he is within the chambers of his own restless mind, is in no way "touched of heaven," and it seems, therefore, not inappropriate that the stern morality of the novel should ordain that he die in the delirium resulting from the fever that possesses him, once he is stricken by the plague brought into the region from abroad by the emperor's returning armies. Marius tenderly nurses him through the final days of his illness, and on his last morning Marius, at about daybreak, asks, " 'Is it a comfort that I shall often come and weep over you?' " To which his dying friend says only, " 'Not unless I be aware, and hear you weeping!' " (1:119). And, with this scene of young Flavian's refusing to go gently into the night ahead, Part I of the novel is brought to a close.

"To Marius, greatly agitated by that event, the earthly end of Flavian," as we are told in the opening paragraph of Part II, comes "like a final revelation of nothing less than the soul's extinction" (1:123). He is so overborne by the spectacle of Flavian's perished body and, after its cremation, of "the little marble chest" carrying the remains of ash that the likelihood of "further stages of being still possible for the soul in some dim journey hence" is suddenly blasted. And the collapse in him of the old hope for some fulfillment beyond the grave brings at last a sense of the untenability of "almost all that remained of the religion of his childhood" (1:123).

Now it is at this point that Marius, at the age of eighteen, begins his journey in quest of some system of meaning wherewith his broken world may once again be knit together, and this is a journey which is to take him from first one and then to another of the great alternatives proposed by the ancient world. He has a natural antipathy toward Platonism, for the indifference it would have the soul cultivate with respect to "its bodily house" strikes him as essentially "inhuman" (1:125). But he has an equally natural inclination to embrace Epicureanism, and thus at first he feels prompted to go back from Epicurus and Lucretius to "the writer who was in a certain sense the teacher of both, Heraclitus of Ionia" (1:128), as well as to Aristippus of Cyrene, who developed and clarified at the level of conduct the practical import of the Heraclitean doctrine of perpetual flux. From Heraclitus he learns that, though "the uncorrected sense gives . . . a false impression of permanence or fixity in things," the world "is in reality full of animation, of vigour, of the fire of life" (1:129), and that the eternal flux controlling all things is but an expression of "the sleepless, ever-sustained, inexhaustible energy of the divine reason itself." Then, from Aristippus of Cyrene, he learns that, since all "things are but shadows, and . . . [since] we, even as they, never continue in one stay" (1:135), we "must maintain a harmony with that soul of motion in things, by constantly renewed mobility of character" (1:139). We must rid ourselves of all such "abstractions as are but the ghosts of bygone impressions" (1:141), approaching experience, as it were, virginally. "Liberty of soul, freedom from all partial and misrepresentative doctrine which does but relieve one element in our experience at the cost of another, freedom from all embarrassment alike of regret for the past and of calculation on the future: this would be but preliminary to the real business of education—insight, insight through culture, into all that the present moment holds in trust for us, as we stand so briefly in its presence" (1:142). In short, *"Be perfect in regard to what is here and now"* (1:145).

Now it is under the influence of this "New Cyrenaicism" that Marius, about a year after Flavian's death, sets out for Rome, a friend of his late father having arranged a secretarial post for him on the staff of the Emperor Marcus Aurelius. And on the seventh evening of his journey, as he is working his way up "the long windings by which the road ascended to the place where that day's stage was to end," a heavy mass of rock is suddenly detached from the steep slope bordering his path and falls to the road, so close behind him that he feels its touch on his heel. By the merest hairbreadth he has escaped being crushed to death, and the shock of the moment, as it discloses how cruelly exposed we are to the buffetings of sheer contingency, makes him realize in the instant the incompetence of his revisionist Epicureanism in relation to such emergencies of life. "His elaborate philosophy had not put beneath his feet the terror of mere bodily evil; much less of 'inexorable fate, and the noise of greedy Acheron' " (1:166).

Then, on the following morning as he is leaving the inn where he has spent the night, scheduled now to take the coming day's journey on horseback, he overtakes shortly after his departure a young Roman soldier of the Twelfth Legion whose name is Cornelius. They break into conversation—which in due course arouses in both "sufficient interest . . . to insure an easy companionship for the remainder of their journey" (1:168) to Rome. Marius does not know that Cornelius is a Christian: he knows only that there is in this young man a blitheness of spirit, a comeliness of manner, an austere kind of dignity, that makes him feel as if he is "face to face, for the first time, with some new knighthood or chivalry, just then coming into the world" (1:170). And,

once they arrive in Rome (" 'The Most Religious City in the World' "),
Marius remarks his friend's indifference not only to all the various
foreign cults and religions to which the city offers hospitality but also to
the effigies and rituals of Roman religion as well.

No sooner does Marius take up his new situation as an amanuensis
on the imperial staff than he finds himself deeply attracted to the majes-
tic figure of Marcus Aurelius, whose Stoicism, in its emphasis on the
brevity of our span and the consequent vanity of all ambition, appears
to offer a kind of invincible nonchalance wherewith to face all the
vicissitudes of life. There is something powerfully appealing in the very
fervor of his disillusion, in the asceticism written not unpleasantly into
the character of his face, in the genial composure of his general de-
meanor, and in his habit of seeming never " 'too much occupied with
important affairs to concede what life with others may hourly demand' " (1:217). There is, in other words, an allure about the man
himself that makes it inevitable that Marius should feel required seriously to reckon with the body of doctrine to which Aurelius gives his
suffrage. And he is led to do so perhaps all the more by the sharpness of
its difference from his former creed. For Cyrenaicism says: " 'The
world, within me and without, flows away like a river; therefore let me
make the most of what is here and now.' " But Stoicism says: " 'The
world and the thinker upon it are consumed like a flame; therefore will
I turn away my eyes from vanity: renounce: withdraw myself alike from
all affections' " (1:201).

There comes a time, however, when this young voyager begins once
again to be doubtful about that which bids for his allegiance. For, when
he finds the emperor sponsoring the terrible spectacles in the city's
amphitheater that involve the torture and slaughter of animals and the
fearfully bloody contests between gladiators, he is repelled. True,
Aurelius tends to avert his eyes from these "manly amusements" by
reading or attending to his correspondence, but that he can patiently
sit through them, in a manner expressing tolerance and indifference,
seems "to Marius to mark Aurelius as his inferior now and for ever on
the question of righteousness; to set them on opposite sides, in some
great conflict, of which that difference was but a single presentment"
(1:241). Moreover, on a later occasion he finds that, when Aurelius is
himself afflicted with adversity, his *apatheia* fails and quite deserts him.
His little son, Annius Verus, is fatally stricken by some obscure illness,
and the child's death plunges him into a desolation which is inconsol-
able, his air being "less of a sanguine and self-reliant leader than of one
. . . defeated" (2:59). So Marius cannot resist concluding that the Stoic

scheme must surely rest on "some flaw of vision," and he feels "a strange pathos" in this whole gospel.

As Part III of the novel gets under way, then, Marius is one for whom both Epicureanism and Stoicism have run aground. And it is the central event in this section of the narrative—the discourse of Cornelius Fronto—that prepares him for the next stage of his progress. It is in the chapter entitled "Stoicism at Court" that Fronto, the emperor's most trusted counselor and the favorite teacher of his youth, presents a discourse on the nature of morality. Fronto, who is generally regarded as Rome's most distinguished rhetorician, makes this presentation on his birthday—to celebrate which Marcus Aurelius has assembled a fashionable audience of "elegant blue-stockings" to savor the old gentleman's ripened wisdom and his exquisite language. And what he wants chiefly to propose is that the moral life has its true foundation in the idea of the world as one great commonwealth or city the conscience of which becomes explicit in "a visible or invisible aristocracy . . . whose actual manners, whose preferences from of old, become now a weighty tradition as to the way in which things should or should not be done" (2:10).

As Marius listens to this urbane old Stoic, his reflections quickly move beyond the actual intentions of the speaker, "not in the direction of any clearer theoretic or abstract definition of that ideal commonwealth, but rather as if in search of its visible locality and abiding-place" (2:11). Fronto, of course, is echoing a theme of Marcus Aurelius himself, who has often spoken of men as holding citizenship in a "*City on high*, of which all other cities are but single habitations" (2:37). And, quite apart from Fronto's particular line of argument, it is simply with this idea of a New Rome, of a Celestial City, an *Urbs Beata*, that Marius suddenly finds himself enchanted. Though, like Aurelius, he suspects that this *City on high* is "incorporate somehow with the actual city whose goodly stones were lying beneath his gaze" (2:37), given his *dis*enchantment now with Stoicism, he is not inclined to expect that it offers any kind of access to this ideal commonwealth. So, as he leaves the assembly that Fronto has addressed, he is haunted by the question as to where this "comely order" may be found. Surely it must have some local habitation, but where? "Where were those elect souls in whom the claim of Humanity became so amiable, winning, persuasive . . . ?" (2:12).

It is Marius's search for the answer to this question that constitutes the central action of Part IV of the novel, and, here, as it turns out, the principal role of Cornelius is to be that of befriending his steps unto that Good Place which is the object of his heart's desire. These two have become good friends in the years that have gone by since Marius first came to Rome, and one afternoon, as they are returning to the city from a visit to a country house, the natural fatigue of the long journey overcomes them quite suddenly about two miles outside the city limits, at which point, "just where a cross-road from the *Latin Way* fell into the *Appian*" (2:94), Cornelius halts at a doorway and, "as if at liberty to enter," opens the door and takes Marius into the garden of a beautiful villa. Throughout these splendidly ordered precincts "the quiet signs of wealth and of a noble taste" (2:95) are to be noticed. The whole place—which belongs to the Roman matron Cecilia—is "like a bride adorned for her husband" (2:97): everywhere there is simplicity, order, peace, and an "air of venerable beauty," especially in the family burial place of the Cecilii which causes Marius to marvel at these people who do not consign their dead to the funeral fire but who bury them, as if by some heavenly alchemy the perished body may be expected to be reconstituted. And, wherever they go on the estate, a most wonderful singing of hymns is to be heard: it is, of course, an underground church assembled for something like a service of Evensong.

The two spend only a few minutes within the precincts of Cecilia's villa and then resume their journey, but Marius has a transporting sense of having encountered, however briefly, a mode of life based on "some fact, or series of facts, in which the old puzzle of life . . . [has] found its solution" (2:105–6).

Now from this point on the pace of the novel noticeably quickens, as it moves toward its imminent climax. Marius has a consuming eagerness to ferret out as much information as he can possibly win about this Christian congregation that meets in Cecilia's house. And gradually, as he learns more and more, he comes to feel "the stirring of some wonderful new hope within himself," for, as it seems to him, this new movement is by way of bringing into existence a "regenerate type of humanity" (2:110). Never, he tells himself, has old Rome so cherished the family as do these people. And what a remarkable solicitousness they represent with respect to children! Moreover, they are a people who cherish industry and honest workmanship. Nor do they harbor any ascetical contempt for the life of the body and the natural order: on the contrary, they declare the sensuous world to be created of God. And he is deeply impressed by the generously humanistic kind of hospitality with which the Church adopts "many of the graces of pagan feeling and pagan custom" (2:125) and gratefully acknowledges its evolution from and indebtedness to the great traditions of Jewish spirituality. At every point, as he feels, this is a community touched by a quite remarkable kind of gaiety and "debonair grace" and (most important of all) chasteness of life.

But, perhaps beyond all else, what Marius is most moved by in the life of the Church is its "unparalleled genius for worship" (2:123). Indeed, it is his experience of a Christmas Mass that seals his commitment to the People of the Catacombs. On a certain winter morning—which he does not know to be the Feast of the Nativity—having decided to leave Rome for a time and wanting Cornelius to know of his whereabouts, he goes to his friend's lodgings. And, not finding him in, he then goes to the Cecilian villa, thinking that Cornelius may be there. He passes through the empty courtyard and into "the vast *Lararium*, or domestic sanctuary, of the Cecilian family" where, as he discovers, a great company of people, "at that moment in absolute silence," is assembled. Then the silence is broken by cries of *Kyrie Eleison! Christe Eleison!*, and the Eucharistic office proceeds on through the *Pro-Anaphora* to the *Anaphora*, the immense absorption and dignity with which the entire company participates in the service suggesting to Marius that "a cleansing and kindling flame" (2:131) is indeed at work amongst them. The local bishop is the celebrant, and, when he begins to recite the great central prayer of consecration, it is "as if he alone possessed the words of the office, and they flowed anew from some permanent source of inspiration within him" (2:136). At its conclusion the faithful approach the altar (which is in fact "the tomb of a youthful 'witness' of the family of the Cecilii") for the administration of the sacrament. Then "the remnants of the feast are borne away" to be administered to the sick. A hymn is sung—after which the young deacons cry out *Ite! Missa est!* And, as the people depart, Marius feels "that he must hereafter experience . . . a kind of thirst for all this, over again" (2:140), for the figure of Christ "towards whom this whole act of worship . . . turned . . . seemed to have absorbed, like some rich tincture in his garment, all that was deep-felt and impassioned in the experiences of the past" (2:134). In short, he is now convinced that here at last in this community he has found that *Urbs Beata*, that wholly inclusive society, for which he has been searching.[73]

This *anima naturaliter Christiana* (as the novel speaks of Marius, echoing the famous phrase in Tertullian's *Apologeticum*) has now reached what is essentially the end of his journey, and it is not at all surprising that his thoughts should begin to turn back to *White-nights*. "Home is where one starts from," says Eliot's *East Coker*: "In my beginning is my end." But certain things must transpire before he returns to his old Tuscan estate. First, he has a long conversation one morning with the writer Lucian, who, confirmed skeptic that he is, insists on the relativity of all doctrines and philosophies. But, though Marius can appreciate a certain cogency in Lucian's agnosticism, it does not finally meet what is for him the crucial exigency—which is (as he says in his diary) that "there is a certain grief in things as they are, in man as he has come to be, as he certainly is, over and above those griefs of circumstance which are in a measure removable" (2:181), and what we need, therefore, for the withstanding of the tragic things in life is not so much schemes of metaphysics (which are all without profit, on Lucian's account) as the assurance that "a certain permanent and general power of compassion" is the "elementary ingredient" of our world. And, since it is the promise of this "ingredient" that he has found in Cecilia's house, he finds himself drawn back again to the underground Church: he listens once more to "the sweet singing of the Eucharist," and, as he follows again the "mystical dialogue" of the Mass, he feels himself to be a part of a great company which, having heard "the sentence of its release from prison," represents now "the whole company of mankind" (2:190). In the course of the service an epistle from the Churches of Lyons and Vienne to " 'their sister,' " the Church of Rome, is read, this epistle recounting the martyrdoms amongst these Christians that Aurelius's legions have exacted. Marius is greatly moved, and it occurs to him that here, indeed, in the kind of testimony made by the willingness of these people to lay down their lives for their faith and for one another, is "that absolute ground amid all the changes of phenomena, such as our philosophers have of late confessed themselves quite unable to discover" (2:184).

Shortly afterward he returns to *White-nights*, his childhood home, and spends eight days there. As he wanders through the family mausoleum, he is distressed by the "odd air of neglect," the faded flowers and the thickness of the fallen dust; and, being struck by a "yearning . . . still to be able to do something for" his own dead, he arranges for the burial of his ancestors' remains, in the Christian way. While he is overseeing this work, his friend Cornelius, having found himself in the neighborhood, stops at *White-nights*, and the two resolve to return to Rome together. But, on their way, they are of a sudden caught in an earthquake at Lucca. The inhabitants superstitiously conceive these strangers, along with certain others, to be the cause of the event, and they are arrested. Marius bribes the guards, however, to release Cornelius, who blithely proceeds on to Rome, it having been so arranged as for him to suppose that Marius will immediately follow. And, before his captors can dispose of him, Marius himself falls ill and is left to die at a farmhouse, under the care of some country people who, as it turns out, are Christians. As he lies on the rough bed provided him, his life rapidly ebbing away, this hierarch of the spirit devotes his last hours to "a conscious effort of recollection." In accord with the ethic of *diaphanéité* he is, of course, one who has always set *seeing* "above the *having*, or even the *doing*, of anything. For, such vision, if received with due attitude on his part, was, in reality, the *being* something" (2:218). And now he thinks "how goodly" the vision has been:

> Throughout that elaborate and lifelong education of his receptive powers, he had ever kept in view the purpose of preparing himself . . . towards some ampler vision. . . . At this moment, his unclouded receptivity of soul, grown so steadily through all those years, from experience to experience, was at its height; the house ready for the possible guest; the tablet of the mind white and smooth, for whatsoever divine fingers might choose to write there. And was not this precisely the condition, the attitude of mind, to which something higher than he, yet akin to him, would be likely to reveal itself; to which that influence he had felt now and again like a friendly hand upon his shoulder, amid the actual obscurities of the world, would be likely to make a further explanation. (2:219–20)

He has not, in other words, directly beheld the naked glory of God himself—which must perhaps remain beyond the reach and ken of any mortal creature: so there are "further explanations," further visions, to be awaited, possibly in some "brave new world" wherein there "is no unrest, no travel, no shipwreck." But, within the range of what is possible in this life, he has had the great thing, for in the New Israel, amidst the People of the Catacombs, he has beheld "Heaven . . . come down among men" (2:214). Which makes it by no means unaccountable that, as he gives up the ghost, the people around his bed should be "praying fervently—*Abi! Abi! Anima Christiana!*" (2:224), for he has surely undergone what the old doctors of the Church called "baptism of desire."

So it is that the book moves, and T. S. Eliot's word about its "incoherence" is utterly astonishing, for its beautifully organized structure does indeed, as Harold Bloom says, present at very nearly every point a thoroughly "unified narrative" whose "four parts are four stages on the life's way of Marius." And, again, though (as he indicated in the letter to Violet Paget cited in note 15) Pater wanted in this book to chart "a . . . sort of religious phase possible for the modern mind," he trifles not at all with anything resembling such an "aesthetic religion" as

Eliot, following the lead of A. C. Benson, imputes to *Marius the Epicurean*. To be sure, Benson claimed that "the weakness of the case [made by the novel] is, that instead of emphasising the power of sympathy, the Christian conception of Love, which differentiates Christianity from all other religious systems, Marius is after all converted, or brought near to the threshold of the faith, more by its sensuous appeal, its liturgical solemnities; the element, that is to say, which Christianity has in common with all religions, and which is essentially human in character."[74] But nothing could be further from the truth, for that which most convinces Marius that the *City on high* for which he has been searching is incorporate within the Church is just the certainty he gradually wins that here, amongst the people he first encounters in the villa of the Cecilii, is a community indwelt by agape.

Benson says that "the sensuous element triumphs over the intellectual,"[75] and this is simply a gross misstatement of things. True, Pater hardly presents at all any explication of Marius's conversion in terms of what his protagonist conceived to be at stake in the way of formal doctrine. And for this there are, I think, two explanations, the first being that, since "Marius attains to Christianity within the primitive church of the apostles and martyrs, not the church of the *Summa Theologiae*, it would be unhistorical to expect from him a theologically reasoned [argument]"[76] of a piece with the expositions of a Calvin or a Schleiermacher or a Newman. But, then, secondly, what it is no doubt even more important to recall in this connection is that "wholesome scepticism" for which Pater gratefully acknowledged his indebtedness to Hume and Mill. Like so many other Victorian intellectuals, he took for granted what Matthew Arnold had enunciated in his book of 1875, *God and the Bible*, that "two things about the Christian religion must surely be clear to anybody with eyes in his head"—the one being that "men cannot do without it; the other, that they cannot do with it as it is."[77] And that which was no longer negotiable was nothing other than the old supernaturalist postulates of classical theism, with their projection of an immutable, impassive, immaterial, self-subsistent Being "up there"—the *ens realissimum*—who, like the elder Lord Shaftesbury, thinks and acts and who governs the universe, intervening here and there to move it in one direction or another. Pater was not himself, of course, a theologian: nor did he have ready at hand, even in the more advanced theology of his time, a language calculated to offer incisive definition of what it was that needed reformulation. So, as in his essay on Coleridge, he could only speak somewhat darkly about the irrelevance of "the absolute" and of "vague scholastic abstractions." But, however awkwardly the essayist may have expressed it, the novelist knew that the *sensus divinitatis* is mediated by way not of dubious metaphysical propositions but of precisely that which A. C. Benson mistakenly declared him to be unmindful of—namely, the encounter with agape. He knew, in other words, that "Love is the unfamiliar name"[78] behind the design of the *civitas terrena*, and thus Marius's conversion to the Christian faith is accounted for not in formal doctrinal terms (since none of those available to Pater, as he in all likelihood felt, were wholly satisfactory) but in terms rather, as Graham Hough says, of "an actual experience, the experience of a society which he can see, whose atmosphere he can feel, in which he has some hope of participating,"[79] and which, in its consecration to the *caritas* made manifest in Christ, represents (as the novel says) "the whole company of mankind." And, as Pater wanted to suggest, a faith thus grounded is of a sort "possible for the modern mind."

It was by way, then, of the elaborate stratagem involved in the writing of *Marius the Epicurean* that Pater hoped to correct or to clarify the Conclusion of *The Renaissance*. Which is to say that *Marius* was intended to be his full statement of where a true *diaphanéité* may be expected to lead. Many had concluded that his earlier plea for "openness" to and "receptivity" of what experience brings represented nothing more than a somewhat oblique apology for a program of hedonistic self-indulgence, and, having suffered at once surprise and distress at this miscomprehension of what he was aiming at, he had withdrawn the Conclusion from the second edition of *The Renaissance*. But, then, restoring it in the third edition of 1888, he said: "I have thought it best to reprint it here. . . . I have dealt more fully in *Marius the Epicurean* with the thoughts suggested by it." And what he trusted his more attentive readers to realize was that *Marius* had indeed made it clear that the ethic of *diaphanéité*, of openness and receptivity, when seriously pursued in relation to *the grief in things*, leads not—far from it!—to any sort of unprincipled *sensualité* but leads, rather, to a search for that which, in releasing us from "the prison" of the single ego's solitariness, confers the kind of beatitude that is found only in a community of Love. In short, to "dwell poetically" is to be poised toward that universal commonwealth which some call "the Kingdom of Christ." So to state the matter is to put it in terms which Pater's reserve would not perhaps have allowed him. (In his "reserve" how much like Keble he is!)[80] But his real intention is fully disclosed in *Marius the Epicurean*.

In the years that remained until his death in 1894 Pater published at intervals in *Macmillan's Magazine* one or another of his short "imaginary portraits" (the brilliant "A Prince of Court Painters" in October of 1885, "Sebastian van Storck" in March of 1886, "Denys l'Auxerrois" in October of 1886, and "Duke Carl of Rosenmold" in May of 1887), and these were issued in a small volume by the Macmillan firm in 1887. A long installment of a semiautobiographical novel, *Gaston de Latour*, was published serially in *Macmillan's Magazine* in 1888. He kept busy also with essays—on Shakespeare, Amiel, Sir Thomas Browne, Browning, and various other figures—many of which he gathered into the collection of 1889 entitled *Appreciations*. And in 1893, the year before his death, he published his *Plato and Platonism*, which was based on a series of lectures he had periodically presented to Brasenose undergraduates. But these and numerous other things, though many of them are impressively touched with Pater's special genius, do not require to be thought of as really major work. Indeed, the ten-volume "New Library Edition" of his writings that Macmillan issued in 1910 carries but two masterpieces (*The Renaissance* and *Marius the Epicurean*), and it makes a considerable irony that Pater should for so long have been thought of in the terms that have been reserved for him—"hedonism," *volupté*, "aestheticism," *décadence*—when *Marius the Epicurean* deserves to be accounted amongst the few great religious classics of the modern period.

To speak of *Marius* as a religious classic is not, of course, to foreclose the possibility of its being regarded in its "doctrine" as something more religiously ambiguous than I have been inclined to suggest. (Indeed, many of those in recent years who have undertaken to deal with it in a serious way have been so eager to multiply ambiguity that their renderings often in no way at all "prove" themselves in relation to one's *immediate* experience of the novel.) It is only to say that—like the poems of Hopkins, like Martin Buber's *I and Thou*, like the books of Simone Weil, like Eliot's *Quartets*—it causes us to question the authenticity of our present mode of being in the world in such a way as, in effect, to make us "retrieve" the religious *possibility*; and, thus, it makes "a nonviolent appeal to our minds, hearts and imaginations, and through them to our wills."[81] Which is in turn to say that Pater's legacy deserves to be accorded a status rather different from that of dusty *school* classics.

5/ Santayana's Poetics of Belief

It is a kind of total grandeur at the end,

. . . .

Total grandeur of a total edifice,
Chosen by an inquisitor of structures.

—Wallace Stevens,
"To an Old Philosopher
in Rome"

Among the great masters in this century of the philosophic vocation—
James, Whitehead, Dewey, Husserl, Wittgenstein, and Heidegger—
there is perhaps none whose legacy is today so indifferently valued as is
George Santayana's. Nor does the inappreciation that generally marks
the prevailing view of his work represent a development that has only
just gradually come to pass in the years since his death in Rome in the
early autumn of 1952. On the contrary, throughout his entire career,
though he was always far from being ignored, he constantly faced an
intellectual community, particularly in the United States, that reserved
sympathies for him that were very imperfect indeed. The "intense mas-
culinity" (as, I believe, Santayana himself somewhere phrases it) of his

own Harvard mentor, William James, was slightly offended by a certain mandarinism and "moribund Latinity" it descried in the young Santayana, offended enough for James to have convinced himself that the early work of his protégé did in fact express what he called "the perfection of rottenness." And something like James's animus (which in his case, to be sure, was mingled with affection) was persistently a part of the response Santayana was offered during his lifetime on the American scene.

The themes of the philosophical disputation that Santayana aroused in the sixty years of his publishing career (from his debut in 1890, with his first major essay in *Mind*, to the appearance in 1951 of his last book, *Dominations and Powers*) are, of course, long since familiar. Many of his contemporaries were not in the first instance easily to be convinced that he was even properly to be regarded as a philosopher at all. Is not this chap who writes so prettily, who takes so manifest a delight in the various gestures his diction and syntax can be made to perform, really a sort of dandy, an *élégant* more fascinated with the pirouettes of his own rhetoric than with the exactions of rigorous analysis? So it was that the impeachment went with numerous pedants who, like their kind generally, supposed that seriousness of thought bears some necessary relation to circuitousness and obscurity. Is he not rather a poet than a philosopher? And, assuredly, the members of his own academic guild in advancing this suggestion were not intending praise.

Moreover, throughout the central period of his working career—the period, let us say, extending from 1905 (when the first volumes of *The Life of Reason* were issued) to 1940 (the year in which the fourth volume of *Realms of Being* appeared)—Santayana's basic conception of philosophy was very much at odds with the reigning doctrines. Viewing the life of culture from the standpoint of a generous democracy that accorded an almost equal weight to religion, art, science, and the counsels of common sense, he felt the philosopher's obligation to be that of building a synoptic vision of the human situation that renders an appropriate justice to all the great ways of man's reckoning with his experience. But most of his immediate contemporaries, having liberated themselves from what they conceived to be the vaporousness of German idealism, were taking it for granted that, now in this late time, the one legitimate role for philosophy is that of extending scientific procedure into every nook and cranny of human life; and such a man as Santayana, who appeared to regard the symbolic forms of science as having no more privileged an ontological status than the symbolic forms of religious faith, struck them as being little more than a professional obscurantist. Whereas by the late 1930s his younger contemporaries, as they began to be stirred up by the new excitements brought onto the Anglo-American scene by the spokesmen for the Vienna Circle, were deciding that philosophy is a procedure of linguistic sanitation, and thus to them Santayana's manifest lack of concern for this whole program made him appear a sort of late Victorian belletrist whose only interest lay in the curious example he presented of a fin-de-siècle Catholic who had lost his faith but who remained a fin-de-siècle Catholic.

Nor did his American confreres ever quite forgive Santayana for the critical assessments he permitted himself of the country that was his host through most of the years from 1872 (when his father brought him from Avila to Boston to take up residence with his mother and the children of her first marriage) to 1912, when he resigned his Harvard professorship for a European life of study and writing. The stringent appraisal he presented in his novel *The Last Puritan* of the distortions of feeling and conscience bequeathed a type of American character by the Puritan tradition, the thrusts he directed at the airy mysticism of the Transcendentalists, his gentle raillery of the pensive and ineffectual agnosticism of our high culture, the ironies he bestowed on "the heartiness of American ways, the feminine gush and the masculine go"— none of this represented anything more severe than the judgments people like Cabot Lodge and Trumbull Stickney and William Vaughan Moody amongst his early Harvard friends would themselves have been inclined to express. And, indeed, the phrase forming the title of one of Santayana's most famous essays, "the genteel tradition," was immediately picked up in the 1930s and converted by Vernon Parrington, Malcolm Cowley, and scores of others into far more of a pejorative than he had ever intended it to be. But *he* was a foreigner, and not an Englishman or a Frenchman but a Spaniard: so his estimate of the American condition, for all its cogency and lack of malice, was felt to represent an egregious condescension, and the impertinence of this "dainty unassimilated man" (as the classicist Paul Shorey spoke of him) was unpardonable. So, though such a figure as Dewey was offered garlands and testimonials on his seventieth, eightieth, eighty-fifth, and ninetieth birthdays and though Santayana "outlived the conventional three score and ten by nearly another score, and many of his contemporaries received public congratulations from their sixty-fifth birthdays on,"[1] there was never any occasion during his long span (as Horace Kallen remarked at the time of the hundredth anniversary of his birth) when a decent tribute was paid this great old Lucretian by those whose philo-sophical tradition he had so greatly dignified. Yet, as he said when he was not far from passing into the ninth decade of his life—with no doubt the bemused smile of one who knew how questionable was his status as a European—"it is as an American writer that I must be counted, if I am counted at all."[2]

But now this man—who was christened Jorge Agustín Nicolás Ruiz de Santayana y Borrás on 1 January 1864 in the parish church of San Marcos in Madrid and whose remains are buried in the *Tomba degli Spagnuoli* of the Verano cemetery in Rome but whose formative years were shaped under American auspices—is virtually unremembered and unspoken of in our intellectual life, despite all that he *added* to our native inheritance. It is a strange and unfortunate circumstance, this inaptitude that we have for practicing the art of anamnesis.

The strangest anomaly, however, that we face in the history of San-tayana's reputation is that it is precisely the element of the most genuine profundity in his thought which has occasioned the most firmly dis-missive charges of "defiant eclecticism."[3] For it is his way of combining a thoroughgoing materialism with a kind of chastened transcendental-ism (which he was as eager to distinguish from Emersonian romanti-cism as from the more classic forms of idealism descending from Kant) that constitutes the special signature of his genius, and yet it is just his hospitality toward these divergent perspectives that has proved most irritating.

But, whatever may be the verdict of his critics, Santayana himself, in his ripe maturity, wanted very emphatically to insist that the real ground of his thought is to be found nowhere else than in his material-ism. "My philosophy," he said, "is not an academic opinion adopted because academic tendencies seemed . . . to favour it. I care very little whether, at any moment, academic tendencies favour one unnecessary opinion or another. I ask myself only what are the fundamental presup-positions that I cannot live without making. And I find that they are summed up in the word materialism."[4] Yet Santayana's materialism hardly proposes any sort of systematic cosmology, and nothing could be more alien to its true import than so quintessentially materialistic a dictum as that which Hobbes lays down in chapter 46 of the *Leviathan*, when he says: "The universe, that is, the whole mass of all things that are, is corporeal, that is to say, body, and hath the dimensions of magni-tude, namely length, breadth, and depth . . . and that which is not body is no part of the universe: and because the universe is all, that which is no part of it is nothing, and consequently nowhere." Indeed, wherever one turns amongst the key statements of his career, whether to *The Life of Reason* or to *Scepticism and Animal Faith* or to *Realms of Being*, Santayana's profession of materialism, far from being inspired by scientific precept and far from claiming that matter and reality are coextensive, would appear to be saying nothing other than that the supporting matrix of the human enterprise formed by all the coherences and continuities of the natural order represents an absolutely recalcitrant kind of otherness which can in no way be thought to be called into being by any creative act of the human spirit itself. He conceives the controlling principle of matter or existence to be the principle of "substance," since substance is that which "actualizes and limits the manifestation of every essence that figures in nature or appears before the mind."[5] And the account in *Realms of Being* of the "presumable properties" of substance makes a nice example of his dialectical powers at full stretch, but the doctrine of substance does, at bottom, want to assert nothing more than the primacy of that aboriginal world which primitive experience and common sense confront "as the condition of mind" and as that which makes us know that "mind . . . [is not] the condition of nature."[6] Man does not dwell, in other words, as Santayana wants to say, in his own brainpan but, rather, in the presence of a world which, in respect to the human agent, is *wholly other*; he is its witness, not its creator; it is to nothing more than this that his materialism comes down in the end, and to conceive it otherwise is to misconceive it.

Santayana's account of the human situation goes on, however, to insist on the dark inscrutability of that order of things *out there* with which we have our daily commerce. His German contemporary Edmund Husserl, to be sure, was launching his whole project of phenomenology with the contention that things are nothing other than what they are as "things of experience" and that the inexperienceable is beyond the domain of both thought and discourse. But to the great innovator at Freiburg Santayana would have been inclined to say: "When I rub my eyes and look at things candidly, it seems evident to me that they stubbornly refuse to be sucked into the immediacies of actual experience." And it was in this conviction that a cardinal premise of his thought was deeply rooted.

That there is a natural world by which we are surrounded and which is peopled with myriad things and creatures—this Santayana took to be a necessary postulate of that "animal faith" which the venture of living requires of us all. And he considered it to be the task of philosophy not so much to justify this assumption as to advertise its presumptiveness, and thus to keep steadily before us the essentially

fideistic basis on which all our transactions with the world are con-
ducted. But, though animal faith must take it for granted *that* the
circumambient world has a genuinely real status in the realm of being,
what the various things and creatures of our experience are, in the
absolute specificity of their actual existence—this, as Santayana insists,
remains forever hidden. The only "givens" that human intelligence has
at hand are its apprehensions of this and that, what he calls "essences."
Yet these data which are immediately present to consciousness are powerless to authenticate their own factuality, and thus Santayana finds
himself driven to his sceptical conclusion, that "nothing given exists."[7]

Santayana's "essence" is not, of course, as he frequently found it
necessary to insist, merely another version of the Platonic Idea, for
Platonism, as he reminds us, materializes the Idea into a supernatural
power capable of acting causatively upon the natural order. In his own
vision of things, however, an essence, since it does not "exist," lacks
any sort of material efficacy. It is simply the indelible impression that a
particular fact, that a particular chunk of reality, scores upon the
mind.[8] Indeed, Santayana's doctrine of essence is not unlike Gerard
Manley Hopkins's doctrine of "inscape." Hopkins considered all things
to be "upheld by instress,"[9] and by "instress" he meant that power and
drive of Being which keeps each created thing from scattering and
dissolving, that ontological energy wherewith a bird or a flower or a
cloud in the sky is *assembled* into the given *Gestalt* which it constitutes
and made to be what it is—rather than another thing. Whereas a thing's
"inscape" is just the pattern or form which its instress rivets upon the
alert witness. And Santayana's essence is, basically, Hopkins's inscape:
it is just that elementary *haecceitas*, that radical particularity, which is
felt in *this* "red wheelbarrow glazed with rain water," in *this* girl's face
when it is touched by the slanting rays of the afternoon sun, in *this*
limestone landscape with its "murmur / Of underground streams"—
when any one of these things manages so to penetrate (in Coleridge's
phrase) "the film of familiarity and selfish solicitude" as to command
upon itself a heedful gaze of the mind. "Whatsoever existing fact we
may think we encounter, there will be obvious features distinguishing
that alleged fact from any dissimilar fact and from nothing. All such
features, discernible in sense, thought, or fancy, are essences; and the
realm of essence which they compose is simply the catalogue, infinitely
extensible, of all characters logically distinct and ideally possible."[10]

The essence, however, in Santayana's conception, is not what traditional empiricism speaks of as sense-datum, for, though his materialism
requires him to regard it as indeed an awareness of *something* and as

thus bringing us tidings of the real, it is not so much an affair of mere unorganized sensory impression as it is a kind of symbolic form which intuition *posits* and which henceforth serves as something like a sign or portent of a certain feature of reality. So, since it is not actually intermingled with that which it exemplifies but stands rather only in a sort of parallel relation to it,[11] he insists that an essence may not be considered to "exist": it is an expression of nothing more than that capacity of the human spirit to reach intentively beyond itself toward its environing world, that capacity which (in his transcendentalist idiom) Santayana speaks of as "spirit."

Yet, however "theoretic" the realm of essence may be, its periphery defines the limit beyond which, in Santayana's sense of things, there is no possibility of extending our cognizance of the world. Which is to say that the realm of the essences offers us our one mode of fathoming that generative order of reality which he calls "the realm of matter." So, to all intents and purposes, we dwell actually in "the realm of spirit"— which is not, as he conceives it, any sort of ghostly heterocosm but simply that region of endeavor in which we seek to organize and integrate our experience by way of religion and science and philosophy and literature and the arts. And, of course, the life of spirit reaches out, eagerly and yearningly, toward that most elusive of all the Realms of Being—namely, "the realm of truth." But essences are the only earnest of reality we can ever win, and, since they do not "exist" and tell therefore no tales about what is *actually* the case, Santayana's account of truth, perhaps expectably, is as elusive as the thing itself. For all the abhorrence he felt for the fundamental worldview of American pragmatism, he was, to be sure, occasionally inclined toward a kind of pragmatic view of our situation as one in which, by way of our dealings with essences, we dream awake and our "dreams are kept relevant to . . . [their] environment . . . only by the external control exercised over them by Punishment, when the accompanying conduct brings ruin, or by Agreement, when it brings prosperity."[12] On other occasions, however, he seems to have been inclined to think of truth as constituted of those essences that find real embodiment in existence—though, since we have immediate contact only with the essence itself and are never therefore able strictly to verify its relation to actuality, he, in accord with his basic premises, considered *knowledge* to be assumptive, a matter of "animal faith" that the data present to the mind are indeed indicative of existing states of affairs.[13] Yet one feels that, finally, the doctrine of truth that Santayana's scepticism found most congenial is nowhere more suggestively and poignantly adumbrated than in the concluding sentence of the Epilogue of his novel *The Last Puritan* which says: "After life is over and the world has gone up in smoke, what realities might the spirit in us still call its own without illusion save the form of those very illusions which have made up our story?"

Nor did he want even in the slightest degree to exempt his own philosophy from the kind of unillusioned stringency expressed in this concluding sentence of *The Last Puritan*. At a certain point he imagines himself being interrogated about the truth-claims he would make in behalf of his own reflections. He says:

> A rationalistic reader might . . . ask: "Is there no truth within your realm of essence? Are not unity and distinctness present in all essences, and is it not true to say so? And all that you yourself have written, here and else-where, about essence, is it not true?" No, I reply, it is not true, nor meant to be true. It is a grammatical or possibly a poetical construction having, like mathematics or theology, a certain internal vitality and interest; but in the direction of truth-finding, such constructions are merely instrumen-tal like any language or any telescope. A man may fall into an error in grammar or in calculation. This is a fault in the practice of his art, at bot-tom a moral defect, a defect in attention, diligence, and capacity: and in my dialectic I have doubtless often clouded my terms with useless or dis-turbing allusions. But when consistently and conscientiously worked out and stripped to their fighting weight, my propositions will be logically necessary, being deducible from the definitions or intuitions of the chosen terms, and especially of this chosen term "essence" itself. But logic is only logic: and the systems of relation discoverable amongst essences do not constitute truths, but only other more comprehensive essences, within which the related essences figure as parts.[14]

We are compassed about, then, by the four realms of matter, es-sence, spirit, and truth. And though, in the order of experience, it is the realm of essence which claims primacy, in the ontological order it is the realm of matter which is the truly aboriginal and generative dimension of reality. But in relation to this region of things we see through a glass darkly and face, for all its pomp and circumstance, unfathomable mys-tery. "The light of the spirit which shines in the darkness cannot see the primeval darkness which begat it and which it dispels."[15] Indeed, San-tayana's vision of the human situation is more than a little touched by a sense of what Martin Heidegger called *Geworfenheit*, by a sense of our having been "thrown" into a world which is not of our own making and which in its sheer givenness, in its sheer thereness, confronts us with a contingency so absolute that we find ourselves staring at "dark abysses before which intelligence must be silent, for fear of going mad."[16] The world in its various concrete aspects is, to be sure, easily perceptible: yet "what is most plain to sense is most puzzling to reason ... and what is intelligible to reason at one level ... may become arbitrary and obscure to a reason that ... asks deeper questions."[17] "The aim of intelligence is to know things as they are."[18] But it finds the universe with which it undertakes to treat to be "a conjunction of things mutually irrelevant, a chapter of accidents, a medley improvised here and now for no reason, to the exclusion of myriad other forces which, so far as their ideal structure is concerned, might have been performed just as well."[19] Ours, in short, is a world that simply cannot be brought to heel and that evokes a great *o altitudo!* of astonishment, as we find ourselves (in a metaphor of Pascal that Santayana could easily have appropriated) "in a vast sphere, ever drifting in uncertainty," where "to attach ourselves to any point and to fasten to it" is to find it wavering and slipping past us and vanishing forever. "This," says the *Pensées*, "is our natural condition, and yet most contrary to our inclination; we burn with desire to find solid ground and an ultimate sure foundation whereon to build a tower reaching to the Infinite. But our whole groundwork cracks, and the earth opens to abysses"[20]— abysses, says Santayana, "before which intelligence must be silent."

Yet, absurd as the world appears to be in the inexplicableness of its sheer factuality, we are nevertheless in thousands of ways dependent upon it for health and sustenance. We need air to breathe and space in which to abide and the nourishment of food and drink and the countless other bounties with which nature ministers to our frailty and makes our sojourning on the earth supportable. And thus, for all the recalcitrancy of the material universe, it would be, as Santayana wants to urge, a foolish mistake for us to permit ourselves any great aversion from the realm of matter, for, were we to hold it in contempt, "it would not be merely ashes or dust that we should be despising, but all natural existence in its abysmal past and in its indefinite fertility; and it would be, not some philosopher's sorry notion of matter that we should be denying, but the reality of our animal being."[21] Indeed, as he insists, if reverence is to be offered anything at all, it ought to be directed not toward "ideal objects" but toward "the realm of matter only,"[22] since, opaque and mysterious though it may be, it is that which chastens and corrects us, which preserves and protects us, and which with its far horizons grants us a place in which to dwell.

Now the form in which Santayana conceives this *pietas* to find its proper expression he frequently speaks of as "pure intuition"—which may not be the happiest locution, since it can suggest what is really contrary to the final drift of his basic meaning: namely, that it is a kind of angelism, the delights of something like a Platonic heaven, at which "spirit" aims. But in *Scepticism and Animal Faith* he speaks of "discernment of spirit" as an affair of "attention" and "wakefulness"[23]—which is no doubt a language more apt, for this is indeed the kind of response that, in his sense of things, a true piety will make toward the world which is at hand: "we may say that for the mind there is a single avenue to essence, namely attention."[24] But even when he speaks in this connection of "intuition," he does not mean any sort of "divination, or a miraculous way of discovering that which sense and intellect cannot disclose. On the contrary," as he is careful to say, "by intuition I mean direct and obvious possession of the apparent."[25] Or, as it might be somewhat differently put, by intuition or wakefulness of attention he means nothing other than a heedful openness toward all the things of earth as, in their concrete particularity, they take on the dimension of *presence*: he means the kind of openness that wants, in Richard Hovey's phrase, to "have business with the grass."

Spirit—"the light which lighteth every man that cometh into the world"—is, of course, for Santayana the name and nature of *humanitas*, of what (had he ever produced an anthropology) he would have declared to be the distinctively human thing itself. And it is simply that capacity for self-transcendence which enables the human creature to hail or salute its world and to be so awake to the furniture of existence as to discern the "inscapes" of its various items. Indeed, "the exercise of sight as distinguished from blindness,"[26] the act whereby we "greet" and pay heed to the things of earth, is precisely that which Santayana considers to be the central act of the human spirit, for it constitutes the agency by means of which "essences are transposed into appearances and things into objects of belief" and both "are raised to a strange actuality in thought."[27] But intuition or wakefulness of attention is not merely an affair of simple awareness, for it is laden with what he (rather obscurely) calls "intent." And by intent he means that leap of animal faith whereby "spirit," though dealing always with essences which do not "exist," nevertheless *posits* a relation between the "given" (essence) and that which is not given (the existing thing)—and not only posits such a relation but holds it to be "true," in the manner of a symbolic form. What intent achieves, in other words, is a grasp of things which is "not true literally, as the fond spirit imagines when it takes some given picture, summary, synthetic, and poetical, for the essence of the world; but true as language may be true, symbolically, pragmatically, and for the range of human experience in that habitat and at that stage in its history."[28]

It is in such terms that Santayana renders the life of spirit, and thus his whole system of reflection represents the truly human mode of being as one involving a very strict kind of receptivity and alertness to the stars of heaven and the winds of earth, to the fowls of the air and the beasts of the field, to mountains and plains, to nights and days, to the high and exalted and the low and downtrodden—indeed, to all the myriad forms of the world that presses in upon us. And, as he suggests, it is only by way of such vigilance and wakefulness of attention that we may escape the grosser forms of egotism and win through to that capaciousness and clarity of vision belonging to "the life of reason."

Nor should it go unremarked that it is just in this connection that Santayana wants to record what it is that he finds irresistibly appealing in the figure of Christ. For spirit "claims nothing, posits nothing, and is nothing in its own eyes, but empties itself completely"[29] into that which it contemplates, and it is precisely this readiness for *kenosis*, this *disponibilité*, that he considers to be "one of the [chief] beauties in the idea of Christ." "In spite of his absolute holiness, or because of it, he shows a spontaneous sympathy, shocking to the Pharisee, with many non-religious sides of life, with little children, with birds and flowers, with common people, with beggars, with sinners, with sufferers of all sorts, even with devils. This is one of the proofs that natural spirit, not indoctrinated or canalised, was speaking in him."[30] And it is, indeed, in the breadth of his sympathies and his quick responsiveness to every slightest bid for his attention that comes from the world about him that Santayana finds also a sort of proof of the fullness of Christ's humanity.

The kind of punctiliousness of attention that marks the life of spirit in its purest modes is, however, a moral achievement by no means easily realized, and, in a manner strikingly reminiscent of Pascal's anatomy of the various forms of *divertissement*, Santayana discriminates the several types of "distraction." "By distraction," he says, "I understand the alien force that drags the spirit away from the spontaneous exercise of its liberty, and holds it down to the rack of care, doubt, pain, hatred, and vice. And I will distinguish the chief agencies in this distraction, after the picturesque manner of Christian wisdom, as the Flesh, the World, and the Devil."[31]

In regard to the carnal passions, it is not, of course, any kind of sour asceticism that Santayana wants to espouse, for he knows that the flesh, forming as it does "the raw material of human nature," cannot be simply discarded and that, indeed, the fleshly impulses, if merely gagged and repressed, will take their revenge, often in cruel and devastating ways. Yet he does want to lay down the necessity of taming and transmuting them in such a fashion that they will warm rather than anarchize the affections, so that spirit may not be distracted from its true vocation.

Nor does he want to preach any fanatical doctrine of contempt for the world, since he takes it for granted that the charms and delights of the world—comfort and security and favorable repute—are well enough, taken simply in and of themselves: "spirit does not come from or demand another world, or reject any form of life as unworthy. It is ready to participate in any undertaking and to rejoice in every achievement."[32] And for him the principle of worldliness stands not for a sober accommodation to the material requirements of earthly life but rather for the kind of entanglement in the cares and trivialities of the quotidian realm that hobbles and restricts the full range of sympathy that spirit might otherwise have for the whole panorama of existence. Which is to say that the worldling's self-preoccupation leads to a certain tragic desuetude of attention: he smokes "his excellent cigar with a calm sense that there is nothing in the world better than what he does,"[33] and the tax that is levied against him for his philistinism is a very great poverty, the poverty of insentience and dullness and ennui.

And, as for the devil, Santayana says that he takes this personage to stand for "an enemy of spirit that is internal to spirit [itself]"[34]—which makes bedevilment the subtlest and most insidious of all the snares we face. Its tempting power arises out of the strange situation in which spirit finds itself, of being committed to the intuition of essences that have no status in existence other than that which animal faith posits and of being, therefore, peculiarly susceptible to a kind of monarchism, to the dream of omniscience. It seems that "either we can know nothing, because confined to our passing dream, or we can know nothing because there is nothing but our passing dream to be known"[35]—and, when the dream of omniscience has taken hold, it is the second alternative that will be embraced, spirit then imagining itself to be absolutely free and absolutely creative. But when spirit in this way denies its dependence on the ancestral order of nature, it is at the point of closing itself in upon itself, of forfeiting precisely that attentive openness toward the circumambient world which is its distinctive genius: its pride in its own creativeness is by way of leading it to assert its essential infinity—and this way madness lies, the kind of madness that Lucifer prepares.

The flesh, the world, and the devil, then—these three—are the great agents of "distraction." But, in so far as the spirit can be preserved from its threefold enemy, it will then proceed to do the work which it is man's special vocation to do, of building up that "ideal," symbolic universe (of science, poetry, art, religion, and metaphysics) which results from the play of the mind on the vast domain of quiddities which is called "the realm of essence." The human situation, as Santayana conceives it, is one of our being placed in a universe which is neither spirit nor spirit's vision of it: so he calls it "the realm of matter." And the vocation of spirit, after keeping for itself a proper piety in recognizing its dependence on this universe, is to *comment* upon it. But the world on which this commentary is made remains forever dark and hidden: "its powers germinate underground, and only its foliage and flowers emerge into clear light."[36] Indeed, its very existence is no more than a postulate of animal faith, for the only terms available to any exploration of it are the essences which belong to an ontological realm wholly other than that generative order of nature which they characterize. Matter, in other words, is absolutely transcendent, for it "is always more and other than the essence which it exemplifies at any point. . . . We may enjoy it, we may enact it, but we cannot conceive it; not because our intellect by accident is inadequate, but because existence . . . is intrinsically a surd."[37] Yet, though we find ourselves enveloped by darkness, we, since we are creatures of spirit, have it as our destiny to try to illumine the darkness—by giving the most careful heed to all the various impressions (or essences) that are scored upon the mind by, as we trust, the world *out there* and by using this material as the basis for a symbolic transformation of the dazzling darkness into those fabrics of meaning that are posited by science, poetry, religion, and art.

Santayana was, of course, reluctant to advance any claim about the veridical capacities of these fabrics of meaning, since they are all wrought out of nothing more than our experience of essences. True, he was prepared occasionally to suggest that the terms of the natural sciences—as compared, say, with those of mythology—are comprised of essences which "are the fruit of a better focussed, more chastened, and more prolonged attention turned upon what actually occurs"[38] and that, therefore, however much faith may be entailed in living by science, "not to live by it is folly."[39] But though, at the level of practice, experience gives a certain urgency to the essences with which physics and biochemistry deal, he was not inclined, finally, to concede that they give us any real "information" about existence: they and all other sciences represent "only a claim . . . put forth, a part of that unfathomable compulsion by force of which we live and hold our painted world together."[40] And it was with a similar agnosticism that Santayana was disposed to respond to any depositions regarding the cognitive import of poetry and the arts and religion, for, in his estimate of things, none of these has any "standing ground in fact": like science, they represent only spirit's attempt at lighting a candle in the dark. Yet, if he ever paid any attention to a brash little manifesto called *Language, Truth and Logic* issued in 1936 by a bright young Englishman named A. J. Ayer, he must surely have felt it to express a particularly repellent kind of coarseness in its relegation of poetic and religious discourse to the province of "nonsense." For Santayana conceived the poetic and the religious imagination to be deeply a part of "the life of reason." Religion and poetry, to be sure, provide us with no information about things (about the realm of "matter")—though (as Santayana would have wanted to say to Mr. Ayer) in this respect, strictly speaking, they are no more impotent than science; but, as he felt, they do hold up "those large ideas tinctured with passion, those supersensible forms shrouded in awe, in which alone a mind of great sweep and vitality can find its congenial objects."[41] Both, as he proposed in his famous formula, "are identical in essence and differ merely in the way in which they are attached to practical affairs. Poetry is called religion when it intervenes in life, and religion, when it merely supervenes upon life, is seen to be nothing but poetry."[42]

For Santayana a very troublesome kind of mischief begins to be made, however, when (as Matthew Arnold put it) religion materializes itself in the fact, in the supposed fact, when it attaches its emotion to the fact[43]—and the same mischief will be made by science and by poetry, whenever they in their way forget the virtuality of their perspectives and seek to impute to spirit the authority of matter by claiming to enunciate something like "absolute truth." What the scientist and the artist need to remember no less than the expositor of sacred mysteries is that "in so far as spirit takes the form of intelligence and of the love of truth . . . it must assume the presence of an alien universe and must humbly explore its ways, bowing to the strong wind of mutation, the better to endure and to profit by that prevailing stress."[44] Indeed, spirit is by way of being betrayed when its devotees forget that all their fashionings are but imaginative projections and then seek to materialize them "in the supposed fact." To try thus to convert spirit into matter is merely to compound illusion with illusion. "Mind was not created for the sake of discovering the absolute truth. The absolute truth has its own intangible reality, and scorns to be known. The function of mind is rather to increase the wealth of the universe in the spiritual dimension, by adding appearance to substance . . . and by creating all those . . . perspectives, and those emotions of wonder, adventure, curiosity, and laughter which omniscience would exclude."[45]

"The light of the spirit which shines in the darkness cannot see the primeval darkness which begat it," but, by the deepest necessities of its own nature, spirit is driven to form by processes of *poiesis* such structures of vision and belief as will permit it to dwell amidst the environing darkness in sanity and peace. These structures—what we call science, religion, poetry, and art—are, of course, grounded in essences which are "the native grammar of the mind," and thus they are not so much "maps" of reality as they are ventures of the imagination at a systematic deciphering of a world which everywhere outruns all our systems of figuration and which asks us therefore not to insist that things are just as we represent them but to say rather of our various schematisms that *something* of the sort may be the case.

So, then, the late Henry Aiken was surely right in suggesting that Santayana "is best understood as a . . . philosopher of symbolic forms,"[46] for this is certainly the field of his most fundamental interest, and thus he deserves to be regarded as one of the great forerunners of what may well turn out to be the decisive enterprise in the intellectual life of our period. But though his idioms made an easily negotiable currency of exchange for the generation of Whitehead and Cassirer, they are no doubt not so readily usable in the age of Roland Barthes and Algirdas Greimas and Gérard Genette. And if one wants summarily to account for what it is in our present situation that makes Santayana's system seem now unnegotiable, one must say that the New Men are bent on hypostatizing "spirit," in a way that would to him have appeared to represent a very strange sort of astigmatism indeed.

The names just mentioned—Barthes, Greimas, and Genette—are cited merely as emblems of that French movement which we speak of (in the loose way in which all "movements" are spoken of) as structuralism and which, as it has drifted onto the Anglo-American scene over the past decade, has increasingly demanded recognition as the reigning accountant now of the *problématique* of symbolic forms. And what perhaps most chiefly distinguishes the present time from that of Santayana is that, whereas then (for such people as Ernst Cassirer, Wilbur Marshall Urban, and Susanne Langer) it was natural to think of the great symbolic forms as structures wherewith human subjectivity constitutes and organizes its experience, today the new dispensation regards them as merely a function of certain governing codes or systems of language and social usage.

Contemporary reflection (Jacques Derrida, Michel Foucault, Tzvetan Todorov, and Julia Kristeva) takes it as its *absolute* presupposition that the symbolic order so absolutely precedes *le signifiant* that its work (*parole*), however elaborate it may be, must be regarded as but a fragmentary expression of the *langue* from which it issues. Indeed, a part of what is anomalous in the whole scheme is that its stress on *le signifiant* is calculated very greatly to devalue the signifier, for the *absolute* presupposition says that, however conveniently first-person verbs may function as a category of reference to the human individual as an agent of certain vocal and bodily acts, the transcendental subject of traditional humanism is in point of fact an invented fiction quite without any substantial nonlinguistic reality. The real situation, in other words, is that the "I" is simply a linguistically encoded stereotype emanating from the cultural matrix by which it was formed—and thus, in the terms of the familiar Saussurean distinction, since *parole* is but an epiphenomenon of *langue*, the truly decisive cultural fact is not the creative power of the autonomous self but the impersonal system of language-structures which shapes and authenticates all human utterance. So it is that "man is dissolved . . . into little more than . . . a speaking pronoun, fixed indecisively in the eternal, ongoing rush of discourse,"[47] one who instead of being the impresario of his language is its slave. And, given this assassination of the subject, the poetries and religions and sciences that he might himself have been thought to have created are seen rather to be merely diverse materializations of that vast superstructure defining the nature and range of linguisticality (and thus of thought and feeling) in a particular cultural situation.

Moreover, trapped as we are within the order of *langue*, it is assumed that nothing could be more misguided than the search after some transitive relation that symbolic forms bear to *le signifié*. So tyrannously, indeed, does this assumption prevail that the symbolic order is itself conceived to be coextensive with all of reality, and nothing is more irritating for the strategists of the *nouvelle critique* than some attempt at resurrecting a metaphysics of "presence," at reviving the notion that univocal substances extrinsic to the symbolic order do in fact exist. For, of course, the new theorists have been taught by Saussure that, even were it analytically possible to isolate *le signifié* as an object of inquiry, it would be found, inevitably and in the nature of the case, to be itself simply another sign-system, since any accessibility it could have to the mind would necessarily be a consequence of its having been organized and constituted by some *signifiant*. So, as it is taken for granted, the symbolic order—that environing superstructure which precedes all particular acts of symbolization—*is* reality, and thus each "text" that we confront, whether it be a poem, a scientific theorem, a theological proposition, a ritual of sport, a style of courtship, or a mode of burying the dead, makes reference to nothing other than that system of *intertextualité* that forms the grid through which it asks to be read and correlatively placed with respect to the other texts to which it is adjacently related. And, therefore, a hermeneutic of culture will entail at bottom an effort of *découpage*, an attempt at cutting through the various epiphenomena of poetry, religion, art, and science to the fundamental linguistic codes by which mind is decisively controlled.

True, traditional humanism (whether by way of the Greeks or of such modern guides as Herder, von Humboldt, Coleridge, and Nietzsche) considers *langue* in all its manifestations—poetic, scientific, religious—to be a foremost case of that creativity wherewith the human spirit gives pattern and order to the multifariousness of experience. But, in these late days of our misery, our present overseers are not inclined to traffic with a "myth of origins": so eager are they to establish the primacy and the exteriority of the symbolic order with respect to *le signifiant* that any attempt at going back behind it to its source in the radical freedom of creative intelligence is deemed a sterile kind of philosophastry. And thus, as the doctrine of imagination is relegated to the discard, a strange anomaly emerges, of what Santayana took to be an expression of "spirit" being so hypostatized now that, far from being thought of as a result of that immanent power of self-transcendence whereby man constitutes his world, it begins to appear as a structure separate from and standing over against him, as indeed coextensive with reality itself.

We ought not to find it surprising, then, given the climate in which humanistic studies must presently be pursued, that, apart from the occasional reference that glances at his influence on Wallace Stevens, the name of Santayana is rarely mentioned today. For the fundamental terms for the author of *Realms of Being* are spirit *and* matter, and the linchpin of his whole concept of the realm of essence is a very large and robust doctrine of the imagination. Yet, despite the velocity with which the winds of change sweep across the contemporary landscape, particularly in the field of literary theory, the principles ultimately controlling the intellectual life are essentially conservative, and we are therefore doubtless always mistaken, when we are quick to conclude that the legacy of so magisterial a thinker as Santayana has been suddenly rendered passé by one or another shift of the *Zeitgeist*. So, as we are seeking today new bearings in theory of interpretation, it may not be unprofitable to turn to major figures of the recent past who are currently neglected, for the sake of appropriating the kind of interrogation of our present moment that they would seem to propose; and, amongst these, Santayana is surely one—and Wilbur Marshall Urban is another—whose testimony, when reconsidered, may have the effect of cross-questioning us into new clarity about the tangled issues facing criticism in our period.

Santayana always stubbornly refused, of course, any pansymbolism of the sort unembarrassedly embraced by his younger German contemporary Ernst Cassirer. In Cassirer's view, the world of symbolic forms stands as "an autonomous creation of the spirit." "The question of what, apart from these . . . [forms], constitutes absolute reality," as he felt, presents us with "an intellectual phantasm."[48] And, thus regarding the search for what may be the relation between symbolic forms and "a self-subsistent world of 'things'" to be misconceived, he forswore any real interest in the issues of ontology. But this was not Santayana's way, since, Lockean though he was in his conviction of the ultimate impenetrability of "matter," he never relaxed his assurance that the great symbolic forms do nonetheless make reference to the realm of matter— that is, to the world *out there*. For, despite the absolute transcendence of the essential interiority of things with respect to human intelligence, they do make their impact in the form of the myriad impressions that they leave as their residue in the mind, and our highest vocation is to keep the strictest possible alertness to these intuitions—and to comment upon them, as we do by way of our science, literature, art, and religion.

True, we can have no certain assurance that the commentary we produce embraces the essential truth, since the mind's transactions are, all of them, restricted to essences, but, by a venture of "animal faith," we wager that we are not altogether misled by the best acts of attention we perform before the great pageantry of the world. And, indeed, our having a "world" at all is a consequence simply of our paying the most careful kind of heed to the "inscapes" of things and to the way in which they bring (as Heidegger would say) "what presences to presence."[49] For the mind not to be focused on the various external influences that are brought to bear upon it and for it not to undertake to build into systems of symbolic forms the various transcripts of reality that the essences convey to us is for it to dwell amidst nothing more than a wilderness of its own contriving. It is, in short, our intuitions of essences and our ordering of these intuitions into the large designs of science and art and religion that give us structures of belief whereby the whole welter of existence can be transformed into what is truly a "world."

For Santayana, however, the imagination is by no means an agency of pure formation that takes reality to be a cliché requiring annulment or redemption, by way of some heterocosmic alternative to the existing world. Indeed, he is quite unprepared to accord (in Henry James's phrase) any "obstinate finality" to consciousness or to endorse the injunction of Emerson's Orphic poet to "build therefore your own world." He does not, in other words, conceive the imagination to possess anything like the aseity that the old doctors of Catholic theology attributed to the Godhead, since, in his sense of things, the principle of ultimacy is to be found only in the Realm of Matter—which constitutes, therefore, that to which the imagination is accountable and to which it owes its final obedience. Indeed, far from being entitled to claim any sort of absolute freedom, the imagination finds itself bidden to reckon with, to be *wakeful* before, that-which-is-at-hand. And thus no symbolic form, however elaborately intricated it may be, can be accorded value by reason of the "reality" it has in its own right or can be assumed to have an intelligibility of a purely intransitive kind. For the languages of the symbolic imagination bring "what presences to presence." "Saying and Being," as Heidegger puts it, "word and thing, belong to each other in a veiled way, a way which . . . is not to be thought out to the end."[50] And Santayana would have wanted to render a similar judgment, given his impatience with the notion that the great symbolic forms present us with closed systems of signification that signify nothing extrinsic to themselves: the degree to which they approximate the things of "matter" may be resolvable only in the terms of animal faith, but they aim at least at some fairly decent ostensiveness— and thus they are betrayed if their intent is taken merely to be self-reflexive.

Those strategists, however, who, under the influence of contemporary structuralism, are charting out a new program for the philosophy of symbolic forms register a great disinclination to make room for what Jacques Derrida calls a "transcendental and privileged signified."[51] Roland Barthes insists, for example, that in the world of the literary imagination language is misconceived altogether if it be thought to involve any kind of reference to "a social, emotional, or poetic 'reality' which pre-exists it, and which it . . . [seeks to] express."[52] Or, again, Michel Foucault even more stringently asserts the "radical intransitivity" of poetic language—which, as he says, "has no other law than that of affirming . . . its own precipitous existence; and so there is nothing for it to do but to curve back in a perpetual return upon itself, as if its discourse could have no other content than the expression of its own form."[53] And it is a similar testimony that is being voiced today by the other leading representatives of the *nouvelle critique* and by their increasingly numerous American discipleship.

So, given Santayana's high doctrine of imagination—of man as the creator of forms—and given his "faith" that these forms do really speak of the world of which we are members, his basic outlook is one that, when juxtaposed against the canons being pressed upon us by the new avant-garde, will surely underscore, by reason of its sharp difference from current orthodoxy, what is most truly fundamental in the assumptions on the basis of which the contemporary movement proposes to reconstruct not only theory of literature but also our way of thinking generally about symbolic forms. This, one suspects, is the chief merit of our undertaking now to remember Santayana's legacy: it is not that a man of his time may be expected to speak in some immediately direct way to the generation of Derrida and Foucault but, rather, that, by making a return to one of the great saints of modern humanism and by confronting the salient antithesis between his testimony and that of the reigning wisdom, we may see more precisely the kind of basic decision that has been made by those in our own period who want to interpret what is at stake in the work which is done by the *animal symbolicum*. And, indeed, this is a juxtaposition that cannot fail to alert us in a newly vivid way to how great is the retreat being arranged by those who seek today to define what it is that man does with his world, for to contemplate their testimony from the perspective of a Santayana is to be reminded that, on their accounting, he does nothing with it at all: he simply accedes to being puppetized by antecedent linguistic codes whose constituent terms refer only to one another and not at all to the circumambient world.

Now it is clear, of course, given the special kind of parochialism generally represented by Continental intellectuals, that the Frenchmen so much in vogue at the moment have never bothered to consult the literature produced by the Anglo-American formalism of a generation ago, and the American epigones of European structuralism are just now so eager to distance themselves from the New Criticism that they are busily forgetting the inheritance bequeathed them by Cleanth Brooks, Allen Tate, W. K. Wimsatt, and the people of their time. But, again, as it would seem, the art of anamnesis very much needs to be freshly cultivated, for the question immediately brought to the fore by our juxtaposition of Santayana and the luminaries of recent structuralism, as to whether the principal modalities of the symbolic imagination (and, most particularly, the great forms of literary art) do indeed make reference to anything beyond themselves—this is a question that was being deeply pondered on the American scene in the period when the New Criticism was at full tide.

The New Critics were not, of course, interested in redeeming mimeticist doctrine, by way of any version of it at all resembling its primitive or classical forms. For they knew that, in our own late post-Kantian time, the grammar of modern intelligence requires us to think of man as dwelling most immediately not in a world of Things but in a world of symbolic forms.[54] Indeed, so far were they from wanting to resurrect for literary theory any simple imitationism that their anxious concern for what was called the "autonomy" of the verbal arts frequently led them to give the impression that they were proposing to sunder the poem qua poem from any and all extramural attachments. It is, as they tended to argue, a structure whose constituent terms behave not ostensively or semantically but reflexively and syntactically, for, however much they may appear by reason of their currency in conventional usage to have some referential bearing on the world of common experience, they do in fact, once they are drawn into the poetic organism, immediately begin to fuse into one another and to gather new meanings that are a function only of the interrelationships whereby they are knitted together into the total pattern that forms the unity of the poem. The terms and "statements" comprising a literary work do not, in other words, refer to anything extrinsic to the work itself but refer, rather, most essentially to one another and thus form an independent system whose organic unity has the effect of shutting off the language of the poem from the "blooming buzzing confusion" of "the ordinary universe." So it was that Brooks, Ransom, Blackmur, and Tate conceived (in René Wellek's phrase) "the mode of existence of a literary work of art."

Yet, for all the apparent inordinacy with which this poetic fenced literature off from the existential world, its major exponents retained a considerable eagerness to accord an important ontological import to the verbal arts and wanted very much to insist that they represent one of the great ways of reckoning with What Is. For, as it was maintained, though the forms of statement employed by the literary imagination do not yield predications of the sort advanced by scientific discourse, nevertheless that pattern of thrust and counterthrust which constitutes the fundamental "tension" and "irony" of poetic art does, in its rich complexity, so fully reflect the complexity of the human world that the poem, closed system though it may be, does at last in analogical fashion prove to be a simulacrum of reality. In short, the poem presents itself as something like "a world enclosed by endlessly faceted mirrors, reflecting and re-reflecting images," but "mirrors [that] somehow become windows opening again upon our everyday world"[55] and granting us an access to it so fresh and full that we find ourselves, as it were for the first time, in possession of "the world's body."

It was in such terms, by way of a by no means simple dialectic, that the New Criticism sought at once to honor the autonomy of the symbolic forms created by the literary imagination and to avow their power to illumine and comment on the instant facts of "the ordinary universe." No doubt the poetic designed to meet this dual purpose represented some incoherence: as one of the strictest arbiters of the whole movement says, the poem "cannot be partly closed, partly open":[56] consistency requires that it be one or the other. Yet the inconsistency in the poetics of the New Criticism represented nothing other than an attempt at dealing candidly with the actualities of that literature on which it was focused—such texts as "The Canonization," *The Tempest*, the Immortality "Ode," *Pride and Prejudice*, *The Possessed*, *The Waste Land*, "Among School Children," *Ulysses*, and *Doctor Faustus*.

The New Criticism could, of course, accord an ontological import to literary art because it harbored no scepticism at all about the objective existence of the poem qua poem. In its impatience with "intentional fallacies," its refusal "to locate the *subject* of a text beyond its particular verbal organizations,"[57] and in its sense of the executive role played by the linguistic medium in the creative process, the school of Blackmur and Brooks and Wimsatt may have been intending, in something like the manner of recent structuralism, that "man the author . . . [should be] unceremoniously deposed."[58] And in this regard certainly this was a poetic requiring to be adjudged highly questionable from the perspective of a Santayana. But at least it never doubted the stoutly perduring thinginess and iconicity of verbal art, and thus, for all its obsession with the autonomy of the literary work, it never ceased to try to reckon with the ways in which the poem may be an instrument of mediation whereby we are given a kind of genuine insight into the essential realities of human existence.

At our present juncture, however, the *nouvelle critique* offers us little more than "a lesson in how to subvert the specificity of literature,"[59] for it is bent on reducing man himself and all the great forms of the symbolic imagination to the status of being simply functions of the linguistic codes and systems that rule us. The language of the poem, we are told, only doubles back on itself and thence on to the language of other poems to which it is related by the logic of *intertextualité*, and thence on to that system of signification of which the poem is merely an epiphenomenon. Which means, therefore, that the function of the literary economy "is not to communicate an objective, external meaning which exists prior to the system but only to create a functioning equilibrium, a movement of signification."[60] The "presence" of the poem, in other words, is displaced by *langue*, and the essence of the poem is to be found simply in the significatory process itself, not in what it signifies.

So, as we are reminded by our new guides, the literary experience is bound to be filled with emptiness and disappointment, for, however much the work of art may seem to promise mediation of the "world," this pledge will at last be found to be spurious, mired as the poem is in a relational universe of linguisticality by which it is ultimately and inevitably devoured. In short, all *tropiques* and *pôles* of the literary universe are *tristes*, since they must all be finally descried to lead into nothing more than "signs" and never into what Santayana's mythography calls "matter." And thus, since the figurative impulse leads nowhere beyond sheer figuration itself and since literary art is therefore quite blind with respect to "the ordinary universe," what M. Derrida calls "the interpretation of interpretation"—which must necessarily claim the paramount interest of the new avant-garde—becomes a strange carnival[61] involving something like the dancing of a jig on the grave of both literature and criticism. Hayden White's summary of it is splendidly comprehensive and concise. He says:

> To see through the figurative to the literal meaning of any effort to seize experience in language is impossible, among other reasons, because there is no "perception" by which "reality" can be distinguished from its various linguistic figurations and the relative truth-content of competing figurations discerned. There is *only figuration.* . . . Being, itself, is absurd. Therefore there is no "meaning," only the ghostly ballet of alternative "meanings" which various modes of figuration provide. We are indentured to an endless series of metaphorical translations from one universe of figuratively provided meaning to another. And they are all equally figurative.[62]

Recent theory of symbolic forms, at least as it is being carried forward within the literary community, signalizes, then, the advent of a strange, new mood that surely deserves to be very carefully pondered. For what it would seem to express on the part of the curators of *litterae humaniores* is an intention to assert the essential emptiness of the verbal arts. Within the terms of Saussure's dualities of *le signifiant* and *le signifié*, of *parole* and *langue*, we are assured by such authorities as Jacques Derrida, Roland Barthes, Michel Foucault, and Paul de Man that the distance between human subjectivity and the world of "things" is so unbridgeable that, as a consequence, all our "signifiers" are without any "signified" and that our gestures in the direction of *parole* are therefore fated to figure forth nothing more than that system of norms and rules constituting the *langue* off which they ricochet. In short, *écriture* is utterly "worldless," being fashioned of "cercles immenses / Dans le néant";[63] and thus it brings us to something like a *degré zéro*, where there is only "the ghostly ballet . . . of figuration"—dancing about the Void. Such is the verdict we are given.

So it is clear, indeed, that the protocols of Santayana's system do not offer an easily negotiable medium of exchange in the context of contemporary reflection on the symbolic process. For, despite all his resolutely sceptical commitments, he conceived man's place to be at a point of juncture between "spirit" *and* "matter": he took it for granted, therefore, that any theory of meaning must embrace *both* dimensions, that it must entail a semantics as well as a semiotics, and the positing of figuration itself as the sole object of figuration would have struck him as being what it surely is, a radically absurd hypostatization of "spirit" alone. Santayana does not, of course, from within the terms of his own thought offer any systematic refutation of the theory of symbolic forms currently in vogue, but the whole drift of his vision, when we undertake today to recover it, may, by its sharp divergence from the reigning doctrine, have the effect of newly putting us in mind of how drastic is the new hermeticism. And it may also bring us to the threshold of a new *decision*, as to whether or not we shall give our suffrage to a poetic that does, at bottom, contend for the essential worthlessness of literary art.

To read Roland Barthes on Racinian tragedy, Gérard Genette on Proust, Tzvetan Todorov on *Les Liaisons dangereuses*, or Michel Foucault on Raymond Roussel is no doubt to be somewhat dazzled, and a little intimidated, by the brilliance of inventiveness and wit that marks their discourse, for they and numerous others of their general party are—let us freely admit it—consummately resourceful performers. But, having duly acknowledged what there may be of ingenuity and even wizardry in the *esprit* brought onto the contemporary scene by the *nouvelle critique*, the question ought not then to be evaded as to whether this is a movement whose doctrine is calculated to support or to subvert what needs to be called (banquet phrase though it may be) the fundamental humanistic enterprise—of exhibiting wherein the work of the literary imagination illumines and helps us to reckon with our fears and hopes, our loves and hates, our deceptions and our self-deceptions, our finitude and our capacity to touch the fringes of eternity. And if it appears that a given poetic, with whatever cleverness it may be espoused, not only abdicates from this whole range of discrimination but positively disavows even its possibility for critical discourse, then, as it would seem, it simply deserves what the poet of the *Commedia* spoke of as *il gran rifiuto* ("the great refusal").

One occasionally hears today nervous declarations about the "crisis" that has overtaken contemporary criticism, and no doubt ours is a period in which the condition of criticism deserves to be so conceived. But it may need to be remembered that "crisis" speaks not merely of a bothersome situation of difficulty but of a situation in which the occasion has arisen for *deciding* whether a given state of things should continue to prevail or should be modified or terminated. And, indeed, if the legacy of a Santayana offers us any kind of tonic just now, perhaps it is one that chiefly consists in a certain invitation this legacy conveys from the Old Philosopher in Rome, who, from "that Platonic heaven to which the circumstances of time are wholly irrelevant,"[64] may be thought to look down upon us with the "smile of Parmenides"[65] on his face, gently voicing an entreaty that we simply decide whether or not in the last analysis we shall cast our vote for the enterprising anti-humanism that presently bids for our allegiance.

6/ Stevens's Route— Transcendence Downward

We often suppose the name of the modern poet to be Orpheus, since in his characteristic manifestations (from Novalis to Mallarmé and Valéry, and from Blake to Rilke and St.-John Perse) he takes it to be within the power of song to assemble—or reassemble—all the *disjecta membra* of the earth and to build a world that will suffice in a time of dearth. And, in the common view, it is Wallace Stevens, the invincible poet of the Supreme Fiction, who brings the whole Orphic venture to its point of culmination. So generous is the hospitality that this Connoisseur of Chaos offers to a wide variety of divergent perspectives and projects that one can, of course, find some basis in the poetry on which to ground any one of a dozen or so quite different views of his basic tendency. But, undoubtedly, the Stevens of *Harmonium* and *Ideas of Order*, of *The Man with the Blue Guitar* and *Parts of a World* and *Transport to Summer*, may be thought of as the last great heir of the ancient Thracian lyrist who, when he touched his frail golden lyre, brought, as it were, "the disparate halves / Of things [that] were waiting in a betrothal"[1] unto marriage.*

The long meditation recorded by his poetry—the meditation extending, say, from "Sunday Morning" (1915) to the great work of his

The Collected Poems of Wallace Stevens will be designated as "CP" in all subsequent citations which will appear in the main body of the text.

last years in *The Auroras of Autumn* (1950) and *The Rock* (1954)—is one whose enabling principle derives from a deep sense of ours being indeed a time of dearth, for this poet takes it for granted that we have seen "the gods dispelled in mid-air and dissolve like clouds"—"as if they had never inhabited the earth."[2] True, when he wrote these words, in an essay called "Two or Three Ideas," he was speaking of "the ancient and the foreign gods" (OP, 205), but, as he says in one of his "Adagia," "The death of one god is the death of all" (OP, 165).* And his recurrent testimony about collapse in the Courts of Heaven is most principally intended to make reference to the death of the *ens realissimum*, the *deus faber*, of old Christendom, for, in his sense of things, this divine *Pantokrator*, this immaterial Person behind the myriad phenomena of existence, has been so laid to rest that it is now only "the last fading smile of a cosmic Cheshire Cat."[3] Like Nietzsche, whose influence may have been less marginal than is commonly supposed,[4] Stevens does not present any systematic argument in support of his conviction that God is dead: it is rather a matter to be reported simply as a datum of immediate experience, of the experience of one who is like "the listener, who listens in the snow, / And, nothing himself, beholds / Nothing that is not there and the nothing that is" (CP, 10). As he says in his "Conversation with Three Women of New England," "The author of man's canons is man, / Not some outer patron" (OP, 109). He conceives himself to dwell in an "island solitude, unsponsored." And this "introspective voyager" concludes, therefore, that something *else* "must take the place / Of empty heaven and its hymns" (CP, 167).

So, given the basic drift of Stevens's thought and feeling, the little tableau that we meet in his early masterpiece, "Sunday Morning," is not at all surprising. As a certain lady one Sabbath morning sits on her sunny porch over her late coffee and oranges, it occurs to her to reflect on how the "pungent fruit" and the "comforts of the sun" and the green cockatoo that adorns her rug "mingle to dissipate / The holy hush of ancient sacrifice" (CP, 66–67). Indeed, she asks herself if these—the "pungent fruit and bright, green wings" and "any balm or beauty of the earth"—shall not be "all of paradise that we shall know":

> She says, "I am content when wakened birds,
> Before they fly, test the reality
> Of misty fields, by their sweet questionings;

*Stevens's *Opus Posthumous* will be designated as "OP" in all subsequent citations which will appear in the main body of the text.

But when the birds are gone, and their warm fields
Return no more, where, then, is paradise?"   (CP, 68)

The Morning Office that she soliloquizes on this Lord's Day is, in other words, a thoroughly pagan rite. Yet, though the day is for her but a *dies solis*, she finds her reverie after breakfast taking her back "to silent Palestine, / Dominion of the blood and sepulchre." But, even so, "the measures destined for her soul" belong to the sensuous world of April's green and swallows' wings and misty fields, and the poem's conclusion is that that "tomb in Palestine" which formed "the grave of Jesus" has no claim upon us ("Why should she give her bounty to the dead?"), that

We live in an old chaos of the sun,
Or old dependency of day and night,
Or island solitude, unsponsored.   (CP, 70)

The "dark / Encroachment of that old catastrophe" (CP, 67)—presumably, the Passion of Christ—has quite lost its power to disturb: not only is old Jove of "inhuman birth" a god now dead, but, since the death of one god is the death of all, the entire structure of the Christian *mythos* has given way as well, and thus at eventide, when "casual flocks of pigeons make / Ambiguous undulations as they sink, / Downward to darkness, on extended wings" (CP, 70), the heavens from which they descend are empty.

Now the poems by which "Sunday Morning" was surrounded in *Harmonium*, Stevens's book of 1923—such poems as "Le Monocle de Mon Oncle," "The Comedian as the Letter C," "Peter Quince at the Clavier," and "Sea Surface Full of Clouds"—have been much talked about in terms of the extravagant gaudiness of imagery and language which they present. But the elaborate dance which these poems perform round sun and moon and snails and pears and plums is calculated in part to say simply that this is all there is and that it is foolish, therefore, to "persist with anecdotal bliss / To make believe a starry *connaissance*" (CP, 13). Indeed, for all its carefully wrought felicities and gorgeous elegance, the general ethos of the poetry making up Stevens's first book is perhaps best instanced by the severe disenchantment of the rarely noticed poem called "Palace of the Babies":

The disbeliever walked the moonlit place,
Outside of gates of hammered serafin,
Observing the moon-blotches on the walls.

The yellow rocked across the still façades,
Or else sat spinning on the pinnacles,
While he imagined humming sounds and sleep.

The walker in the moonlight walked alone,
And each blank window of the building balked
His loneliness and what was in his mind:

If in a shimmering room the babies came,
Drawn close by dreams of fledgling wing,
It was because night nursed them in its fold.

Night nursed not him in whose dark mind
The clambering wings of birds of black revolved,
Making harsh torment of the solitude.

The walker in the moonlight walked alone,
And in his heart his disbelief lay cold.
His broad-brimmed hat came close upon his eyes.   (CP, 77)

But, now, if the whole structure of the *philosophia perennis* and the Christian system has dropped away, what, then, remains for this walker in the moonlight whose solitude makes a harsh torment? The answer which Stevens was to give to this question is, of course, already being hinted at in one of the most famous poems in *Harmonium*, the "Anecdote of the Jar":

I placed a jar in Tennessee,
And round it was, upon a hill.
It made the slovenly wilderness
Surround that hill.

The wilderness rose up to it,
And sprawled around, no longer wild.
The jar was round upon the ground
And tall and of a port in air.

It took dominion everywhere.   (CP, 76)

The jar, as it stands here amidst this desolate Tennessee landscape, proves itself capable of ordering and subduing its slovenly environment simply by dint of its nature as a work of artifice, for, as such, it substantializes a form round which the formlessness of this wilderness can assemble itself into a scene less formless than that which would appear were the jar not there. Which is to say that the jar is an emblem of the imagination and of its power to take dominion of the world. And it was just in this capacity of the imagination to create out of the sheer fecundity of its own inventiveness new patterns of order that Stevens found a sovereign principle for reckoning with a world from which the gods have been dispelled. As he says in one of the "Adagia," "in the absence of a belief in God, the mind turns to its own creations and examines them . . . for what they reveal, for what they validate and invalidate, for the support that they give" (OP, 159).

Nowhere perhaps does he more beautifully evoke the transforming and creative power of the imagination than in the great poem in his book of 1935, *Ideas of Order*, the poem called "The Idea of Order at Key West," where we meet a girl singing by the sea:

> It may be that in all her phrases stirred
> The grinding water and the gasping wind;
> But it was she and not the sea we heard.
>
> For she was the maker of the song she sang.
>   . . . .
>
> She was the single artificer of the world
> In which she sang. And when she sang, the sea,
> Whatever self it had, became the self
> That was her song, for she was the maker. Then we,
> As we beheld her striding there alone,
> Knew that there never was a world for her
> Except the one she sang and, singing, made.
>   . . . .
>
> Oh! Blessed rage for order.   (CP, 129–30)

And the triumphalist imperialism that belongs to the "doctrine" of the imagination expressed in the Key West poem is being sounded again and again in many of Stevens's most frequently cited poems—in, for example, "Tea at the Palaz of Hoon," "To the One of Fictive Music," and "Sea Surface Full of Clouds" in *Harmonium*, in many of the poems in *Ideas of Order*, in "The Man with the Blue Guitar" (1937), in "Connoisseur of Chaos" and "Of Modern Poetry" and "Mrs. Alfred Uruguay" in *Parts of a World* (1942), and, of course, in "Notes toward a Supreme Fiction," which was written in the first months of 1942 and which presents his fullest statement in this vein. Moreover, the essays gathered in *The Necessary Angel* and in Samuel French Morse's edition of the *Opus Posthumous* are also, many of them, striking that Coleridgean note which figures so prominently in Stevens's testimony, that it is the imagination which "struggles to idealize and to unify" and that it is "essentially *vital*, even as all objects (*as* objects) are essentially fixed and dead."[5] Indeed, says the poet of "Final Soliloquy of the Interior Paramour," "The world imagined is the ultimate good":

> We say God and the imagination are one . . .
> How high that highest candle lights the dark.
>
> Out of this same light, out of the central mind,
> We make a dwelling in the evening air,
> In which being there together is enough.   (CP, 524)

But not even in the world as it is *post mortem Dei* may the imagination arrogate to itself any sort of absolute autonomy, for, unless it holds itself accountable to what Stevens calls "reality," it will inevitably come to represent a principle of frivolity, of caprice, of irresponsible vagary. And Stevens's "reality" in much of the work of his early and middle period is essentially the universe being plotted in Santayana's *Scepticism and Animal Faith* and *Realms of Being*. Which is to say that that aboriginal otherness which the imagination faces is simply the order of nature, what Santayana called "the realm of matter"; and it often appears to Stevens to be something as opaque and impenetrable as it seemed to be from Santayana's standpoint.

The imagination—which is, says Stevens, his term for "the sum of our faculties"[6]—wants to "step barefoot into reality" (CP, 423), but reality proves to be our "inescapable and ever-present difficulty and inamorata" (OP, 241). The poet—"meaning by the poet," he says, "any man of imagination"[7]—hopes to find ways of so taking hold of the world that we may find ourselves "Within the very object that we seek, / Participants of its being" (CP, 463). But the things and creatures of earth are fugitive and evanescent, as we are being reminded, for example, in one of his early poems, "Earthy Anecdote," where a little tale is told about a herd of bucks clattering across an Oklahoma landscape while being chased by something called a firecat—which is, presumably, the poem's emblem of the imagination. The bucks—which are Stevens's image of things "earthy"—swerve in "a swift, circular line /

To the right," or they swerve in "a swift, circular line / To the left" (CP, 3), depending on the direction in which they are prodded by the bristling firecat, but their galloping does not cease. At last, says the "Anecdote," the firecat closes his bright eyes and goes to sleep, and the poem invites us to suppose that the bucks continue on in their headlong, clattering flight across the plains: the firecat's rage for order notwithstanding, they cannot be stilled, in the way that the flux of existence must somehow be arrested if the imagination is to win that immediacy of contact with reality for which it yearns. "The squirming facts exceed the squamous mind" (CP, 215), as many of his focal poems are often remarking with dismay.

But the facts surpass the grasping power of the imagination not only because of the restless dynamism that keeps reality forever in transit, forever in motion. As the poem called "Someone Puts a Pineapple Together" (NA, 83–87) poignantly reminds us, their elusiveness is also occasioned by "the irreducible X" (NA, 83) in the *Ding an sich* which remains forever hidden: the absolute noumenality of things is not, in other words, endowed with a candor that permits any sort of easy apprehension of "The angel at the center of the rind" (NA, 83), when we confront a pineapple on a table.*

The poet wants, of course, to render things in their pristine transparency, and this, says Stevens, must involve a certain process of "decreation" (NA, 174–75). The term is one which he borrows from Simone Weil, who says that decreation is "to make something created pass into the uncreated."[8] And her point is that "decreation" defines the discipline whereby the creature nullifies itself in order that it may enter into the eternal life offered by the divine Creator. But Stevens appropriates the term for his own purposes and makes it stand for that whole effort to "see the very thing and nothing else," and to "see it with the hottest fire of sight." "Burn everything not part of it to ash" (CP, 373), he says. Or, as he phrases it in another formulation, you must

> Throw away the lights, the definitions,
> And say of what you see in the dark
>
> That it is this or that it is that,
> But do not use the rotted names. (CP, 183)

---

*From this point on Stevens's *The Necessary Angel* is designated as "NA" in all citations which will appear in the main body of the text.

And the process whereby we dispose of "the rotted names" in order to reach things in their "pure reality, untouched / By trope or deviation" (CP, 471), he calls "decreation."

The counsel being offered to a young poet ("ephebe") in the opening lines of "Notes toward a Supreme Fiction" suggests something of what Stevens takes the discipline of decreation to entail. In the headnote presiding over the first section of the tripartite structure of the poem he lays it down that "It Must Be Abstract." And then he says:

> Begin, ephebe, by perceiving the idea
> Of this invention, this invented world,
> The inconceivable idea of the sun.
>
> You must become an ignorant man again
> And see the sun again with an ignorant eye
> And see it clearly in the idea of it.   (CP, 380)

Now Stevens's language here is curious indeed, for one might well suppose that, if the young poet is really to see the sun, he would want to concentrate his attention not on the "idea of the sun," not on any sort of "abstraction," but on the sun itself. And the inattentive reader of the poem might well conclude with the English critic A. Alvarez that Stevens's "method is the exact reverse of the slogan William Carlos Williams uses in his epic *Paterson*," that "instead of Williams' axiom, 'No ideas but in things,' Stevens . . . [is proposing] 'No things but in ideas.' "[9] But so to interpret his meaning is quite radically to misinterpret it. As Joseph Riddel wisely says in this connection, "there are abstractions and abstractions":[10] some, in other words, are different from others—and, for Stevens, the abstractive process involves not the contraction of reality into some notional, theoretic construct but, rather, its disimprisonment from within all such constructs. The poet must abstract the sun from all the old "rotten names" for the sun, from all the old mythologies of the sun, from all the clichés of science and religion: from all this the sun must be "abstracted," if it is to be simply beheld in its naked celestial glory. And then, as Stevens wants to say, when it is so beheld, it will be seen "in the idea of it"—not, that is, in the Platonic sense of idea as general or ideal form but in the archaic sense of the term as (in the *O.E.D.*'s definition) "the original of which something else is a copy." As he once remarked in a letter (28 October 1942) to his friend Henry Church, "If you take the varnish and dirt of generations off a picture, you see it in its first idea. If you think about the world without its varnish and dirt, you are a thinker of the first idea."[11] And it is such a thinker that he would have a young poet aim to be, for, thinking in this way, he will be able to do what it is the poet's principal obligation to do: he will perform the act of decreation, facing *this* or *that* in its "first idea," everything else having been burned to ash.

Yet Stevens finds it difficult to rest even in the "idea" of the sun, and it sometimes appears that his sense of the "idea," of what Henry James called the "direct impression," is of something not much different from Santayana's "essence." For Santayana, of course, the great world by which we are surrounded, a world of a well-nigh infinite variety of things and creatures, must simply be *postulated* as a matter of "animal faith," since, Lockean that he was, he could not be persuaded that, given the ultimate inaccessibility of this world in its primitive quiddity, we have actually at hand anything more than *our* apprehensions of things—which cannot in the nature of the case be in any way absolutely authenticated as to their factuality. And these apprehensions he called "essences." Essences do not "exist": they in their totality are what the mind, after its encounter with "matter," *posits*, as a kind of rough chart or map of the world—which, happily, turns out generally to afford a reliable basis for the conduct of life. But, strictly considered, the essence is only a postulate of the imagination, as it reaches out toward "the realm of matter," and Santayana envisages no possibility of our transcending what the phenomenologists call the dimension of "intentionality." Which would seem to be the kind of impasse that occasions in Stevens a very profound disquiet. For his "idea" strikes him often as being nothing other than what Santayana took his "essence" to be: it is simply *our* apprehension of this and that, so that the disillusion of that agnostic "walker in the moonlight" ("Palace of the Babies") appears to be only

> the last illusion,
> Reality as a thing seen by the mind,
>
> Not that which is but that which is apprehended,
> A mirror, a lake of reflections in a room,
> A glassy ocean lying at the door.   (CP, 468)

In short, as he is to be found sadly remarking again and again, we seem fated tragically to fail in our effort to grasp "Not the symbol but that for which the symbol stands, / The vivid thing in the air that never changes, / Though the air change" (CP, 238).

Indeed, the encystment of the mind within its own concepts and categories does at times appear to be so unbreakable that Stevens is occasionally, as it would seem, at the point of regarding "reality" as but an epiphenomenon of the mind itself—as when, for example, he tells us that the imagination is "the one reality / In this imagined world" (CP, 25). As he says in one of the "Adagia," "There is nothing in life except what one thinks of it" (OP, 162), and the kind of primitive idealism expressed in this word forms a note that he recurrently strikes. "We live in the mind" (OP, 164)—and thus the world that is built by the imagination is "indistinguishable from the world in which we live, or," as he says he ought to put it, "from the world in which we shall come to live, since what makes the poet the potent figure that he is . . . is that he creates the world to which we turn incessantly and without knowing it and that he gives to life the supreme fictions without which we are unable to conceive of it" (NA, 31). "Reality . . . [is] a thing seen by the mind, / Not that which is but that which is apprehended" (CP, 468)— and so on and so on. "Imagination is the only genius" (OP, 179).

But the fullest weight of Stevens's testimony inescapably conveys the impression that his most central and *final* sense of things is not of our being locked up within our own brainpan but of the mind's having to confront and reckon with that which is *totaliter aliter*, which is wholly other, than itself. As he said in a letter to Bernard Heringman in 1951 (20 March), "Sometimes I believe most in the imagination for a long time and then, without reasoning about it, turn to reality and believe in that and that alone. But both of these things project themselves endlessly and I want them to do just that" (L, 710).* And, in the end, he seems never to be able quite to persuade himself that "the mind in the act of finding / What will suffice" (CP, 239) need only explore its own interiority, since "the imagination [always finds itself] pressing back against the pressure of reality" (NA, 36). In, for example, the late poem called "Saint John and the Back-Ache," the Back-Ache's contention that "The mind is the terriblest force in the world" prompts in Saint John a riposte that is brief and brusque: "The world is presence . . . / Presence is not mind" (CP, 436). So, veiled though the essential nature of things seems to be, Stevens, like Santayana, nevertheless stubbornly posits—by something like a kind of "animal faith"—the eternal perdurance of the rock of reality. It is

> The starting point of the human and the end,
> That in which space itself is contained, the gate
> To the enclosure, day, the things illumined

---

*From this point on the *Letters of Wallace Stevens* is designated as "L" in all citations which will appear in the main body of the text.

> By day, night and that which night illumines,
> Night and its midnight-minting fragrances.   (CP, 528)

"The real will from its crude compoundings come," however, only as we "hear / The luminous melody of proper sound" (CP, 404): "man is the intelligence of his soil" (CP, 27), and reality "untuned by the imagination is not enough: the green day must be played by a blue guitar."[12] True, " 'Things as they are / Are changed upon the blue guitar.' " Yet they must not be so changed that, finally, the musician (or the poet) fails to play " 'A tune upon the blue guitar / Of things exactly as they are' " (CP, 165).

Stevens desires, in other words, a constant commerce between the imagination and reality. But he does not expect this to be anything swift and easy, given that tragic principle deeply inwrought into the nature of things which is an affair of nothing less than a fundamental "maladjustment between the imagination and reality" (NA, 33). He often wants to think of "the imagination and reality as equals" (NA, 27), but the mind in its search for the real finds itself over and again frustrated by a strange perversity in things which leads them to withdraw so deeply into their own otherness as to make the bridging of the chasm between them and the human spirit appear to be something that "could occupy a school of rabbis for the next few generations" (L, 435). Reality, in short, confers no cheap grace, and so elusive, so inaccessible indeed, does it prove to be that Stevens concludes at last that the rigors of the quest for "what will suffice" can be borne only by him whom in "Notes toward a Supreme Fiction" he calls "major man."

The major man is a "figure of capable imagination" (CP, 249), one

> who has had the time to think enough,
> The central man, the human globe, responsive
> As a mirror with a voice, the man of glass,
> Who in a million diamonds sums us up
>
> He is the transparence of the place in which
> He is and in his poems we find peace.   (CP, 250–51)

As we are told in the ninth canto of "Examination of the Hero in a Time of War," the central man or the major man

> seems
> To stand taller than a person stands, has
> A wider brow, large and less human
> Eyes and bruted ears: the man-like body

Of a primitive. He walks with a defter
And lither stride. His arms are heavy
And his breast is greatness. All his speeches
Are prodigies in longer phrases.
His thoughts begotten at clear sources,
Apparently in air, fall from him
Like chantering from an abundant
Poet, as if he thought gladly, being
Compelled thereto by an innate music.   (CP, 277)

It is

As if, as if, as if the disparate halves
Of things were waiting in a betrothal known
To none, awaiting espousal to the sound

Of right joining, a music of ideas, the burning
And breeding and bearing birth of harmony,
The final relation, the marriage of the rest.   (CP, 464–65)

And the major man is the priest who solemnizes this marriage, who brings to pass this mysterious conjunction of reality and the imagination.

Yet, though he seems to stand taller than most of us, the major man is not to be regarded as any *simple* analogue of Nietzsche's *Übermensch*, for, as Stevens says in the fifth canto of the "Examination,"

The common man is the common hero.
The common hero is the hero.   (CP, 275)

Which is to say that the central man is not a "heroic" figure. He is "Without panache, without cockade": he is "With all his attributes no god but man" (CP, 185–86), one indeed who in his external ordinariness is something like Kierkegaard's "knight of faith"—a chap who of a given afternoon

                         may be seated in
A café. There may be a dish of country cheese
And a pineapple on the table. It must be so.   (CP, 335)

Major men, in other words, are not world-historical figures who alter the course of the kinds of events that are reported in our daily newspapers: the central man is, rather,

> The pensive man . . . He sees that eagle float
> For which the intricate Alps are a single nest.   (CP, 216)

His pensiveness, to be sure, is, paradoxically, a kind of ignorance, for he knows that, in order to see the sun "in the idea of it,"

> You must become an ignorant man again
> And see the sun again with an ignorant eye.   (CP, 380)

But the special kind of ignorance he cultivates is not that of the "anti-master-man, [the] floribund ascetic," who (as Stevens says in "Landscape with Boat") would reach the center of reality by brushing away the thunder and the clouds, "by rejecting what he saw / And denying what he heard," by choosing

> not to live, to walk in the dark,
> To be projected by one void into
> Another.   (CP, 242)

No, the major man knows that all the things of earth may be parts of "the heraldic center of the world" (CP, 172)—

> the irregular turquoise, part, the perceptible blue
> Grown denser, part, the eye so touched, so played
> Upon by clouds, the ear so magnified
> By thunder, parts, and all these things together,
> Parts, and more things, parts.   (CP, 242)

So he does not elect any *via negativa*: his is rather the Way of Affirmation, and, through—let us use Whitehead's term—his "prehensions" of things, he seeks, in relation to his fellows, "to make his imagination theirs," to make it "become the light in the minds of others. His role, in short, is to help people to live their lives" (NA, 29).

The major man—whose image in Stevens's poetry is but one of the conceits wherewith he proposes to talk about the imagination—the major man is, of course, an adept in the art of decreation. His principal concern, indeed, is to cast aside the old "rotted names" and to try to see everything in its "first idea": he is committed to that "difficultest rigor [which] is forthwith / On the image of what we see, to catch from that / Irrational moment its unreasoning" (CP, 398). And the morality, the ethic, the *ascêsis*, to which the major man is dedicated forms one of the leading themes of the great poem of 1942, "Notes toward a Su-

preme Fiction," the long first section of which is devoted to what Stevens calls "abstraction," which is his term for that whole process
whereby all the old rotted names and conventional schemes of interpretation are so "bracketed" (by something like the Husserlian *epoché*)
that their "ravishments of truth, so fatal to / The truth itself" (CP, 381),
are rendered inefficacious. Then it is, after the poetic imagination performs the phenomenological reduction (or "abstraction"), after it puts
aside all those concepts and sentiments that are the result of routinized
modes of thought and perception—then it is that at last it begins to
discover the "candor" in things, the munificence with which they show
themselves forth as what they irrevocably and most essentially are, and

> the candor of them is the strong exhilaration
> Of what we feel from what we think, of thought
> Beating in the heart, as if blood newly came,
>
> An elixir, an excitation, a pure power.
> The poem, through candor, brings back a power again
> That gives a candid kind to everything.   (CP, 382)

It is, in other words, in the moment of what the Greeks called
aletheia, in the moment of revelation, when the candor in things leads
them to unveil themselves, that we find ourselves savoring that "bou-
quet of being" (OP, 109) which reaches us when we begin to notice
how, as Hopkins says,

> Each mortal thing does one thing and the same:
>   Deals out that being indoors each one dwells;
>   Selves—goes itself; *myself* it speaks and spells,
> Crying *What I do is me: for that I came.*[13]

To win the great gift of *aletheia* there must, of course, be a right disposition of the mind and heart, such as the disciplines of decreation and
abstraction prepare. But, once this *habitus* has been achieved, we discover (in Hopkins's words) that

> These things, these things were here and but the beholder
> Wanting.[14]

Or, as Stevens puts it in the "Notes," to have begun to encounter the
things of earth in their "first idea" is to realize that

>   The clouds preceded us.
>
> There was a muddy centre before we breathed.
> There was a myth before the myth began,
> Venerable and articulate and complete.
>
> From this the poem springs: that we live in a place
> That is not our own and, much more, not ourselves
> And hard it is in spite of blazoned days.   (CP, 383)

Which is to say that the aboriginal reality is not the isolate self but a prior otherness with which the self must reckon, "a place / That is not our own," the "muddy centre [that was] before we breathed." True, Stevens appears to postulate an aboriginal Fall, for, as he says, "Adam / In Eden was the father of Descartes / And Eve made air the mirrors of herself" (CP, 383). No sooner, in other words, did man enter the world than he was displacing the "first idea" of this and that by his own concepts and perspectives and categories: he was by way of making the world but a mirror of himself and was thus presuming to dwell, as it were, in a palace of the mind. But "The clouds preceded us. / There was a muddy centre before we breathed. . . . we live in a place / That is not our own"—and it is "From this the poem springs," or ought to spring. "The poem refreshes life so that we share, / For a moment, the first idea" (CP, 382).

So, in the lesson being laid down for the young poet in the long and difficult opening section of "Notes toward a Supreme Fiction," Stevens wants to say that in a time *post mortem Dei*, however we define the ultimate belief now possible for us, "It Must Be Abstract": it must be calculated, that is, to rescue us from all the superstructures thrown up by the mind between the imagination and the "first idea," in order that efficacy may once again be restored to the primordial bond uniting us with the *milieu ontologique*.

But not only must "It" be abstract: the headnote presiding over the second section of the "Notes" declares, "It Must Change." Which is to say that any ultimate structure of belief must take full account of the impermanencies and mutabilities that are everywhere a part of the on-going life of the world. And thus the poetic imagination must "move to and fro," must be "a luminous flittering" (CP, 396), in all its solicitations of this "universe of inconstancy." So it is no wonder, as the poem remarks, that the great equestrian "statue of the General Du Puy" seems to be mere "rubbish in the end," for, in its massive bronze fixity, it is something wholly stiff and unpliant and inflexible:

The right, uplifted foreleg of the horse
Suggested that, at the final funeral,
The music halted and the horse stood still.

On Sundays, lawyers in their promenades
Approached this strongly-heightened effigy
To study the past, and doctors, having bathed

Themselves with care, sought out the nerveless frame
Of a suspension, a permanence, so rigid
That it made the General a bit absurd,

Changed his true flesh to an inhuman bronze.
There never had been, never could be, such
A man.   (CP, 391)

"The great statue of the General Du Puy / Rested immobile"—and precisely for this reason it has the effect not of enlivening the past but of
divesting it of any merest semblance of life. And, like Coleridge, Stevens, through all the complex tropes and fables making up the second
section of the "Notes," wants to insist that the imagination cannot
reckon with this various world by way of "fixities and definites."[15] "It
Must Change."

Then, as the heading of the final section of the poem says, "It Must
Give Pleasure." By which Stevens means that the Supreme Fiction—or
whatever it is that may suffice in the way of a final structure of belief—
should make people happy. But he is immediately at pains to speak of
the kind of rejoicing and exultation that will not do; he wants not to
endorse the old stylized festivities of traditional religious piety:

To sing jubilas at exact, accustomed times,
To be crested and wear the mane of a multitude
And so, as part, to exult with its great throat,

To speak of joy and to sing of it, borne on
The shoulders of joyous men, to feel the heart
That is the common, the bravest fundament,

This is a facile exercise.   (CP, 398)

Whereas Stevens, as against this "facile exercise," wants to commend
"the difficultest rigor"—which is

> forthwith,
> On the image of what we see, to catch from that
>
> Irrational moment its unreasoning,
> As when the sun comes rising, when the sea
> Clears deeply, when the moon hangs on the wall
>
> Of heaven-haven. These are not things transformed.
> Yet we are shaken by them as if they were.
> We reason about them with a later reason.   (CP, 398–99)

It is, in short, the pleasure consequent upon a naked, "unreasoning" confrontation with the things of earth that will be known by the major man—who in this final section of the poem is imaged forth in the figure of Canon Aspirin.

Though the Canon likes to drink Meursault and to eat "lobster Bombay with mango / Chutney," he is far from being any sort of unthinking hedonist: indeed, he is one who (as Stevens said in a letter to Hi Simons, 29 March 1943) "has explored all the projections of the mind, his own particularly": yet he has won no "sufficing fiction" (L, 445). When we meet him, he has returned to the "sensible ecstasy" of his widowed sister's house where she dwells with her two little daughters in what appears to be a kind of retirement from the world, "rejecting dreams" and demanding of sleep only "the unmuddled self of sleep" (CP, 402). But at midnight, when "normal things had yawned themselves away," there is no unmuddled sleep for the Canon who remains wakeful and who finds himself facing a nothingness which is "a nakedness, a point, / Beyond which fact could not progress as fact" (CP, 402). Presumably, this nocturnal reverie on "the finality and limitation of fact" (L, 445) is prompted by a depressing sense he has of a certain poverty in his sister's defeatist rejection of all dreams. In any event, as he lies on his bed and thinks of how beyond a point fact as sheer fact takes one nowhere at all, he begins to let his imagination play on fact, on the darkness, on "night's pale illuminations, gold / Beneath, far underneath, the surface of / His eye and audible in the mountain of / His ear":

> Straight to the utmost crown of night he flew.
> The nothingness was a nakedness, a point
>
> Beyond which thought could not progress as thought.   (CP, 403)

The Canon has arrived, then, at two extremities—the point beyond which fact cannot progress as fact and the point beyond which thought cannot progress as thought. Neither reality nor imagination, in other words, can be sufficient unto itself. And, for a time, in his exasperation he simply

> imposes orders as he thinks of them,
> As the fox and snake do.
> Next he builds capitols and in their corridors,
>
> Whiter than wax, sonorous, fame as it is,
> He establishes statues of reasonable men.   (CP, 403)

He forgets, it seems, that "to impose is not / To discover." But, as Stevens declares,

> To discover an order as of
> A season, to discover summer and know it,
>
> To discover winter and know it well, to find,
> Not to impose, not to have reasoned at all,
> Out of nothing to have come on major weather,
>
> It is possible, possible, possible. It must
> Be possible.   (CP, 403–4)

The dialectic of the poem wants, then, to suggest two things at once—that, on the one hand, reality untuned by the imagination's guitar is something barren and unprofitable (since fact as fact can progress only so far and no farther); and that, on the other hand, the imagination must not deal so aggressively with reality as simply to impose upon it its own "fictive coverings." What is to be desired is that there should be a true marriage of the one with the other, since only out of this can come any full "discovery" of "the whole, / The Complicate, the amassing harmony." Indeed, it would seem that the Canon is beginning at last to see this, is beginning to see that, choosing not *between* imagination and reality but choosing rather "to include the things / That in each other are included," there will be "an hour / Filled with expressible bliss, in which I have / No need, am happy, forget need's golden hand, / Am satisfied without solacing majesty" (CP, 404–5). And thus the poem moves toward its final doxology, about the "thing final in itself and, therefore, good"—the "Fat girl, terrestrial, my summer, my night." But, as we may perhaps gloss Stevens's resolutely opaque lines, the final thing—the fat girl, the terrestrial—is good in part because its "candor" is just enough to permit the imagination to dance round it, "round and round, the merely going round, / Until merely going round is [itself] a final good" (CP, 405). "In short," to allow Stevens now his own gloss, "a man with a taste for Meursault, and lobster Bombay, who has a sensible sister and who, for himself, thinks to the very material of his mind, doesn't have much choice about yielding to 'the complicate, the amassing harmony.'" But, then, as he adds in a parenthesis, "How he ever became a Canon is the real problem" (L, 445). And, though it may not be anything like *the* problem in what is one of the most difficult poems of the modern period, it does undoubtedly remain a small bafflement (which is in no way clarified by Harold Bloom's energetic fidgetings over it, though his suggestion that the Canon is intended to figure forth a "cure for our headache of unreality" is appealing).[16]

Now it is the beautifully doxological reflections on the final goodness of things predominating in the closing cantos of the "Notes" that look toward the central themes in the rich and inexhaustible poems of Stevens's last years, the poems making up *The Auroras of Autumn* (1950) and *The Rock* (that body of new work forming the last section of *The Collected Poems* of 1954). At the end of a poem in *The Auroras of Autumn* called "The Ultimate Poem is Abstract," Stevens says:

> It would be enough
> If we were ever, just once, at the middle, fixed
> In This Beautiful World of Ours and not as now,
>
> Helplessly at the edge, enough to be
> Complete, because at the middle, if only in sense,
> And in that enormous sense, merely enjoy.   (CP, 430)

And this is where the great poems of his final period want to take us— to the middle, to the very center of reality: they want to present nothing less than "The outlines of being and its expressings, the syllables of its law" (CP, 424). The poet of *The Auroras* and *The Rock* wants to explore that

> huge, high harmony that sounds
> A little and a little, suddenly,

By means of a separate sense. It is and it
Is not and, therefore, is.

(CP, 440)

What he is struggling toward is "the central poem," and, as he says (in "A Primitive Like an Orb"), the central poem is

a poem of
The whole, the essential compact of the parts,
The roundness that pulls tight the final ring

And that which in an altitude would soar,
A vis, a principle . . .
Or else an inherent order active to be
Itself, a nature to its natives all
Beneficence, a repose, utmost repose,
The muscles of a magnet aptly felt.

(CP, 442)

This "principle" or "inherent order," this "essential compact of [all] the parts" making up "the whole," is, of course, nothing other than Being itself. And in these late days of our post-Wittgensteinian misery nothing is more likely to strain the patience of the cognoscenti than the very notion of Being—which, as the English philosopher A. J. Ayer was telling us a generation ago, presents an instance merely of "the way in which a consideration of grammar leads to metaphysics." That is to say, we are afflicted by "the superstition . . . that, to every word or phrase that can be the grammatical subject of a sentence, there must somewhere be a real entity corresponding."[17] So, since we have in our inherited language the participle *being* that may also function as a noun, we mistakenly suppose that there is some discriminable entity to which the noun refers. But, as Mr. Ayer and numerous other philosophers of his general persuasion would insist, in point of hard fact no such entity exists.

Stevens's usages, however, make it fully apparent that it never occurs to him to think of Being as simply one item amongst those belonging to the category of "things." He stands indeed in the line of Aristotle and Aquinas and Kant and all the great strategists of Western metaphysics in taking it for granted that Being is not *a* being but, rather, that informing *élan* or power, that "dearest freshness deep down things,"[18] that enables all the various particular things of earth to be what their inner entelechies intend them to be. One does not see it as one sees a rose; it is not *here* or *there*; yet it is the "insolid billowing of the solid" (OP, 111); it is nothing other than that ontological energy wherewith a bird or a flower or a cloud in the sky is assembled into the given *Gestalt* which it constitutes and made to be what it is—rather than another thing. But, since it is not one thing amongst other things and since it is nowhere to be encountered simply in its naked isolateness, Stevens often speaks of it apophatically—as when, for example, he tells us, "It is and it / Is not and, therefore, is" (CP, 440), or when he says:

> If
> It was nowhere else, it was there and because
> It was nowhere else, its place had to be supposed,
> Itself had to be supposed, a thing supposed
> In a place supposed. (CP, 242)

Which led the late Randall Jarrell irritatedly to mutter that all this was the "spun-sugar" of a "pastry-cook"—or, rather perhaps, something like "G. E. Moore at the spinet."[19] But what Jarrell was very probably quite unaware of is that the language of apophasis forms one of the great classical idioms for discourse about Being—in Dionysius the Areopagite, in Eckhart, in Boehme, in Schelling, and in many others in the Western tradition who unintentionally echo the "*neti, neti*" of Hinduism ("Not this! Not this!"). In any event, though Stevens is not *finally* an adherent of the *via negationis*, he keeps a certain reluctance to speak "univocally" about Being, since it is perceptible nowhere in and by itself alone and is, therefore, like "beasts that one never sees, / Moving so that the foot-falls are slight and almost nothing" (CP, 337).

At times the course of Stevens's thought seems curiously to have paralleled in some degree that of Martin Heidegger, and, particularly in one respect, to remark the parallel is perhaps to clarify a certain phase of Stevens's poetic procedure that may otherwise appear hopelessly oblique. One turns here not to the later Heidegger, the Heidegger of the *Brief über den Humanismus* (1947), the *Holzwege* (1950), *Was heisst Denken?* (1954), and *Gelassenheit* (1959)—between whom and the later Stevens there are, to be sure, many fascinating convergences—but to the early Heidegger of *Sein und Zeit* (*Being and Time*, 1927), one of whose major presuppositions was that "Being" is accessible only by way of a very strict analysis of the *human* modes of being. That is to say, since that which "assembles" everything that exists does not itself belong to the category of things and is therefore "above" the ordinary categories of reflection, Heidegger reasoned that it needs to be approached not theoretically but existentially, by way of the one creature whose relation to it is that of conscious participant—namely, man himself. Since man, by the inner dynamism of his own nature, is driven to search out the ultimate ground of his existence, Heidegger decided that the appropriate technical term, indeed, for the distinctively human mode of being is *Dasein*, which means literally *being-there*. "*Dasein*," as he said, "is an entity for which, in its Being, that Being is an issue."[20] And thus he concluded that our best path into Being-itself is one that leads through those structures of existence that belong to the particular being whose unique vocation it is to be obsessed with the question concerning what it means to *be*. As he laid it down, to do "fundamental ontology" is to seek after not a "transcendental analytic" but an "existential analytic," and such was the undertaking to which he dedicated his brilliantly original book of 1927.

Now it would seem to be some such intuition as this, of the relation of *Dasein* to Being-itself, that underlies Stevens's penchant in many of his poems for imaging forth Being anthropomorphically. True, Being is a "transcendental," is "above" the ordinary categories of reflection, and cannot be properly spoken of univocally: indeed, when it is thought of in relation to the world of particular beings, Being, since it is not *a* being, may seem to require that we consider it to be "that-which-is not." But the kind of discourse that a poet supervises cannot be wholly an affair of negatives, of "not this" and "not that." Moreover, as we may take Stevens to have reasoned, since Being is inherent in man and may be thought to attain self-consciousness in man alone, it is surely not illicit for the poet to regard his "license" as entitling him to give Being a human form (this being understood to be a purely tropological maneuver). And the preeminent case in point is the beautiful poem in *Transport to Summer* entitled "Chocorua to Its Neighbor," which, in its meditation on the mystery of Being, looks forward to the great statements being made in this vein by many of the last poems.

Mount Chocorua belongs to the chain of the White Mountains in New Hampshire, and she is imagined in the poem as speaking quietly to some neighboring mount. Hers is, of course, a great eminence from the perspective of which the wars between cities far below appear to be merely "a gesticulation of forms, / A swarming of number over number." But her great elevation is not so lofty that she fails to be deeply stirred by what happened "At the end of night last night," when, as she says,

> a crystal star,
> The crystal-pointed star of morning, rose
> And lit the snow to a light congenial
> To this prodigious shadow, who then came
> In an elemental freedom, sharp and cold.

The feeling of him was the feel of day,
And of a day as yet unseen, in which
To see was to be.   (CP, 296–97)

"He was not man, yet he was nothing else," and so huge was he (with "more than muscular shoulders, arms and chest") that, says Chocorua, "Upon my top he breathed the pointed dark." And, as she reports to her neighbor, she heard him say: " 'I hear the motions of the spirit and the sound / Of what is secret becomes, for me, a voice / That is my own voice speaking in my ear.' "

"Now," says Chocorua, "I . . . speak of this shadow as / A human thing," but this "eminence," as she suggests, is really "the common self" that potentializes and gives character to all the things and creatures of earth, "So that, where he was, there is an enkindling, where / He is, the air changes and grows fresh to breathe." And thus she speaks of this prodigious presence as "the collective being" of whom captains, cardinals, heroes, mothers, and scholars are but embodiments, "True transfigurers fetched out of the human mountain." So it is that Chocorua's *Benedicite* goes, and, despite all the majesty that she can herself claim, her great hymn in praise of Being ends on a note of utmost humility:

How singular he was as man, how large,
If nothing more than that, for the moment, large
In my presence, the companion of presences
Greater than mine, of his demanding, head
And, of human realizings, rugged roy.   (CP, 302)

Stevens says in his "Adagia": "A poem is a meteor" (OP, 158). Which invites one to think of the arc described by the meteor of "Chocorua" as reaching directly towards "An Ordinary Evening in New Haven," the dominating masterpiece in his book of 1950, *The Auroras of Autumn*. For this is the poem which, perhaps more than any other, fully effectuates the shift in his late poetry from his earlier view of the imagination as the principle of ultimacy to his final view of ultimacy as resident in nothing less than Being itself. As in "Chocorua to Its Neighbor" and "Credences of Summer" (with its great sixth canto on "the rock [that] cannot be broken") in *Transport to Summer*, Stevens in "An Ordinary Evening in New Haven" keeps "coming back and coming back / To the real: to the hotel instead of the hymns / That fall upon it out of the wind. We seek," he says, "The poem of pure reality, untouched / By trope or deviation" (CP, 471). And, of course, at the end Stevens can so resolutely give his suffrage to a reality untouched by trope because of the conviction he had won in working through "Notes toward a Supreme Fiction" that "the whole, / The Complicate, the amassing harmony," solicits and sanctions a true marriage between reality and the imagination, such a marriage indeed as allows the poetry of the imagination to be at last "Part of the res itself and not about it" (CP, 473).

"An Ordinary Evening in New Haven" in its first version (a sequence of eleven rather than of the thirty-one poems comprising the final version) was prepared in fulfillment of a commission Stevens had been given to prepare a poem commemorating the one-thousandth meeting of the Connecticut Academy of Arts and Sciences (4 November 1949), and in due course he read the new work before that gathering. While it was in preparation he, in a letter (3 May 1949) to Bernard Heringman, spoke of the project and of his "interest . . . [in trying] to get as close to the ordinary, the commonplace and the ugly as it is possible for a poet to get. It is not," he said, "a question of grim reality but of plain reality" (L, 636). And it is indeed "The eye's plain version" of things, what he calls "The vulgate of experience" (CP, 465), that the poem wants to render.

Stevens begins a little self-mockingly:

> The eye's plain version is a thing apart,
> The vulgate of experience. Of this,
> A few words, an and yet, and yet, and yet—
>
> As part of the never-ending meditation.   (CP, 465)

The poem is being written in his seventieth year, and, being filled with age, he is wryly acknowledging that he has an old man's inclination toward garrulity, that with him "a few words" are likely to be an affair of yakking on and on, with one "and yet" following another, and it being followed by still another. And, for all its richness, his discourse here does indeed prove to be very much like this, the poem seeming, despite its thirty-one long cantos, never really to want to come to an end. It is wonderfully sinuous and wrought with the craft of a master, but it is the poem of an old man, one for whom "the wind whimpers oldly of old age / In the western night" (CP, 477).

So it is not surprising that the evening of which Stevens writes is an evening in the autumn of the year, when the cycle of the seasons is just at the point of winding down into the death of winter. The town and the weather are "a casual litter" of whirling leaves and mud and squirrels huddled together "in tree-caves," and drenching everything is "the repugnant rain" that constantly "falls with a ramshackle sound" (CP, 475). The scene is one of bleakness and dilapidation. "The wind has blown the silence of summer away"—and "The last leaf that is going to fall has fallen":

> The barrenness that appears is an exposing.
> It is not part of what is absent, a halt
> For farewells, a sad hanging on for remembrances.
>
> It is a coming on and a coming forth.   (CP, 487)

It is a "plain version" of things that the poem presents, but it is a savage kind of plainness—as Stevens says, "the last plainness of a man who has fought / Against illusion" (CP, 467).

Yet he calls the dark, wind-swept streets of the town "metaphysical streets," since it is just amidst their dilapidated ordinariness that we, when thinking deeply, may realize that they do not in any final sense imprison us, that we do most truly reside

> In a permanence composed of impermanence,
> In a faithfulness as against the lunar light,
>
> So that morning and evening are like promises kept,
> So that the approaching sun and its arrival,
> Its evening feast and the following festival,
>
> This faithfulness of reality, this mode,
> This tendance and venerable holding-in
> Make gay the hallucinations in surfaces.   (CP, 472)

And thus, given this "faithfulness of reality," given the steadfastness and graciousness of that uncreated power of Being which gathers all things into themselves, the poet—"Professor Eucalyptus of New Haven," scholar of the ordinary and the commonplace—as he sits in his hotel room, does not expect to find God "in the rainy cloud" but, rather,

> seeks him
> In New Haven with an eye that does not look

Beyond the object. He sits in his room, beside
The window, close to the ramshackle spout in which
The rain falls with a ramshackle sound. He seeks

God in the object itself, without much choice.   (CP, 475)

Professor Eucalyptus says:

"The search
For reality is as momentous as
The search for god." It is the philosopher's search

For an interior made exterior
And the poet's search for the same exterior made
Interior.   (CP, 481)

"After the leaves have fallen, we return / To a plain sense of things"
(CP, 502)—and "a plain sense of things" seeks

Nothing beyond reality. Within it,

Everything, the spirit's alchemicana
Included, the spirit that goes roundabout
And through included, not merely the visible,

The solid, but the movable, the moment,
The coming on of feasts and the habits of saints,
The pattern of the heavens and high, night air.   (CP, 471–72)

The "poem of pure reality," in other words, wants to define "a fresh
spiritual"—which concerns nothing other than the "essential integrity"
of "The actual landscape with its actual horns / Of baker and butcher
blowing" (CP, 474, 475).

As "An Ordinary Evening in New Haven" slowly and reluctantly
moves toward its close Stevens says in the twenty-eighth canto:

This endlessly elaborating poem
Displays the theory of poetry,
As the life of poetry. A more severe,

More harassing master would extemporize
Subtler, more urgent proof that the theory
Of poetry is the theory of life,

As it is, in the intricate evasions of as,
In things seen and unseen, created from nothingness,
The heavens, the hells, the worlds, the longed-for lands.   (CP, 486)

But, indeed, he is nothing if not a severe and harassing master, and the whole intention of his work in its final phase is to persuade us that the theory of poetry is the theory of life. Stevens wants, of course, to propose that we think of the poet as (in Martin Heidegger's phrase) a "shepherd of Being," but, more basically even, he (like Heidegger)[21] wants us to think of man as a "shepherd of Being," the poet therefore offering only an ideal *exemplum* of the quintessentially human vocation. It is in this way that his theory of poetry is also his theory of life.

True, the poet is most immediately distinguished by his adeptness in the art of supervising the word, but, when he rightly understands the poetic office, his most fundamental purpose is so to supervise the word as to show forth the things and creatures of earth "in the starkness and strangeness of their being what they are."[22] He teaches us how to revel in their particularity, in their *presence*, in the marvelous inner cohesion whereby they manage to be what they are, rather than something else. And thus, by inviting an attitude of enthrallment before the various concrete realities of the world, he prepares us to be laid hold of by that wherewith these things are inwardly constituted and enabled to be what they are—which is none other than Being itself. The great gift, in other words, that he confers is what Wordsworth in Book 2 of *The Prelude* calls "the sentiment of Being."

Now, in inviting us to offer a kind of *Amen* to the various finite realities that make up the earth since they are themselves instinct with Being, Stevens is in effect attributing to Being the character of holiness. Which is to say that, for him, Being is the primary focus of a radically religious faith. And, here, we are bound to be put in mind of two words that he addressed to Sister M. Bernetta Quinn—the one in a letter of 7 April 1948 which said, "Your mind is too much like my own for it to seem to be an evasion on my part to say merely that I do seek a centre and expect to go on seeking it" (L, 584); and the other in a Christmas letter of 1951 (21 December) which said, "I am not an atheist although I do not believe to-day in the same God in whom I believed when I was a boy" (L, 735). But, of course, conventional opinion amongst Stevens's interpreters represents a great disinclination to take him at his word when he forswears any sort of allegiance to atheism. How, it will be asked, can any other position be attributed to one who proclaimed so imperatively the death of all the gods and who, now that "the phan-

toms are gone," conceived himself to be a "shaken realist" committed
to "the imagination's new beginning" (CP, 320)? Or, if it be granted
that the position expressed in the poetry of his final period is in some
sort religious, it will then be asked how this *mystique* of Being can be
considered to be anything other than a kind of pantheism.

These are difficult questions, and questions it is well-nigh impossible to answer to the satisfaction of the kind of *simplicitas* about religious discriminations that normally belongs to the literary community.
For, there, it is the common tendency to suppose either that the term
"God" refers to *a* being such as archaic mythology represented as
"dwelling" at the summit of a mountain or somewhere in the skies, or
that it refers to that metaphysical entity conceived by classical theism to
be a person "dwelling" incorporeally beyond the world. And, accord-
ingly, it is assumed that to refuse, as Stevens most assuredly does, "the
gods" of ancient mythology and the God-thing of traditional theism is
to embrace what amounts to atheism. Indeed, Heidegger himself, who
reinstated the doctrine of Being more powerfully than any other philosopher of the modern period, seems to have been so convinced of the
term "God" ineradicably carrying the implication of *a* being over and
above the world that he was always careful to insist on the impropriety
of equating "Being" with "God,"[23] for he knew that even to appear to
be postulating *a* being "above" or "beyond" the world that is studied
by empirical science is to violate the grammar of modern intelligence to
a degree intolerable by the people of our age.

But, though the categories of classical theism (in so far as they posit
a supreme being above or beyond the world) may no longer represent a
negotiable currency, it remains the case today as much as ever before
that the religious imagination finds itself wanting to regard the world as
charged with "a kind of total grandeur at the end" (CP, 510) and as
tabernacling grace and glory. True, it may not any longer feel it to be
possible to articulate such a vision by making reference to some exalted
supernatural Person—the divine *Pantokrator*—whose "existence" and
whose interventions in the world have the effect of validating or sancti-
fying the significant realities of nature and history. Yet it may, by a
decision of faith, choose to regard as essentially trustworthy, as indeed
holy and gracious, that mysterious *dynamis* that simply lets all the
particular beings of earth *be*. Which would seem to be precisely the
kind of vision at work in the late poetry of Stevens, where all its
"edgings and inchings" appear to be calculated at the end to speak of
the "final goodness" of things. And, of course, when, in an attitude of
faith, we regard as *holy* the Incomparable that "lets-be" all the things

and creatures of this world, then Being itself begins to take on something of the status assigned by traditional theism to "God." Such a God, to be sure, is not "the same God in whom [Stevens] believed when [he] was a boy," though he was surely justified, nevertheless, in asserting to Sister M. Bernetta Quinn that "I am not an atheist." Traditional atheism has undoubtedly directed its polemic at a different God, but to give one's suffrage to such a God as Stevens appears to have embraced is not to assert that *a* particular being dwells in some invisible realm above or beyond the phenomenal world. It is, rather, to declare, as a matter of radical faith, that Being itself is steadfast, reliable, gracious, and deserves our trust: it is to say that the Wholly Other, the uncreated Rock of reality, is *for* us, not against us.

Still, it will be asked if the equation of Being with God does not present what is at bottom only another version of pantheist theosophy—and, as it will be further asked, disbelievingly, is *this* what Stevens is up to? Such a question, however, will be prompted by a very great misunderstanding, for Being, as it is envisaged by Stevens, is no more the sum or the totality of all beings than it is *a* particular being *in addition to* all the other beings that make up our world. Being is, rather, that *transcendens* which, as the enabling condition of everything that exists, is "wholly other" than and distinct from all particular beings, even in their totality. And nowhere in Stevens's poetry is there to be found the merest hint of any sort of pantheistic mysticism.

In one of his "Adagia" he says: "The poet is the priest of the invisible" (OP, 169). But he does not, of course, conceive the "invisible" of which he speaks to be any sort of sheer blankness, and to recall the late poem entitled "Of Mere Being" is to feel, indeed, that, had he taken thought, it is of this that he would perhaps have wanted to say that the poet is a priest—mere Being (which is, to be sure, itself invisible). The poem goes like this:

> The palm at the end of the mind,
> Beyond the last thought, rises
> In the bronze distance,
>
> A gold-feathered bird
> Sings in the palm, without human meaning,
> Without human feeling, a foreign song.
>
> You know then that it is not the reason
> That makes us happy or unhappy.
> The bird sings. Its feathers shine.

> The palm stands on the edge of space.
> The wind moves slowly in the branches.
> The bird's fire-fangled feathers dangle down.   (OP, 117–18)

Here, then, are the tree and the bird—which simply sings because it is its nature to sing; it is "without why," without "care"; it does not fret about the enabling conditions of its existence, and, with its fire-fangled feathers dangling down, it sings for the sake of nothing other than its song. Dylan Thomas says: "The force that through the green fuse drives the flower / Drives my green age. . . . The force that drives the water through the rocks / Drives my red blood."²⁴ And, in its innocent openness to this "force," the bird stands for Stevens as something like a sacrament of the mystery of Being—"mere Being," which is that

> life brighter than this present splendor,
> Brighter, perfected and distant away,
> Not to be reached but to be known,
> Not an attainment of the will
> But something illogically received.   (OP, 101)

So, for all the testimony to the contrary that comes from many of his principal interpreters, Stevens is a profoundly religious poet. But he exemplifies a kind of sensibility for which the direction, as it were, of transcendence is not upward but downward. That is to say, the transcendentality of Being is apprehended as given in and with and under the immanent. For Stevens, the universe is not a two-storied affair, with the realm of the divine above nature and history, to be reached by way of some *scala sacra* leading up beyond the phenomenal world into the timelessness of eternity. On the contrary: the sense of reality controlling his theory of poetry and his own poetic utterance tells him that we dwell in *one* world, not at a point of juncture between two worlds. And thus he finds the transcendent in the most intimate neighborhood of our experience: he finds it (in Teilhard de Chardin's phrasing) to be the "within" of all things, "shining forth from the depths of every event, every element."²⁵ He finds grace, in other words, not overhead but in the world,²⁶ in (as Meister Eckhart would say) the *Is-ness* of everything that exists—in "The actual landscape with its actual horns / Of baker and butcher blowing."

This "inquisitor of structures" (CP, 510) does, then, through his "poem of pure reality," through his "Whole Harmonium,"²⁷ define what is indeed "a fresh spiritual"—which speaks of "that nobility which is our spiritual height and depth. . . . Nothing could be more evasive and inaccessible. . . . But there it is. . . . If it is defined, it will be fixed and it must not be fixed. . . . To fix it is to put an end to it" (NA, 33–34). So he does indeed find, as he says in his great tribute to Santayana ("To an Old Philosopher in Rome"),

> a kind of total grandeur at the end,
> With every visible thing enlarged and yet
> No more than a bed, a chair and moving nuns,
> The immensest theatre, the pillared porch,
> The book and candle in your ambered room.   (CP, 510)

His ultimate apostrophe, in other words, is to "mere Being," "the human end in the spirit's greatest reach" (CP, 508).

It was within the terms of such a vision of the world as this that Wallace Stevens, lawyer and vice-president of the Hartford Accident and Indemnity Co., dwelt poetically in Connecticut from the spring of 1916 till his death in the summer of 1955. "He dwelt in Connecticut," says Frank Kermode, "as Santayana dwelt in the head of the world, as if it were origin as well as threshold."[28]

7/ Epilogue– Heidegger's Vision of Poetry as Ontology

The intellectual career of Martin Heidegger (1889–1976) has sometimes been associated with that family of thought called existentialism, in part no doubt because one of the principal strategists of the existentialist project, Jean-Paul Sartre, did so insistently claim Heidegger as one of his chief mentors. But he himself was somewhat embarrassed by Sartre's homage and steadfastly disowned any affiliation with this whole line of thought, since the question by which he found himself to be haunted beyond all others concerned not so much the nature of human existence as the nature of Being as such. And thus the immense prestige that has gathered about the legacy of this last great genius of philosophy in our period may at first appear to present something of a puzzle, for nothing, as it would seem, is less likely to appeal to modern sensibility than inquiries into the nature of Being. The very notion of Being, as it will be argued, posits something whose existence cannot, in the nature of the case, be established by those procedures of verification which are decisive for our predominantly empiricist mentality. And certainly it has been the testimony of the reigning school of contemporary philosophy that the concept of Being affords an instance of nothing more substantial than "the way in which a consideration of grammar leads to metaphysics." That is to say, "infected [as we are] by the primitive superstition that to every name a single real entity must correspond,"[1] we assume that the participial noun *being* refers to some discriminable thing which actually exists—but, as recent analytic philosophy maintains, this is an assumption fed only by the sheerest delusion. And at the point at which, with a great flourish, this lesson is laid down by A. J. Ayer in his famous book, *Language, Truth and Logic*, his way of alluding to Heidegger makes it clear that he regards such arguments as he brings forward to be an effective broom with which the mind may be swept clean of the heavy confusions which derive from this German metaphysician.

In this connection, however, it needs to be said in Heidegger's defense that, unlike many of his Anglo-American contemporaries, it never occurred to him to suppose that that which is constantly present in all the things of this world does itself belong to the category of "things." Indeed, he was often at pains to remind us that Being is quite radically misconceived if it is thought of as any sort of "object" (*Gegenstand*) standing over against the human "subject"; and in the "Letter on Humanism" (*Brief über den Humanismus*) of 1947 he declared quite explicitly that "Being is wider than every particular being and is yet closer to man than every being, whether it be a rock, an animal, a work of art, a machine, an angel."[2] Which is to say that we do not confront Being as we confront a table or a tree, since it is that which enables all the particular things and creatures of the world to be whatever it is for which they are destined by their inner constitution.

Yet so to speak of Being is not to assign it the status of a universal attribute belonging to every particular being, for Kant's lesson of long ago (in Book 2 of *The Critique of Pure Reason*) is not to be forgotten—that, unlike the predication of redness or roundness about a thing, we do not in any way increase what is known about it when we simply declare that it exists. To say that a thing *is* is not to have specified one of its distinguishing properties; and thus, since being is not a stipulable property of things, the logic of classes forbids its being conceived as constituting any sort of genus. For, since the notion of being implies no distinction among already existing things, it would be merely tautologous to regard it as designating the only kind of class which it might reasonably be considered to denote—namely, that comprising all things which do exist.

Yet the inevitable negativity in what must initially be one's approach to the concept of Being need not be taken as confirming the essential emptiness which is imputed to the concept by philosophic scepticism.

And it is a part of Heidegger's distinction to have shown that conceiving of Being as an entity or substance or attribute or class does not by any means exhaust the conceptual possibilities. His method of discourse makes it clear that Being is for him what the language of traditional philosophy calls a transcendental—namely, a reality which is to be reached only, as it were, by moving through the contingent realities of nature and history and which is therefore "above" the ordinary categories of reflection. But his great book of 1927, *Being and Time* (*Sein und Zeit*), makes it equally clear that he did not regard the path to Being as one which proceeds from the indigence of finitude toward a rational demonstration—by way of inference and the principle of causality—of something like the Absolute of Idealist philosophy.

Indeed, it might be said that, for the Heidegger of *Being and Time*, Being is to be approached not at all theoretically but existentially, since Being is not that which man stands out from or over against. On the contrary, it is that in which he most deeply participates, that by which he is most deeply grasped. Thus the cognitive relation in which he stands with respect to Being is, as we are reminded in the opening pages of *Being and Time*, an affair of a "hermeneutical circle"—which is to say that the interpreter is already a part of that which is to be interpreted, so that the process of interpretation must involve a circular reasoning, since, in the nature of the case, the interpreter begins his task with some inward grasp of that which awaits elucidation. So, instead of involving some theoretical process of deduction, the intellectual act whereby one takes hold of the nature of Being involves a descent into the depths of one's own humanity. The cognitive effort entails, in other words, not a "transcendental analytic" but an "existential analytic," and it is this to which the book of 1927 is very largely given over.

Here, in *Being and Time*, it is *Dasein* which is one of the decisive terms of Heidegger's argument. This Germanism—which means literally *being-there* and is not customarily translated in non-German discussions of Heidegger's thought—is his technical term for the human mode of being: he considers man's distinctive passion to be so much one for interrogating the nature of his existence that he deserves, indeed, simply to be regarded himself as *Dasein*. "*Dasein*," as he says, "is an entity for which, in its Being, that Being is an issue."[3] And since it is in the human quest for Being that we have our most immediate access to Being, it is the exploration of *Dasein* to which the book of 1927 is largely devoted. For Heidegger's most basic supposition in this period of his career appears to have been that the path to Being is one that leads through an analysis of those structures of existence belonging to the particular being whose nature requires him to raise the question of

Being. It was, in short, the study of *Dasein* which he regarded as constituting what he called "fundamental ontology," and the profoundly
original and exciting inquiry that was carried forward in this vein—into
the nature of anxiety (*Angst*), care (*Sorge*), transcendence (*Transzen-
denz*), temporality (*Zeitlichkeit*), the experience of death, and the
meaning of authenticity (*Eigentlichkeit*)—makes it not unreasonable to
think of *Being and Time* as one of the great classic monuments in the
literature of modern existentialism, Heidegger's own discomfort at being so regarded notwithstanding.

Almost immediately after the appearance of this book, however, it
would seem that his thought underwent a certain reversal (*Kehre*), and
this "turning" is to be detected already in the inaugural lecture ("What
Is Metaphysics?")[4] which he delivered in 1929 on succeeding Edmund
Husserl in the chair of philosophy at the University of Freiburg. Here,
as he confronted Freiburg colleagues representing the various faculties
and sciences making up the university, Heidegger chose to attack the
most difficult question with which a philosopher might wrestle before
such an audience—namely, the question as to whether there is anything
at all remaining for the philosopher to do, after the practitioners of the
several scientific disciplines have begun their diverse labors. With a
strange kind of bravado, he proceeded in effect quickly to grant that,
indeed, once the established sciences have launched all their various
inquiries into the nature of the existing world, "nothing" is left over.
But, then, in a brilliant tour de force, he declared this very nothingness
to be the ultimate subject of philosophy.

The lecture makes it clear, however, that this nothingness which is
to be addressed by metaphysical philosophy is no mere logical conun-
drum but is, rather, an existential datum of the most concrete sort. For
man (as it had been argued in *Being and Time*) is a creature who finds
his life encircled by darkness: the human adventure begins by our being
"thrown" into a world which is not of our making, and the transiency
of our life looks only toward the final certitude of death. So man is an
anxious creature because he is aware of the radical finitude of his existence. True, he may be conscious of his anxiety only intermittently and
at rare intervals, since we are normally caught up in all those inconse-
quential routines of daily life that tend to obscure what is fundamen-
tally hazardous in our condition. But, when we are stung by the terrible
dread that comes as we begin to reflect on the oblivion that ultimately
awaits us, then, immediately—as we feel ourselves to be moving merely
from "thrownness" (*Geworfenheit*) to death—the world sinks into a
profound kind of insignificance, and the only thing that remains is the
primordial Nothingness.

Yet, as Heidegger argues in the Freiburg lecture, it is precisely the unhinging encounter with Nothing that enlivens the mind's awareness of our being compassed round about by something more than mere Nothingness—namely, by the multiplicity of actual beings that make up our world-environment. "Only because Nothing is revealed in the very basis of our *Dasein*," he says, "is it possible for the utter strangeness of what-is to dawn on us."[5] It is, in other words, the threatening specter of Nothing which awakens in us that ontological shock wherewith we notice that, indeed, we face not Nothing but *something*. So he suggests that the old proposition *ex nihilo nihil fit* ought perhaps to be made to say *ex nihilo omne ens qua ens fit*.

Now it may, of course, at first appear that the Freiburg lecture is espousing the purest sort of nihilism; but, as Heidegger makes plain in the "Postscript" of 1943, the metaphysic of Nothingness was intended only to be a propaedeutic looking toward a metaphysic of Being. His "Postscript" wants in effect to say that, if in that lecture he seemed to be equating Being with Nothing, this was done only in the manner of a conceit—but a conceit, as he would insist, which is not itself essentially illicit. For, like "Nothing," Being itself is not *a* being; and since it is a non-entity, it is, like "Nothing," *absolutely* different from all beings. Which means that it cannot be fitted into any of the categories of existence. It is, in short, a "transcendental" which we begin to approach when the question is asked, "Why is there anything at all, rather than nothing?"

Just two years after the appearance of *Being and Time* Heidegger was, in other words, already committing himself to what was to become the great quest of his career and one of the great quests of modern intellectual life. For he was now a man in pursuit of the last objective which beckons the philosophical imagination and which is none other than Being itself. But though by the early 1930s his principal concern was no longer the kind of analysis of the human condition which he had undertaken in *Being and Time*, the tendency of many recent interpreters to emphasize very sharply this "turning" in his development ought now perhaps to be somewhat curtailed. For, even in the earlier phase of his career, the study of *Dasein* was conceived primarily to be a way of proceeding toward the question of Being; and though his early work has a notably existentialist slant which is, to be sure, distinguishable from the predominantly ontological emphasis of his later writing, he was himself by no means unjustified in his insistence that, early and late, it had indeed been the question of Being which was the overriding concern of his thought. Above all else, as he contended, it was for this that he sought a new hearing.[6]

Over the last decades of his career, however, Heidegger went about his elected task with an abiding sense of facing into enormously resistant head winds. For, as he frequently reminded us, we in the modern West are a people so committed to the superstitions of positivism and to "the humanization of truth" that we have virtually lost any capacity for performing an act of true attention before the sheer ontological weight and depth of the world. So ours, in Heidegger's reading of it, is an open situation, in the sense of our dwelling in a great intervenient space, in a great *Between*. As he says, in the clumsy stiltedness of manner so typical of his strange yet curiously moving rhetoric, ours "is the time of the gods that have fled *and* of the god that is coming. It is the time of *need*, because it lies under a double lack and a double Not: the No-more of the gods that have fled and the Not-yet of the god that is coming."[7]

The proposal that ours is a time of privation and dearth, of *need*, occurs toward the end of an essay on Hölderlin and reflects Heidegger's fascination with the special sort of eschatological sensibility controlling Hölderlin's poetry. But it also reflects, of course, his equal fascination with that other mad eschatologist in modern German tradition, born in the year following Hölderlin's death, who brusquely proclaimed the death of God (or at least of all the old names and conceptualizations of God) in a book of 1882 curiously entitled *Die Fröliche Wissenschaft* (*The Gay Science*). Indeed, it is Friedrich Nietzsche who marks for Heidegger one of the great decisive turning points in the history of what he speaks of as "the humanization of truth."[8]

The humanization of truth—the doctrine that truth resides in some human perspective rather than in Being itself—is, for Heidegger, the great disaster involved in Western intellectual history, because it entails a sundering of the primordial bond between the human spirit and what (by adapting a phrase of Teilhard de Chardin) might be called the *milieu ontologique*. To be sure, in *Being and Time* he had declared "world"—that entire complex of unitive images and analogies and principles through which the whole welter of existence becomes the integral field of reality in which man actually dwells—to be an achievement of *Dasein*; and such an epistemology would itself seem to have entailed a perspectivist concept of truth. But within a few years after the appearance of this book he appears to have concluded that its account of the relation between *Dasein* and Being was applicable only in a very rough sort of way to the more perfunctory transactions of everyday that man has with reality; whereas, in the great decisive and extreme situations of human existence, it is not in man but in Being itself that truth is found to be resident. So, in a series of works belonging to the 1940s,[9] he began to launch a fierce polemic against the whole heresy of "humanism," wanting now most emphatically to insist upon the nonhumanistic orientation of his own thought.

In this period Heidegger's basic conviction came to be that all encounters between the Self and the Not-self—the terms are not his—occur, inevitably, within the environing milieu of Being, and that all the referential thrusts of human intelligence outward beyond itself are confirmable only in consequence of this encompassing *Plenum* whose "unhiddenness" does indeed make it possible for the Self to meet the Not-self in an act of cognition. The locus of truth, in other words, is not in this or that perspective (or category, or proposition, or system) that may be imposed upon reality, but is rather in the "unhiddenness" or transparency of Being: which is to say that truth is not an achievement but a gift, something granted and received.

But, as Heidegger argued, the assumption perennially informing the Western tradition has been that truth is resident in the schemata of human intelligence. The project of "humanizing" truth was first launched by the Greeks, preeminently by Plato, whose theory of Ideas did in effect attribute ultimate reality to what were nothing more than projections of human reason. The traditional Platonist will no doubt be scandalized by his insistence that the Platonic Idea is nothing more than a concept; but—conventional textbook scholarship to the contrary (and Heidegger needed no instruction in this mode)—this, nevertheless, was his claim, that it is simply an audacious postulate, reified into Eternity. And thus, in his estimate of things, the great bequest of Platonism to Western mentality has been the superstition that truth follows upon a proper deployment by the intellect of its own counters and that, in the ascending scale of ontological priority, certain human principles and idealities hold the sovereign place.

Heidegger found an essentially identical error in medieval Scholasticism, where (as in Aquinas) truth is understood to consist in the "adequation" of the intellect to things as they are. Moreover, this same view of truth as an achievement of human intelligence he found being carried into the early modern period by Descartes, whose *Cogito* only signalized again how persistently the philosophic tradition remains (as Alfred North Whitehead long ago remarked, though from a standpoint rather different from Heidegger's) but "a series of footnotes to Plato."

In Heidegger's reading of the Western tradition, this anthropocentric account of the world as an essentially human "project" gained even more emphatic expression in the critical philosophy of Kant which, after denying the possibility of our knowing things in themselves, went on to locate the ground of all objectivity in the synthetic categories with which the self orders its experience, thus making man himself the final and absolute measure of all truth. And so it comes to be that, for Heidegger, it is but a step from Kant to Nietzsche—and to the end of the whole Western experiment in humanization. For he who in 1882 announced the death of God was in effect embracing, in a violently strident way, what the whole antecedent tradition had been moving toward—namely, the impertinence of regarding the world as itself simply an image of man. Nietzsche's according an ultimate status in reality to "the will to power"—to the principle of human assertiveness—did, in other words, entail, most essentially, nothing more than a radicalization of what since Plato had been perennially inherent in the tradition, for the whole drive of the *philosophia perennis* is toward the assertion that man dwells, uncompanioned and alone, in a universe that is very largely of his own creation. Nor is this assessment of the meaning of our received tradition, for Heidegger, merely something which it is interesting for intellectual historians to contemplate. For on his account it is precisely in the humanization of reality in the West that we may find the explanation of the great malaise that blights the world now, at the end of the modern period—which is a disquiet arising out of the discovery that the triumphs of our scientific technology have been purchased by such an unbridling of "the will to power" as has sundered our most elemental bonds with nature and resulted in a wholly artificial environment for human life.

Indeed, at the heart of our culture there is, Heidegger suggests, a profound perversion, a great imbalance, that needs correction. At the end now of (as he nominates it) the History of Being in the West, what is lost is simply Being itself, and the great task awaiting the imagination is the recovery of a range of sympathy and conscience that will permit us to deal with the world in terms other than those simply of aggressive action. Our traditional habits of preference for what is assertive and bold and aggressive and our inveterate penchant for "calculative thinking" (*rechnendes Denken*)[10] do, to be sure, account for much that is distinctively a part of the impressive Western achievement. And, undoubtedly, man's conduct of his affairs does on certain levels require the instrumentalist orientation of calculative thinking. Yet such an orientation, as it feeds our passion to arrange and organize, to regulate and turn things to practical account, prompts the assumption that reality is wholly coextensive with the world of public operables, with the things that can be weighed and measured and manipulated. And though dealing with the world from the standpoint of this general kind of hermeneutic may enable us to control our external environment with great sophistication, it does, nevertheless, exact a great cost, in the degree to which it tends to shut us up in that cruelest of jails which is established by the limits of commonsense rationality. And it is Heidegger's contention that, until this jail is broken out of, we do not give ourselves any chance to hear the call of Being. For when the things of earth are approached in that grasping, manipulative spirit of the calculative reason and when our sole intention is to make them obedient to some enterprise of science or engineering—when they are simply considered to be material for one or another kind of observation and experiment and use—then they become inert and fall silent.

In such an advanced technological culture as our own, this "silence" of Being is, as Heidegger proposed, to be alleviated only by what is perhaps the most extraordinary feat of imagination that technological man can perform, of managing for a time to shut down all the well-driven machines of his science and his engineering. For it is only when the world begins no longer to be approached merely as something to be "attacked"[11] in the manner of a technological project—it is only when we consent to approach it in the spirit of what Heidegger calls *Gelassenheit* (that is, surrender, abandonment, acquiescence)—it is only then that the "voice" of Being begins to be heard. What is required is a throttling of our great consuming passion to invade every nook and cranny of the world with our concepts and categories and schemes of manipulation. For, until we have learned again the discipline of "letting-be,"[12] we shall not achieve that condition of what he calls "releasement toward things"[13] which is nothing other than an attitude of simple enthrallment before the sheer specificity of all the various givens of the earth.

This is, however, an attitude, a way of *receiving* the world, that rests on quite a different sort of rationality from that which customarily prevails in our culture. For the mind does not become alive to what is most primitively marvelous in the affairs of life until it subordinates calculative thinking to what Heidegger speaks of as "meditative thinking"—by which, as he says, he means utter "openness" to radical mystery, to the mystery of there being *something* rather than nothing.[14] Meditative thinking is a thinking in which the originating force proceeds, as it were, not so much from the mind itself as from that under which it stands, so that we feel a claim being laid upon us, a demand being levied against us. The meditative thinker knows himself to be addressed by something transcendent, by something wholly other than himself; and he is not so much acting on as he is being acted upon, so that the knowledge which is brought to him as a result of his "medita-tion" is something like a gift. Yet he is by no means wholly inactive, for taking up an attitude of meditative openness to the world means "pay-ing heed" to the strange kind of stoutness by which its things and creatures are steadied and supported. And it is by this most exacting labor of imagination that at last we are brought into the neighborhood of Being.

But what is Being? In his writings of the last thirty-five years of his career, it is this ultimate question which Heidegger may often seem to have been evading as constantly as he was raising it, for again and again it slides into view and then quickly slips lizardlike away, leaving only its tail in our hands. On one point, to be sure, he is quite emphatic, that "Being is not God."[15] For the God of traditional metaphysics, or of what he calls "onto-theo-logy," is *an* entity or object, a particular being, albeit the Highest or the Supreme being—but Being itself is not *a* being, not even the totality of all beings. Indeed, when thought of in relation to the world of particular beings, it must be considered to be "that-which-is not," or Nothing. Yet (as he says in the "Postscript" to "What Is Metaphysics?") this Nothing "is not a nugatory Nothing," since its vastness is precisely "that which gives every being the warrant to be."[16] Which is to say that it is nothing less than Being itself.

Nor are Heidegger's negatives in regard to Being confined to the issue of its definability in theistic terms, though these negatives become somewhat less absolute when he begins to examine Being in relation to those modalities which would, formally, appear to be quite distinct from it. In his *Introduction to Metaphysics* (*Einführung in die Meta-physik*),[17] for example, he considers Being in relation to becoming and in relation to appearance (that which "seems-to-be"). And though he wants finally to say that Being is neither becoming nor appearance, his negative is a qualified negative. For since becoming is a process whereby something more fully develops into itself, that which becomes does in some sense already exist; and, therefore, becoming cannot be considered as absolutely antithetical to Being. Yet Being, though it in-cludes within itself a dynamic element, is not mere process, mere per-mutation, mere becoming. Similarly, that which "seems-to-be" could not in any way at all submit itself to our inspection if it did not in some sense truly exist; and furthermore, since Being is a transcendental, it must always be approached mediately, by way of the particular phe-nomena that make up the world of appearance. Yet, though Being is always given in, with, and through its appearances, it is not itself sim-ply appearance, since it is that which enables things, as it were, to be gathered together and to stand before us: so it must in some sense be concealed.

Now these are but the merest handful of the negatives with which the Heideggerian literature is strewn on the question of Being, and they convey something of the extreme reticence which Heidegger very carefully keeps about man's most primal encounter with reality. Yet his final intention is not that of invoking any *via negationis*, for he conceives Being to have a veritable "mission" to the world of earth, and to this he wants to give as positive an utterance as our human language will permit.

Already in his book of 1929 on Kant[18] Heidegger was beginning to speak of the foundation of ontological inquiry as that "pure horizon" of intelligibility "in which the Being of beings becomes antecedently discernible." And it was such a nonobjectifying idiom that he consistently employed in his later writings—in, for example, the "Letter on Humanism"; in the essays on Hölderlin;[19] in the *Introduction to Metaphysics*; in the book of 1954, *What Is Called Thinking? (Was heisst Denken?)*;[20] and in the two books of 1957, *The Principle of Ground (Der Satz vom Grund)*[21] and *Identity and Difference (Identität und Differenz)*.[22]

The testimony being made in these and numerous other works seems calculated to suggest that it is the mission of Being to establish the possibility of *presence* for all particular beings. Being is that primal energy which gathers things into themselves and so keeps them thus assembled that they can stand out before the gaze of intelligence. A being might be said to be simply that-which-is-present, that-which-is-in-the-open; whereas Being itself *is* that Openness which lights up the things of earth, which enables us to behold them in their radical actuality, and which is never itself, therefore, conceivable as *a* being. One suspects that Heidegger would have been inclined to say that the very question "What is Being?" expresses the profoundest misconception that the mind can entertain, for its presupposition is that Being is, indeed, objectively definable. But, as one of his interpreters reminds us, "Being is beyond all 'whats' and 'whiches,' all separations and distinctions."[23] One cannot point to it as one points to a table or a gazelle, for it is itself precisely that which makes it possible for all objects to have objectivity. And, inevitably, that by which all things are lighted up and shown forth must, in its own absolute interiority, remain hidden.

Yet, though Being is hidden and far away because it is the source (*Ursprung*) of all reality, it nevertheless—as Heidegger liked to say— "hails" us, and this hailing consists simply in the generosity with which it permits the things of earth to "come-to-presence."[24] Their presence, in other words, *is* the hail, the salutation, which Being addresses to us; and, since they are present only because Being has imparted itself to them in the manner of a gift, any truly meditative thinking must, in effect, be an act of thanksgiving. For thinking of the most fundamental kind involves our "hailing" Being: which is to say that we respond to its primary hail by receiving and accepting the plenitude which it bestows upon us. And since we know this plenitude to be not of our own creation, since we recognize it to be in no way a part of ourselves, since it is the sheer otherness of Being itself and of its self-giving, genuinely meditative thinking becomes, inevitably, an affair of thanksgiving for the incalculable munificence with which Being lets things be.

Indeed, it is just at this point that we have at last before us the terms which Heidegger doubtless preferred above all others when Being is to be spoken of. For the formula which seems more adequate to his vision than any other is that which is suggested by the phrase "letting-be" (*Seinlassen*), and this, in the final analysis, is what he conceives to be the mission and the very essence of Being—"the letting-be of beings" (*das Seinlassen von Seiendem*). Here, as he wanted to say, is the ultimate mystery of Being, and the mystery which it is the peculiar privilege of man to contemplate, that Being does not hoard up its plenitude within itself (as, conceivably, it might) but rather, with an infinite liberality, takes as its mission the bestowal of itself upon the world of time and finitude and contingency. In short, Being "gives" itself to the world of beings; and it is this primordial dispensation, Heidegger believed, which constitutes the alpha and omega of any truly meditative thought.

But when Being has come to be "forgotten," as in the technological ethos of the modern West, how can we bring the usual traffic of our acting and thinking to a stop, in order that we may deepen ourselves down into the kind of profound repose and expectancy that will permit our becoming permeable again by the integral reality of the world? This is for Heidegger, one feels, the central question needing to be raised in our own late and problematic time, and it is just as the issue begins to be posed by the logic of his own thought that his answer begins already to be in view. For, untroubled by the sense of scandal that he may thereby give to his fellow philosophers, the remarkable position taken by this audacious thinker is that it is precisely the vocation of the poet to bring us once again into the region of fundamental reality.

The epigones like now to make arcane distinctions between the earlier Heidegger (of *Being and Time*) and "the later Heidegger," between the phenomenologist of *Dasein* and the metaphysician for whom the primary reality is no longer *Dasein* but Being. And nothing could be more manifest than that for "the later Heidegger" the principal fact about our culture concerns its dominance by technology. In his view of the modern situation, the sovereign passion controlling our period is one which prompts a great effort at winning mastery of the world: it is a passion to control and to manipulate both nature and human life itself, and this technological orientation is something long prepared for by a culture whose philosophic strategists so "humanized" the predominant conception of reality that Being came to be regarded as that which is to be seized and regulated and put to use. The consequence is that we now find ourselves—in a way, like Mary Shelley's Frankenstein—at the behest of a "second nature" of our own creation which is comprised of the wholly artificial environment technological enterprise throws round human life. And in this extremity, as Heidegger suggests, any profound renewal of the human spirit will require that it unlearn its habit of approaching the world primarily with the intention to exploit, as if it were merely waiting to be raped. What must be learned again is the discipline of "letting-be" What Is, of throttling *the will to will* and of *surrendering* to the radically immanent presence of Being.

Now it is in just this discipline that the poet, as Heidegger maintains, offers a unique and an indispensable tutelage, for his whole purpose is to stir and quicken within us an awareness of the irrevocability by which the things of this world are as they are. In the last three or four decades of his life much of Heidegger's writing was integrally related to his theory of literature, even when, in a given work, his immediate theme happened in no way to touch explicitly on the subject of poetry; but, for a reconstruction of this phase of his thought, the most crucial documents are two collections of essays, the *Erläuterungen zu Hölderlins Dichtung* and the book called *Holzwege* (*Paths in the Forest*).[25] The language of these essays—like that of the entire oeuvre to which they belong—is, in its obscurity and elusiveness, an achievement remarkable even in the German tradition (whose systematic thinkers have rarely been notable for their stylistic clarity). But, in so far as the true intention of this strange rhetoric is discernible at all, it would seem that, for Heidegger, it is most especially the distinctive office of the poet to make us look at the various concrete realities of experience with the kind of wakeful attentiveness that will permit their being disclosed in the radical specificity of what they are. The artist seeks to bring us into a relationship of intense intimacy with a given event, with some quite specific phenomenon. What he invites is an attitude of enthrallment before the sheer singularity of whatever may be the object which he is holding up for attention. The poetic world—that is, the world of literary art in general—is rooted in the concrete particularity of lived experience. Whereas the scientific view of the world is ultimately predatory,

driving toward possession and mastery and control, the poetic imagination in its fascination with the concrete, with the individual qua individual, wants, as Heidegger would say, simply to let things be. The poet
does not want, as it were, to put things on their good behavior by
making them obedient to the well-driven machine of the Idea; rather,
he wants to reconstitute our perceptual habits in a way that will restore
to us the innocence which is simply enthralled by the bright actuality of
the things of earth.

The poet, then, in Heidegger's view, might be said to be an adept in
the art of "paying heed"—which is why he can say in the *Holzwege*
that, in a work of art, "truth is at work."[26] Truth is at work, because
the carefulness with which the poet pays heed to the things of earth has
the effect of bringing them "into the Open." Which is to say, in Heidegger's terminology, that the poet is he who "hails" Being, since Being
itself is nothing other than "the Open"—that immediate and luminous
presence constituting the inner cohesion whereby things are enabled
simply to be what they are.

In the essay on "The Origin of the Work of Art" ("Der Ursprung
des Kunstwerkes") in the *Holzwege*, for example, Heidegger speaks of
a Van Gogh painting of a pair of farm shoes, and he invites us to
compare the artifact with the shoes themselves. The actual shoes are
merely a piece of what he calls "equipment," and the "equipmental
being" of the shoes consists, he says, in their "serviceability." The old
peasant woman who uses them, who trudges in them day by day
through the dampness of the soil and the furrows of her fields, knows
these shoes in their equipmental being, and knows them without having
to take thought. But we, as we look at the shoes, do not begin to
comprehend their essential nature—how they vibrate with "the silent
call of the earth," how they slide along "the loneliness of the field-path
as evening declines," how they are pervaded by "the wordless joy" of
"ripening corn"—until Van Gogh's painting opens them up out of their
captivity unto themselves and into what they most emphatically are in
their radical actuality. It is the work of art that brings into the open that
which has "withdrawn" behind the shoes but which, once it is fully
revealed, is seen to be that which in truth imparts "presence" to the
shoes—and this is nothing other than Being itself whose location is
necessarily always in finite things behind which it withdraws. When
these things are truly paid heed to, so that they are brought into the
open, what is then in view is nothing less than Being itself, for that is
what Being is: it is simply that effulgence wherewith the things of earth
are enabled to have an emphatic and persisting presence.

So poetic art, because it renders us alert to the concrete realities of the world in the dimension of presence, brings us into the region of Being, since Being itself is nothing other than Presence. In performing this kind of function, however, poetry is for Heidegger but the crucial instance of language in general, since, as he says in the *Holzwege*, the primary task of language is not merely to be a technique of signification but "to bring beings as such for the first time into the Open."[27] Indeed, man does not have a "world," does not have any sort of unified matrix of meanings and relations in which to dwell, unless he has a language, a way of declaring what things "appear to be as they come into the Open."[28] This, one imagines, is the insight that he takes to be implicit in the saying of Hölderlin for which he has such a great liking, that "poetically, / Man dwells upon the earth." Man dwells upon the earth —in a really human way—only in so far as he transforms "earth" into "world," and he can have a world only if he has language, only if he has a way of being open to Being and of naming the things of earth in which Being resides: which is to say that he can have a world only as he manages in some manner to be a "poet."

But, of course, though our human situation requires us to dwell poetically on the earth, in the ordinary, day-by-day transactions of life, we become creatures of routinized modes of thought and feeling that permit only just so much attentiveness to reality as is requisite for the immediate fulfillment of our practical purposes. We hasten to and fro in the world, from day to day, from one occasion to another, hearing only so much of this and seeing only so much of that as the urgencies of our common affairs allow. The environing world in which we are set is rarely perceived as anything primitively arresting or marvelous: things are merely cues for action or signals of desire—the bare minimum of all that would be there, were we to take the trouble of paying heed. And thus everything becomes, as it were, incidental and pragmatic, gross and philistine.

Moreover, this impoverishment that is normally a part of ordinary experience is, in Heidegger's sense of things, very greatly deepened in a technological culture such as our own, where inorganic nature becomes merely an affair of pointer-readings and human biology itself becomes the experimental material of a casually deliberate medical science, and where a great screen is thrown up—by all our gadgets and artifacts— between man and the primitive realities of the earth. Indeed, it is in such a climate that human life begins to descend into a most radical "godlessness."

Recurrently in his later writings, and most especially in the essays on Hölderlin, Heidegger speaks in a curiously veiled and gnomic way about "the gods." He says, for example, that we dwell in a period between that in which the gods "fled" and that in which they will return, and he seems to regard it as one of the chief signs of the authentic poet that he should have a very profound sense of this present time as a time betwixt and between. He defines the poet as "one who has been cast out . . . into [this] . . . *Between*, between gods and men."[29] He speaks of the poet as one who consents to take his stand in the presence of the gods and who *names* the gods. And similarly cryptic references to gods appear in various other contexts. But, ambiguously as the term behaves in the logic of Heidegger's thought, its effect has been sufficiently tantalizing to lead some of his theological interpreters apparently to assume that it is merely a somewhat eccentric locution carrying, at bottom, a traditionally monotheistic meaning. Yet so to construe the import of his testimony is surely to misconstrue it; for, despite the short shrift he gives any sort of conventional atheism and despite the deeply religious tenor of his entire work, his basic intentions were not those of Christian apologetics, as he was himself at pains to remind us on more than one occasion. So it is surely an illicit maneuver to singularize Heidegger's "gods" and then to interpret what he says about their "return" as simply his figurative way of anticipating the coming end of Nietzschean nihilism, when the God of traditional Christian experience will no longer be absent and will once again return in power and glory.

But if the term "gods" is not translatable as God, how, then, is it to be understood within the framework of Heidegger's thought? The issue is not to be easily resolved, for the term does, of course, function figuratively and may not, therefore, be fully reducible at all to any definition of a univocal sort. But perhaps it may be hazarded that the basic consistencies of his vision are least violated when, by "gods," he is taken to mean whatever it is that holds the world together and "assembles" it into a stable unity. By "gods" we may assume that he means those ultimate *powers* of Being which permit things to sojourn on the earth and which guarantee to reality the character of permanence and stability and trustworthiness.[30] And his affirming it to be a part of the poet's office to *name* the gods is but his oblique manner of reasserting the radically cognitive way in which the literary experience thrusts outward, beyond itself, toward those realities that, in the most basic way, encompass the human enterprise.

So "godlessness" in Heidegger's lexicon is not properly equated with something like Nietzsche's "death of God." It speaks, rather, of that profound inattentiveness to the essential fabric and texture of the things of earth which becomes epidemic in a technological culture, where everything that faces man is approached with an intention simply to control and manipulate and where, as a consequence, nothing is seen or experienced in the dimension of Holiness. The Holy (*das Heilige*) makes its way into Heidegger's thought through his meditation on that untitled poem of Hölderlin's which begins "Wie wenn am Feiertage . . ."—"As when on a holiday. . . ."[31] He takes it to be a term required of Hölderlin himself by his fidelity to the sheer presence of Being in the finite realities of the earth. And this is precisely what Holiness means for Heidegger: it is that power and form wherewith a thing is what it is—whose penumbra of mystery naturally evokes an attitude of awe and astonishment.

Martin Buber reminds us that we may consider a tree as though it were merely a stiff column against a background of delicate blue and silver in a picture; or we can perceive it as an affair of vital movement, in its "ceaseless commerce with earth and air"; or we may simply regard a given tree, in its formation and structure, as an instance of a species; or we may "subdue its actual presence and form so sternly" as to recognize it only as an expression of certain laws governing the ways in which "the component substances mingle and separate"; or, again, the particular tree may be so subsumed under a given type that it is thought of only as belonging to some scheme of numerical relations. But, then, as he also reminds us, we may be so seized by "the power of exclusiveness" in the given tree that we find "everything, picture and movement, species and type, law and number, indivisibly united"[32] in the one tree that stands before the eye. And if we can manage not to regard the land in which the tree is rooted as merely a piece of real estate, to be cleared perhaps for a suburban housing development; if we can manage not to regard the tree as merely a piece of timber to be cut down and converted to some useful purpose; if we can manage so to subdue *the will to will* as to confront this tree in an attitude of "letting-be," so that we can really be laid hold of by the sheer presence of Being in the tree, then, as Heidegger would say, we shall find that what indeed we are most essentially seized by is that which is Holy in the tree—for the Holy, he declares, is simply the "advent" (*Kommen*) of Being itself.

When, however, man becomes so enwrapt in the spirit of modern technological enterprise that he loses any capacity for reverential awe before the radical holiness of Creation, then human life begins to descend into the Profane, into that condition in which our commitment to manipulative and predatory ways of dealing with the world defraud us of the power to marvel at the generosity with which things are steadied and supported by the power and presence of Being. But to whatever extent a person fails to be attentive to what Gerard Manley Hopkins called that "pitch of self" which distinguishes each bird, each tree, each flowing stream, each bit of Creation, then he is, of course, to that extent by way of losing any full sense of that pitch of self which distinguishes his own reality—as Hopkins put it, "that taste of myself, of *I* and *me* above and in all things, which is more distinctive than the taste of ale or alum, more distinctive than the smell of walnutleaf or camphor."[33] When there is no longer any sense of grandeur in the "shining from shook foil," or of splendor in "the ooze of oil / Crushed," when there is no longer any lively sense of "the dearest freshness deep down things,"[34] then a great descent has begun—into that deprived condition that Martin Heidegger would nominate as "godlessness."

In such a time—of dearth, of inanition, of godlessness—Heidegger considers it inevitable that the vocation of the poet should become something pastoral and priestly. It is, of course, most especially the mission of the poet to be a watchman (*Wächter*) or shepherd (*Hirt*) of Being, as it emerges in the things of earth.[35] And his meditations on the poems of Hölderlin that speak of the poet as a wanderer journeying homeward[36]—"Heimkunft / An die Verwandten" ("Homecoming / To the Kinsmen") and "Andenken" ("Remembrance")—lead him to conclude that, when "forgetfulness" of Being has become the primary apostasy, then the poet must undertake to initiate in us a process of "remembrance" and to lead us homeward, back into "proximity to the Source."[37]

In the logic of Heidegger's metaphor, the process whereby the imagination recovers (in Wordsworth's phrase) "the sentiment of Being" entails a "journey" because Being is "distant" and far away (*fern*).[38] It is far away simply because it is never to be encountered nakedly and in itself, but only in and through the things of earth which it supports and whose presence it establishes. Yet, though Being is in this way "withdrawn," it is, paradoxically, also "near," since its immanence within the things of our immediate experience is precisely that which enables them to *be*, and thus to be *near*. Hence it is, as Heidegger sees it, that, in a time of dearth, the renewal of the life of the imagination can be conceived to involve a kind of journey. The journey is back to the "Source" (*Ursprung*), since that is what Being is; and to return into proximity to the Source is to be once again "at home," since Being is nothing other than the original and proper domain of the human spirit. And since to be brought back into the neighborhood of Being is to have been put in mind again of that which had been forgotten, the journey homewards is also conceived to be a process of anamnesis or recollection.

In the contemporary world of Anglo-American poetics, given its impatience with any sort of Longinian aesthetic of elevation and transport, the whole tenor of Heidegger's reflections may seem excessively inflated and hyperbolic. But, always, he does in fact have in view the concrete actuality of *poiesis*, and everything that he has to say about the poet's openness to the Holy, about his "naming the gods" and his bringing us homeward to the Source, is but his way of asserting that the poet supervises language with such cogency and adroitness that we find ourselves being thrust onto new levels of heightened perception, where we no longer simply take for granted the common things of earth and where, performing again an act of genuine attention before the world that confronts us, we recover what is perhaps the most primitive of all sensations—namely, the sense of astonishment that there is *something* rather than *nothing*.

In his book of a generation ago, *Arts and the Man*, the late Irwin Edman recalls a story of Stephen Crane's ("The Open Boat") about four shipwrecked seamen adrift in a small boat waveringly breasting agitated waters—and Crane's opening sentence says: "None of them knew the color of the sky." "So intent were they," says Edman, "upon the possibilities of being saved that they had no time, interest, or impulse for seeing the color of the sky above them."[39] But what Heidegger wants to assert is that the whole job of the poet—in his office as priest—is so to intensify our awareness, our vision, of the concrete realities surrounding us that, instead of moving constantly "among the abstract possibilities of action,"[40] human sensibility may be reinstated into a kind of pure alertness to the ontological depth and amplitude of the actual world. "I require of you only to look," says St. Teresa—and it is, says Heidegger, by making us gaze, by making us truly look, at the things of earth that the artist disarms us of that penchant for manipulation and use characteristic of the predatory spirit in which we normally approach the world: he invites us instead to approach it in the spirit of *letting-be*, to offer a kind of *Amen* to the various finite realities that make up the earth, since, in so far as they are truly present to us, their presence is seen to be consequent upon their being rooted in the creative Ground of Being itself. Using a phrase that John Crowe Ransom once bestowed upon a collection of his essays, we might say that Heidegger's testimony—and in this he adumbrates, in his own quite special way, a perennial axiom—is simply that it is the function of literary art to enliven and deepen our cognizance of "the world's body,"[41] to the point of enabling it to become for us a "glass of vision."[42] This, as he maintains, is what it is uniquely within the power of the literary imagination to confer upon us in a time of dearth.

Then, there is a final emphasis which deserves to be thought of as also a part of Heidegger's theory of literature, though, in his own writings, it actually figures not so much as a part of his account of *poiesis* as it does as a part of his account of the drama of *thought*. What is here in view is the duality he posits between the two great roles that are enacted in the adventure of man's encounter with Being—the role of the poet (*der Dichter*) and the role of the thinker (*der Denker*). That is to say, the path into Being may be by way either of poetic art or of systematic thought. But Heidegger's whole style of reflection tends so much, in effect, to convert the philosophic enterprise itself into a kind of poetry that it is difficult to identify clearly the precise difference being drawn between poet and thinker. Presumably, of course, the task of the thinker qua thinker is to win as large a competence as possible in supervising the procedures of discursive reason and dialectical argument; whereas the task of the poet qua poet is that of winning the greatest possible precision and resourcefulness in those ways of metaphor and analogy that are most distinctively native to the creative imagination. But, like the poet, the thinker, too, does not possess any legislative prerogatives in regard to primal reality. Systematic thought is bound to be something crippled and misshapen unless it originates in a "willingness . . . to be the enemy of nothing that is,—actual or possible, contingent or necessary, animate or inanimate, natural, human, or divine."[43] In the presence of Being, the attitude of both the poet and the thinker needs to be that of docility and submissiveness, for that very presence is a gift. And unless it is patiently hearkened to, in a spirit of acquiescence and gratitude, there can be no good result for either poetry or thought; for vision, whether poetic or metaphysical, requires that there be something to be seen—and something which we consent to be reached by, which we consent to accept as a gift.

Indeed, at whatever point Heidegger launches into an analysis of the nature of thought—whether in the essay "On the Essence of Truth"[44] ("Vom Wesen der Wahrheit") or the "Postscript" to the essay "What Is Metaphysics?" or his book *What Is Called Thinking?*—he is to be found stressing the impertinence of any attempt on the part of the thinker to seize reality by direct assault, since, before the thinker can even begin to undertake his various labors, he must wait for the "advent" of Being, for the advent of the Holy. Though this theme figures most immediately in Heidegger's meditations on the nature of the philosophic enterprise, it is yet so integral to the whole body of his thought, and the line of demarcation between poet and thinker is everywhere so lightly drawn in his work that we may, therefore, consider all that he has to say in this connection as bearing just as immediately on his theory of poetry as on his theory of the philosophic act itself. Both the poet and the thinker, in other words, are adepts in the art of paying heed to Being, and both, therefore, teach us something about what is involved in the discipline of waiting.

It is in the book of 1957, *Der Satz vom Grund* (*The Principle of Ground*), and the book of 1959, *Gelassenheit* (entitled in its English version *Discourse on Thinking*), that Heidegger presents some of his most suggestive statements on this issue. And since everything that he says here about the thinker as one who *waits* pertains equally as much to his understanding of the poet, the appropriate transposition may be made as though it had been explicitly made by Heidegger himself.

The basic presupposition of the little book of 1959 is—as it is said by the Teacher in his conversation with the Scholar and the Scientist—that "we are to do nothing but wait."[45] And nothing else is to be done, since, in all our transactions with the world, what comes *to* us is not a *re*-presentation of something which has already emerged out of ourselves but is rather something *wholly other*; indeed, to suppose the contrary to be the case is to have submitted all over again to the old wrongheadedness of attempting to "humanize" reality. The basic ontological situation is simply that of man-in-the-neighborhood-of-Being, and, since Being is not a human property at man's disposal, there is nothing to be done but to await its coming-to-presence. And it is just here that we may identify the nature of the discipline which the poet enjoins upon us; for it is a great part of his distinctive office to teach us how to wait, to teach us how to approach the environing reality of the world in a spirit of meditative openness (in the spirit of *Gelassenheit*, of surrender, of abandonment) to the manifold influxions of Being. The poet—that is, the artist in words, whether in verse or drama or prose fiction—so deploys his sounds and images and dramatic situations that we are compelled to recognize how gross and inadequate are the various concepts and counters with which we customarily order and interpret experience, and how reductive and distorting they often are of our actual life-world. Thus, in effect, he invites us, as we approach the world, to hold these concepts and counters in a state of suspension, to "leave open what we are waiting for,"[46] in order that our waiting may release itself into the openness of Being without violating that openness. This is indeed, for Heidegger, the true meaning of *Gelassenheit*: it consists in nothing other than our consenting to let things be and to dwell on the earth without restlessly searching all the time for ways of domesticating reality within a framework of human design and purpose.

Gelassenheit, in other words, is simply openness to the Mystery of Being. And it is hinted in *Der Satz vom Grund* that, when *the will to will* in a man has been thus quieted and subdued, he may be found to be like that rose which is spoken of by the German mystical poet of the seventeenth century, Johannes Scheffler. Scheffler, generally known as Angelus Silesius (the name he gave himself after his conversion to the Roman Catholic Church), in one of the poems in his book *The Cherubinic Wanderer* (*Der Cherubinische Wandersmann*) declares:

> The rose is without why; it blooms because it blooms,
> It cares not for itself, asks not if it is seen.

This saying very greatly fascinated Heidegger. For a rose that does not fret about the enabling conditions of its existence, that is not constantly attacking the world and seeking to contain it within its own scheme of concepts and categories, that simply blooms because it blooms, being quite content to be "without why"—such a rose, in its undemanding openness to the Mystery, to the Ground of Being, became for Heidegger a kind of sign, an emblem of what man himself is like when he is most truly human. Because—like the rose—he, too, if he is to be truly *gelassen* before the spectacle of the world and thus genuinely open to the influx of Being, must learn to bloom simply for the sake of blooming, must learn to live without "care," without predatoriness, without anxiety, "without why." Which is to say that he must learn how to wait, and even how to wait without needing to know precisely what it is he waits for, since, if we are to "abandon ourselves to the game"[47] of existence, we must make up our minds to the fact that there is no way of aprioristically charting and conceptualizing the miracle of Being. "We are to do nothing but wait." And this is the great lesson that we are taught by poetry.

By now, then, it should be apparent that Heidegger's is a theory of the poetic imagination that bespeaks a very profound kind of piety toward all the wondrous works of Creation—toward the outgoings of the morning and evening, toward the north and the south, toward the lion and the adder and the children of men, toward all the round world and they that dwell therein; for, in all this, if we consent patiently and reverently to wait, the advent of Being may be descried. What is at work is an immense sensitivity of ecological conscience that prompts this thinker to regard the whole of reality as sacramental, in the sense that the true identity of everything that exists is considered to reside in its way of showing forth the Mystery of Being. Everything is, therefore—as it was for Blake—instinct with holiness. And thus to move down into the deep inwardness of things is to know that they are not just so many dead appurtenances of the human enterprise but that they are, rather, awakened into reality by nothing less than the power and presence of Being itself. The disclosure of this great fact is what Heidegger takes to be the principal mission of the poetic imagination, and his argument in this connection presents a massive summary of much that is either being presupposed or is at the fore in the testimony presented by the figures to whom this book has been devoted.

Notes

1/Introduction

1. This remark of Stevens's appeared on the wrapper of *The Man with the Blue Guitar and Other Poems* (New York: Alfred A. Knopf, 1937).
2. See James Engell, *The Creative Imagination: Enlightenment to Romanticism* (Cambridge: Harvard University Press, 1981).
3. William Wordsworth, *The Prelude* (the 1799, 1805, and 1850 texts), ed. Jonathan Wordsworth, M. H. Abrams, and Stephen Gill (New York: W. W. Norton, 1979), bk. 13, ll. 190–92 (1805 text), p. 468.
4. Wallace Stevens, "Final Soliloquy of the Interior Paramour," in *The Collected Poems of Wallace Stevens* (New York: Alfred A. Knopf, 1954), p. 524.
5. See T. S. Eliot, "The Metaphysical Poets," in *Selected Essays: 1917–1932* (New York: Harcourt, Brace and Co., 1932), pp. 241–50.
6. Thomas Sprat, *History of the Royal Society*, ed. Jackson I. Cope and Harold Whitmore Jones (St. Louis: Washington University Studies, 1958), p. 113.
7. Thomas Hobbes, *Leviathan*, ed. A. R. Waller (Cambridge: Cambridge University Press, 1935), pt. 1, chap. 8, p. 42.
8. Thomas Hobbes, "Answer to Davenant's Preface to *Gondibert*," in *Critical Essays of the Seventeenth Century*, ed. J. E. Spingarn, vol. 2 (Oxford: Clarendon Press, 1908), p. 59.
9. John Dryden, "Epistle Dedicatory of *The Rival Ladies*," in *Essays of John Dryden*, vol. 1, ed. W. P. Ker (New York: Russell and Russell, 1961), p. 8.
10. John Locke, *An Essay Concerning Human Understanding*, vol. 1, ed. Alexander Campbell Fraser (Oxford: Clarendon Press, 1894), bk. 2, chap. 11, p. 203.
11. Ibid., p. 204.
12. David Hume, *A Treatise of Human Nature*, ed. L. A. Selby-Bigge (Oxford: Clarendon Press, 1888), bk. 1, pt. 3, sec. 10, p. 123.
13. Ibid., p. 121.
14. David Hume, *Essays Moral, Political, and Literary*, vol. 1, ed. T. H. Green and T. H. Grose (London: Longmans, Green, and Co., 1882), p. 93.

15. See Gilbert Ryle, *The Concept of Mind* (London: Hutchinson and Co., 1949), chap. 8.
16. Michel Foucault, *The Order of Things: An Archaeology of the Human Sciences*, an anonymous translation of *Les Mots et les choses* (New York: Pantheon Books, 1970), p. 298.
17. See Ferdinand de Saussure, *Course in General Linguistics*, trans. Wade Baskin (New York: McGraw-Hill, 1966).
18. Victor Turner, *Dramas, Fields, and Metaphors* (Ithaca: Cornell University Press, 1974), p. 233.
19. See Victor Turner, *The Ritual Process* (Ithaca: Cornell University Press, 1977, reprint), p. 127.
20. Ibid., p. 128.
21. Philip Wheelwright, *The Burning Fountain: A Study in the Language of Symbolism* (Bloomington: Indiana University Press, 1954), p. 8.
22. Roger Hazelton, *God's Way with Man: Variations on the Theme of Providence* (New York-Nashville: Abingdon Press, 1956), p. 101.
23. Julián Marías, *Reason and Life*, trans. Kenneth S. Reid and Edward Sarmiento (New Haven: Yale University Press, 1956), p. 27.
24. Wheelwright, *The Burning Fountain*, rev. ed. (Bloomington: Indiana University Press, 1968), p. 21.
25. Ibid., p. 22.
26. Ibid., p. 26.
27. Abraham J. Heschel, *Between God and Man*, ed. Fritz A. Rothschild (New York: Harper and Row, 1959), p. 38.
28. Maurice Merleau-Ponty, *Phenomenology of Perception*, trans. Colin Smith (London: Routledge and Kegan Paul, 1962), p. 62.
29. Heschel, *Between God and Man*, p. 54.
30. Ibid., p. 45.
31. Theodore M. Greene, "The Ontological Dimension of Experience," *Thought*, vol. 29, no. 114 (Autumn, 1954), p. 374.
32. Heschel, *Between God and Man*, p. 56.
33. Blaise Pascal, *Pensées*, trans. William Finlayson Trotter (New York: E. P. Dutton, 1943), Fragment 210 (based on the order of the Brunschvicg ed.), p. 61.
34. Ibid., Fragment 347, p. 97.
35. Reinhold Niebuhr, *The Nature and Destiny of Man*, vol. 1 (New York: Charles Scribner's Sons, 1943), p. 162.
36. This term is used in the sense given currency by Brentano and Husserl—in the sense, that is, of "intention" as the act whereby consciousness directs itself upon things toward the end of apprehending the "meanings" which they adumbrate. The term "intention" in this lexicon speaks, in other words, not of practical aims or purposes but of mental activity in its referential mode, as it *tends toward* those meanings hinted at by the particularities of experience. See Franz Brentano, *Psychology from an Empirical Standpoint*, trans. A. C. Rancurello et al. (London: Routledge

and Kegan Paul, 1973); and see also Edmund Husserl, *Ideas: General Introduction to Pure Phenomenology*, trans. W. R. Boyce Gibson (London: George Allen and Unwin, 1952).

37. Wheelwright, *The Burning Fountain* (1954 ed.), p. 17.
38. See Martin Heidegger, *What Is Called Thinking?*, trans. J. Glenn Gray and F. Wieck (New York: Harper and Row, 1968), pt. 2, lecture 3, pp. 138–47.
39. Wheelwright, *The Burning Fountain* (1968 ed.), pp. 33–34.
40. H. D. Lewis, "Revelation and Art," in *Morals and Revelation* (London: George Allen and Unwin, 1951), p. 212.
41. Hugh McCarron, *Realization: A Philosophy of Poetry* (London: Sheed and Ward, 1937), p. 73.
42. *The Poetical Works of William Wordsworth*, vol. 2, ed. Ernest de Selincourt (London: Oxford University Press, 1952), p. 438.
43. S. T. Coleridge, *Biographia Literaria*, vol. 2, ed. J. Shawcross (London: Oxford University Press, 1907), chap. 14, p. 12.
44. Edward Bullough, " 'Psychical Distance' as a Factor in Art and an Aesthetic Principle," in *Critical Theory Since Plato*, ed. Hazard Adams (New York: Harcourt, Brace, Jovanovich, 1971), p. 756.
45. Ibid., pp. 756–57.
46. Wheelwright, *The Burning Fountain* (1968 ed.), p. 44.
47. Stevens, "Credences of Summer," in *The Collected Poems*, p. 373.
48. See Mircea Eliade, *Patterns in Comparative Religion*, trans. Rosemary Sheed (New York: Sheed and Ward, 1958).
49. Samuel Johnson, *The Rambler*, vol. 2 in *The Yale Edition of the Works of Samuel Johnson*, ed. W. J. Bate and Albrecht B. Strauss (New Haven: Yale University Press, 1969), no. 125, p. 300.
50. Both Nicolas Berdyaev and Paul Tillich had a good deal to say about literature and the arts, as barometers of the cultural situation requiring to be addressed by Christian theology; but they did not take them in any important sense to be fecundating material for theological reflection.
51. Brian Wicker, *The Story-Shaped World* (Notre Dame: University of Notre Dame Press, 1975), p. 72.
52. Elizabeth Sewell, *The Orphic Voice: Poetry and Natural History* (New Haven: Yale University Press, 1960), p. 19.
53. William Blake, "Jerusalem," chap. 3, pl. 74, in *The Complete Writings of William Blake*, ed. Geoffrey Keynes (London: The Nonesuch Press, 1957), p. 714.
54. Ibid., chap. 1, pl. 10, p. 629.
55. Ibid., "A Vision of the Last Judgment," pp. 605–6.
56. Percy Bysshe Shelley, "A Defense of Poetry," in *Critical Theory Since Plato*, ed. Hazard Adams, p. 513.
57. Thomas Love Peacock, "The Four Ages of Poetry," in *Critical Theory Since Plato*, ed. Hazard Adams, pp. 496–97.
58. From a letter (22 November 1802) to Thomas Butts, in *The Letters of*

William Blake, ed. Geoffrey Keynes (Cambridge: Harvard University Press, 1968), p. 62.

59. Josef Pieper, *Leisure: The Basis of Culture*, trans. Alexander Dru (New York: New American Library, a Mentor-Omega Book, 1963), p. 26.

60. The chapter on Heidegger, in the total design, is carried as an epilogue, for the reason that he stands outside the Anglo-American orbit to which the other figures belong—and that he presents a massive kind of conspectus of their common tendency.

61. Stevens, "Esthétique du Mal," in *The Collected Poems*, p. 322.

62. Ibid., "Repetitions of a Young Captain," p. 306.

63. Ibid., "Notes toward a Supreme Fiction," p. 382.

64. See Martin Heidegger, "Memorial Address," in his *Discourse on Thinking*, trans. John M. Anderson and E. Hans Freund (New York: Harper and Row, 1966), pp. 43–57.

65. Heidegger, "The Origin of the Work of Art," in *Poetry, Language, Thought*, trans. Albert Hofstadter (New York: Harper and Row, 1971), p. 72.

66. See Heidegger, "On the Essence of Truth," trans. R. F. C. Hull and Alan Crick, in *Existence and Being*, trans. Douglas Scott et al. (Chicago: Henry Regnery Co., 1949), pp. 319–51.

67. See Heidegger, "Hölderlin and the Essence of Poetry," trans. Douglas Scott, in *Existence and Being*, pp. 293–315; and see " '. . . Poetically Man Dwells . . .' " in *Poetry, Language, Thought*, trans. Albert Hofstadter, pp. 213–29.

2/Coleridge on the Dignity of the Poetic Imagination

1. *The Notebooks of Samuel Taylor Coleridge*, vol. 3, ed. Kathleen Coburn (Princeton: Princeton University Press, 1973), Entry No. 4066.

2. T. S. Eliot, *The Use of Poetry and the Use of Criticism* (London: Faber and Faber, 1933), p. 67.

3. René Wellek, *A History of Modern Criticism: 1750–1950*, vol. 2 (New Haven: Yale University Press, 1955), p. 152.

4. Norman Fruman, *Coleridge, the Damaged Archangel* (New York: George Braziller, 1971).

5. Thomas McFarland, *Coleridge and the Pantheist Tradition* (Oxford: Clarendon Press, 1969), p. 28.

6. Ibid., p. 45.

7. Ernst Cassirer, *The Philosophy of the Enlightenment*, trans. Fritz C. A. Koelln and J. P. Pettegrove (Princeton: Princeton University Press, 1951), pp. 357–58.

8. McFarland, *Coleridge*, p. 46.

9. "Note D" of Sir William Hamilton's "Supplementary Dissertations, or Excursive Notes, Critical and Historical," in *The Works of Thomas Reid, D.D.*, ed. Sir William Hamilton, vol. 2, 7th ed. (Edinburgh: MacLachlan and Stewart, 1875), p. 890.

10. John Stuart Mill, *An Examination of Sir William Hamilton's Philosophy*, vol. 2 (New York: Henry Holt and Co., 1874), pp. 346–47.

11. Ibid., pp. 340–41.

12. McFarland, *Coleridge*, p. 48.

13. Ibid., p. 49.

14. *The Notebooks of Samuel Taylor Coleridge*, vol. 2, ed. Kathleen Coburn (New York: Pantheon Books, 1961), Entry No. 2375.

15. John Stuart Mill, "Bentham," *Essays on Ethics, Religion and Society*, vol. 10 in *Collected Works of John Stuart Mill*, ed. J. M. Robson (Toronto: University of Toronto Press, 1969), p. 77.

16. Ibid., "Coleridge," p. 125.

17. *Collected Letters of Samuel Taylor Coleridge*, vol. 1, ed. Earl Leslie Griggs (Oxford: Clarendon Press, 1956), p. 137.

18. Ibid., 2:706.

19. S. T. Coleridge, *Biographia Literaria*, vol. 1, ed. J. Shawcross (London: Oxford University Press, 1907), chap. 4, pp. 58–59.

20. Ibid., p. 60.

21. Ibid., p. 202.

22. Ibid.

23. John H. Muirhead, *Coleridge as Philosopher* (New York: Macmillan, 1930), p. 41.

24. Bertrand Russell, *A History of Western Philosophy* (New York: Simon and Schuster, 1945), p. 774.

25. *Collected Letters*, 1:429.

26. Ibid., pp. 453–54.

27. Ibid., p. 519.

28. Coleridge, *Biographia Literaria*, 1:99.

29. David Hartley, *Observations on Man*, 5th ed. (London: Wilkie and Robinson, 1810), vol. 1, sect. 2, prop. 7, p. 58.

30. Ibid., prop. 9, p. 60.
31. Ibid., prop. 10, p. 67.
32. Ibid., prop. 12, p. 75.
33. *Collected Letters*, 2:709.
34. See Norman Kemp Smith, *A Commentary to Kant's "Critique of Pure Reason,"* 2d ed. (London: Macmillan, 1930), pp. 77, 225, 265.
35. *Collected Letters*, 1:209.
36. *Collected Letters*, 2:709.
37. See James Volant Baker, *The Sacred River: Coleridge's Theory of the Imagination* (Baton Rouge: Louisiana State University Press, 1957), p. 99.
38. Coleridge, *Biographia Literaria*, 1:82.
39. *The Statesman's Manual*, Appendix C, in *Lay Sermons*, vol. 6 of *The Collected Works of Samuel Taylor Coleridge*, ed. R. J. White (Princeton: Princeton University Press, 1972), p. 89.
40. "Dejection: An Ode," in *The Complete Poetical Works of Samuel Taylor Coleridge*, vol. 1, ed. Ernest Hartley Coleridge (Oxford: Clarendon Press, 1912), p. 365.
41. Ibid.
42. William Wordsworth, *The Prelude* (the 1799, 1805, and 1850 texts), ed. Jonathan Wordsworth, M. H. Abrams, and Stephen Gill (New York: W. W. Norton, 1979), bk. 13, ll. 375, 376 (1850 text), p. 457.
43. *The Statesman's Manual*, p. 29.
44. Coleridge, *Biographia Literaria*, 1:110.
45. Samuel Taylor Coleridge, *The Friend*, vol. 1, ed. Barbara E. Rooke (Princeton: Princeton University Press, 1969), pp. 155–56.
46. Ibid., p. 158.
47. Ibid., pp. 520–21.
48. See Walter Jackson Bate, "Coleridge on the Function of Art," in *Perspectives of Criticism*, ed. Harry Levin (Cambridge: Harvard University Press, 1950), pp. 141–42.
49. Coleridge, *Biographia Literaria*, 2:12.
50. Ibid., 1:202.
51. Basil Willey, *Nineteenth Century Studies* (London: Chatto and Windus, 1949), p. 13.
52. I. A. Richards, *Coleridge on Imagination* (New York: Harcourt, Brace and Co., 1935), p. 58.
53. Willey, *Nineteenth Century Studies*, pp. 13–14.
54. Coleridge, "On Poesy or Art," *Biographia Literaria*, 2:259.
55. Ibid., 1:202.
56. Irwin Edman, *Arts and the Man: A Short Introduction to Aesthetics* (New York: W. W. Norton, 1939), pp. 16–17.
57. Samuel Taylor Coleridge, *Shakespearean Criticism*, vol. 1, ed. Thomas Middleton Raysor (London: J. M. Dent, Everyman's Library, 1960), p. 189.

58. Coleridge, *Biographia Literaria*, 2:6.
59. Ibid., p. 8.
60. Bate, "Coleridge on the Function of Art," p. 145.
61. Coleridge, "On Poesy or Art," *Biographia Literaria*, 2:257.
62. Ibid., p. 258.
63. Ibid., p. 257.
64. *The Notebooks of Samuel Taylor Coleridge*, vol. 1, ed. Kathleen Coburn, Entry No. 921.
65. "The Rime of the Ancient Mariner," in *The Complete Poetical Works of Samuel Taylor Coleridge*, p. 198.
66. Robert Penn Warren, "A Poem of Pure Imagination," in *Selected Essays* (New York: Random House, 1958), p. 255.
67. *The Notebooks of Samuel Taylor Coleridge*, vol. 1, Entry No. 921.
68. "Dejection: An Ode," in *The Complete Poetical Works of Samuel Taylor Coleridge*, p. 366.
69. Dorothy M. Emmet, "Coleridge on the Growth of the Mind," *Bulletin of the John Rylands Library*, vol. 34, no. 2 (March 1952): 295.
70. *The Notebooks of Samuel Taylor Coleridge*, vol. 3, Entry No. 3401.
71. "The Eolian Harp," in *The Complete Poetical Works of Samuel Taylor Coleridge*, p. 101.
72. *The Notebooks of Samuel Taylor Coleridge*, vol. 1, Entry No. 556.
73. *Collected Letters*, 2:864.
74. Coleridge, *The Friend*, 1:514.
75. See Paul Tillich, *Systematic Theology*, vol. 1 (Chicago: University of Chicago Press, 1951), pp. 110, 113, 115, 163, 186.
76. Ibid., p. 163.
77. Coleridge, *The Friend*, 1:514.
78. Ibid., pp. 515–16.
79. H. D. Traill, *Coleridge* (New York: Harper and Bros., 1884), chap. 11.
80. See D. M. MacKinnon, "Coleridge and Kant," in *Coleridge's Variety: Bicentenary Studies*, ed. John Beer (London: Macmillan, 1974), pp. 183–203.
81. See McFarland, *Coleridge*, chap. 3.
82. Quoted from the folio of an as yet unpublished Notebook in James D. Boulger, *Coleridge as Religious Thinker* (New Haven: Yale University Press, 1961), p. 129.
83. *The Notebooks of Samuel Taylor Coleridge*, vol. 1, Entry No. 922.
84. W. G. T. Shedd, "Introductory Essay," in vol. 1 of *The Complete Works of Samuel Taylor Coleridge*, ed. W. G. T. Shedd (New York: Harper and Bros., 1871), p. 44.
85. Ibid.
86. Ibid.
87. John Macquarrie, *Principles of Christian Theology* (New York: Charles Scribner's Sons, 1966), p. 180.
88. Ibid., p. 101.

89. Ibid., p. 181.
90. Ibid., p. 176.
91. *Opus Maximum* is the title conventionally assigned to the three manuscript volumes on which Coleridge was at work in his last years and which he intended to be his theological *Summa*. This work, though unfinished, is being prepared for publication by Thomas McFarland as a part of *The Collected Works*, under the general editorship of Professor Kathleen Coburn. Two quarto volumes of the manuscript are in the Coleridge collection at Victoria College of the University of Toronto, and the third is in the Huntington Library at San Marino, California.
92. See W. B. Yeats, *A Vision* (New York: Macmillan, 1956), pp. 273–76, where Yeats is describing the kind of "administrative mind" and "alert attention" represented by the Romans that drove out the "uncommitted energy" that he considers to have been so much of the essence of the Greek genius.

3/Arnold's Version of Transcendence— The *Via Poetica*

1. See Paul Ricoeur, *Freud and Philosophy*, trans. Denis Savage (New Haven: Yale University Press, 1970), pp. 27–36.
2. Matthew Arnold, "The Study of Poetry," in *Essays in Criticism*, 2d series (London: Macmillan and Co., 1896), p. 1.
3. Matthew Arnold, "Preface," *God and the Bible* (New York: Macmillan Co., 1913), p. xli.
4. Nathan A. Scott, Jr., "Introduction: Theology and the Literary Imagination," in *Adversity and Grace: Studies in Recent American Literature*, ed. Nathan A. Scott, Jr. (Chicago: University of Chicago Press, 1968), p. 4.
5. See F. H. Bradley, *Ethical Studies*, 2d rev. ed. with additional notes (Oxford: Clarendon Press, 1927), pp. 315–17.
6. T. S. Eliot, *The Use of Poetry and the Use of Criticism* (London: Faber and Faber, 1933), p. 116.
7. Matthew Arnold, "Memorial Verses," in *Poetical Works of Matthew Arnold* (London: Macmillan and Co., 1901), p. 290.

8. Arnold, "The Study of Poetry," p. 1.
9. Matthew Arnold, "Stanzas from the Grande Chartreuse," in *Poetical Works*, p. 321.
10. Arnold, "Preface," *God and the Bible*, p. xi.
11. Basil Willey, *Nineteenth Century Studies* (London: Chatto and Windus, 1949), p. 252.
12. Ibid.
13. Matthew Arnold, *Literature and Dogma* (New York: Macmillan and Co., 1896), p. 283.
14. Matthew Arnold, *St. Paul and Protestantism* (New York: Macmillan and Co., 1894), p. 9.
15. Arnold, *Literature and Dogma*, p. 282.
16. Ibid., pp. 287–88.
17. Arnold, *St. Paul and Protestantism*, p. 62.
18. Arnold, *Literature and Dogma*, p. 296.
19. Ibid., p. 295.
20. Arnold, *St. Paul and Protestantism*, p. 7.
21. Arnold, *Literature and Dogma*, p. 283.
22. Ibid., pp. 9–11.
23. Ibid., p. 12.
24. See Matthew Arnold, "The Bishop and the Philosopher," *Macmillan's Magazine*, vol. 7, no. 39 (January 1863).
25. Ibid., p. 241.
26. Philip Wheelwright, *The Burning Fountain: A Study in the Language of Symbolism* (Bloomington: Indiana University Press, 1954), p. 25.
27. Arnold, *St. Paul and Protestantism*, p. 2.
28. Ibid.
29. Ibid., p. 14.
30. Ibid., p. 24.
31. Ibid., pp. 25–26.
32. Wilbur Marshall Urban, *Language and Reality* (London: George Allen and Unwin, 1939), p. 575.
33. Arnold, *Literature and Dogma*, p. 36.
34. Ibid., pp. 10–11.
35. Ibid., p. 12.
36. See Rudolf Otto, *The Idea of the Holy*, trans. John W. Harvey (London: Oxford University Press, 1923).
37. Arnold, *Literature and Dogma*, p. 29.
38. Ibid., p. 37.
39. See *The Statesman's Manual* in *Lay Sermons*, vol. 6 of *The Collected Works of Samuel Taylor Coleridge*, ed. R. J. White (Princeton: Princeton University Press, 1972), p. 29.
40. The term is Stanley Romaine Hopper's. See his "Introduction" in *Interpretation: The Poetry of Meaning*, ed. Stanley Romaine Hopper and David L. Miller (New York: Harcourt, Brace and World, 1967), p. xix.

41. Arnold, *Literature and Dogma*, p. 70.
42. Stephen Prickett, *Romanticism and Religion: The Tradition of Coleridge and Wordsworth in the Victorian Church* (Cambridge: Cambridge University Press, 1976), p. 221.
43. Ibid., p. 222.
44. Susan Sontag, *Against Interpretation* (New York: Farrar, Straus and Giroux, 1966), p. 7.
45. Ibid., p. 14.
46. I am here, of course, rephrasing the old maxim in Kant's *Critique of Judgment* that Paul Ricoeur has lately given currency in many of his writings—"The symbol gives rise to thought."
47. Paul Ricoeur, *Freud and Philosophy*, p. 39.
48. The phrase is Paul Ricoeur's, and it is used recurrently in *The Symbolism of Evil* and *Freud and Philosophy*.
49. Paul Ricoeur, *The Symbolism of Evil*, trans. Emerson Buchanan (New York: Harper and Row, 1967), p. 352.
50. Ibid.
51. Ibid., p. 350.
52. Arnold, *Literature and Dogma*, p. 52.
53. Paul Ricoeur, *The Conflict of Interpretations: Essays in Hermeneutics*, ed. Don Ihde (Evanston: Northwestern University Press, 1974), p. 289.
54. Arnold, *Literature and Dogma*, p. xxvii.
55. Matthew Arnold,. "Introduction," in *The Hundred Greatest Men* (London: Sampson Low, Marston, Searle, Rivington, 1879).
56. Prickett, *Romanticism and Religion*, p. 220.
57. The term is Philip Wheelwright's. See his *The Burning Fountain* (1954 ed.), pp. 27–28.
58. See William A. Madden, *Matthew Arnold: A Study of the Aesthetic Temperament in Victorian England* (Bloomington: Indiana University Press, 1967).
59. Arnold, "The Study of Poetry," p. 1.
60. Matthew Arnold, *Discourses in America* (New York: Macmillan Co., 1902), p. 123.
61. T. S. Eliot, *Selected Essays: 1917-1932* (New York: Harcourt, Brace and Co., 1932), p. 349.
62. Lionel Trilling, *Matthew Arnold* (New York: Columbia University Press, 1949), p. 364.
63. George Santayana, *Winds of Doctrine* (New York: Charles Scribner's Sons, 1926), p. 49.
64. See Willey, *Nineteenth Century Studies*, chap. 10.
65. See Basil Willey, "Arnold and Religious Thought," in *Matthew Arnold*, ed. Kenneth Allott (London: G. Bell and Sons, 1975), p. 245.
66. See I. A. Richards, *Science and Poetry* (New York: W. W. Norton, 1926).
67. Ibid., p. 70.
68. Arnold, *St. Paul and Protestantism*, p. 164.

69. Ibid., p. 177.
70. For sensitive comment on this and related matters, see James C. Livingston, "Matthew Arnold and His Critics on the Truth of Christianity," in *Journal of the American Academy of Religion*, vol. 41, no. 3 (September 1973): 386–401. Though highly limited in scope, Mr. Livingston's essay is one of the finest accounts in recent literature of Arnold's religious position.
71. Arnold, *St. Paul and Protestantism*, p. 304. Arnold appropriates the phrase from Butler's *Analogy*.
72. William Robbins, *The Ethical Idealism of Matthew Arnold* (Toronto: University of Toronto Press, 1959), p. 95.
73. Arnold, *Literature and Dogma*, pp. 292–93.
74. Bradley, *Ethical Studies*.
75. Robbins, *The Ethical Idealism of Matthew Arnold*, pp. 87–88.
76. Reinhold Niebuhr, *The Nature and Destiny of Man*, vol. 2 (New York: Charles Scribner's Sons, 1943), p. 50.
77. See Livingston, "Matthew Arnold and His Critics," pp. 398–99.
78. R. B. Braithwaite, *An Empiricist's View of the Nature of Religious Belief* (Cambridge: Cambridge University Press, 1955), p. 32.
79. Arnold, *Literature and Dogma*, p. 13.
80. Ibid., p. 18.
81. Ibid., p. 16.
82. Ibid., p. 23.
83. Ibid., p. 76.
84. Ibid., pp. 80–81.
85. Ibid., p. 82.
86. Ibid., p. 172.
87. Ibid., p. 174.
88. Ibid., p. 176.
89. Ibid.
90. Ibid., p. 184.
91. Ibid., pp. 200–201.
92. Ibid., p. 204.
93. Ibid., p. 217.
94. Ibid., p. 218.
95. Ibid.
96. Ibid., p. 221.
97. Ibid., pp. 249–50.
98. Ibid., p. 275.
99. Ibid., p. 251.
100. Ibid., pp. 262–63.
101. See Walther Eichrodt, *Theology of the Old Testament*, vol. 2, trans. J. A. Baker (Philadelphia: Westminster Press, 1967), chaps. 12–15.
102. Norman Perrin, *Rediscovering the Teaching of Jesus* (New York: Harper and Row, 1967), p. 55.

103. Quoted in William Robbins, *The Ethical Idealism of Matthew Arnold*, p. 210.
104. Renford Bambrough, *Reason, Truth and God* (London: Methuen and Co., 1969), p. 84.
105. Arnold, *Literature and Dogma*, p. 282.
106. Willey, *Nineteenth Century Studies*, p. 278.
107. Ibid.
108. Wallace Stevens, "Large Red Man Reading," in *The Collected Poems of Wallace Stevens* (New York: Alfred A. Knopf, 1955), p. 423.

4/Pater's Imperative— To Dwell Poetically

1. J. Hillis Miller, "Walter Pater: A Partial Portrait," *Daedalus*, vol. 105, no. 1 (Winter 1976): 97.
2. The preceding chapter indicates why it is that "coarseness" needs to be spoken of in this connection.
3. See T. S. Eliot, *Selected Essays: 1917–1932* (New York: Harcourt, Brace and Co., 1932), pp. 346–57.
4. Walter Pater, *Appreciations* (New York: Macmillan Co., 1910), p. 207.
5. For these notations I am indebted to Gerald Monsman. See his *Walter Pater* (Boston: Twayne Publishers, 1977), pp. 185–86.
6. Lord David Cecil, *Walter Pater* (Cambridge: Cambridge University Press, 1955), p. 20.
7. C. J. Holmes, *Self & Partners (Mostly Self)* (New York: Macmillan Co., 1936), p. 102.
8. Percy Lubbock, ed., *The Letters of Henry James*, vol. 1 (New York: Charles Scribner's Sons, 1920), p. 222.
9. W. K. Clifford, *Lectures and Essays*, ed. Leslie Stephen and Frederick Pollock, 2d ed. (London: Macmillan Co., 1886), p. 389.
10. [Walter Pater], "Coleridge's Writings," *The Westminster Review*, vol. 85 (January 1866), American ed., pp. 49–50. The essay was published anonymously.
11. Walter Pater, Preface, *The Renaissance: Studies in Art and Poetry* (the 1893 text), ed. Donald L. Hill (Berkeley-Los Angeles: University of California Press, 1980), p. xx.

12. Walter Pater, *Plato and Platonism* (London: Macmillan Co., 1925), p. 31.

13. Pater, "Wordsworth," in *Appreciations*, pp. 62, 61.

14. Pater, *The Renaissance*, p. 181.

15. *Letters of Walter Pater*, ed. Lawrence Evans (Oxford: Clarendon Press, 1970), p. 52.

16. Strangely, Pater, despite his excellent command of French, omitted the acute accent over the first "e" and placed a grave accent over the second "e."

17. See Martin Heidegger, "On the Essence of Truth," in *Existence and Being*, ed. Werner Brock and trans. R. F. C. Hull et al. (Chicago: Henry Regnery Co., 1949), pp. 319–51.

18. *The Journals and Papers of Gerard Manley Hopkins*, ed. Humphry House and Graham Storey (London: Oxford University Press, 1959), p. 127.

19. In Heidegger's lexicon the term *Gelassenheit* speaks of a meditative openness and surrender to that mysterious surplusage of meaning that indwells all things: see his *Gelassenheit* (Pfullingen: Verlag Günther Neske, 1959) which is available in an English translation by John M. Anderson and E. Hans Freund under the title *Discourse on Thinking* (New York: Harper and Row, 1966).

20. "God's Grandeur," in *The Poems of Gerard Manley Hopkins*, ed. W. H. Gardner and N. H. Mackenzie, 4th ed. (London: Oxford University Press, 1967), p. 66.

21. See Walter Pater, "Diaphaneitè" [*sic*], in *Miscellaneous Studies* (New York: Macmillan Co., 1900), pp. 215–22.

22. In her review prepared for the April 1873 issue of *The Westminster Review*, Mrs. Mark Pattison insisted that the title was "misleading," rightly maintaining that the book does not in any real way present a *history* of the Renaissance but rather simply a series of studies of a few representative figures. Pater quickly took her point, and, from 1877 on, all subsequent editions have borne the title *The Renaissance: Studies in Art and Poetry*.

23. This is the term used by Thomas Wright, Pater's first biographer, for the Diaphanous Personality. See his *The Life of Walter Pater*, vol. 1 (1907; reprint, New York: Haskell House Publishers, 1969), pp. 216–18.

24. Pater, *The Renaissance*, p. 187.

25. Ibid., p. xix.

26. Pater, *Plato and Platonism*, p. 19.

27. Walter Pater, *Marius the Epicurean*, vol. 1 (London: Macmillan Co., 1910), pp. 130–31.

28. Pater, *Plato and Platonism*, pp. 17–18.

29. Pater, *The Renaissance*, p. 189.

30. Psalm 148 (King James Version).

31. Pater, *The Renaissance*, pp. xx–xxi.

32. Ibid., p. 189.

33. Ibid., p. xx.

34. Ibid., p. 52.
35. Pater, *Appreciations*, p. 6.
36. Pater, *The Renaissance*, p. 190.
37. In *The Renaissance* Pater speaks of music only to say that all art, in its desire to obliterate the distinction between matter and form, "aspires towards the condition of music" (p. 106).
38. Ibid., p. 188.
39. Ibid., p. 189.
40. Michael Levey, *The Case of Walter Pater* (London: Thames and Hudson, 1978), p. 141.
41. The letter (dated 17 March 1873) is in *Walter Pater: The Critical Heritage*, ed. R. M. Seiler (London: Routledge and Kegan Paul, 1980), pp. 61–62.
42. Wright, *The Life of Walter Pater*, 1:255–56.
43. See Levey, *The Case of Walter Pater*, p. 143.
44. See *Walter Pater: The Critical Heritage*, ed. R. M. Seiler, pp. 85–91.
45. Ibid., p. 92.
46. Friedrich Hölderlin, "In Lieblicher Bläue," in *Sämtliche Werke*, 2/1 (Stuttgart: W. Kohlhammer Verlag, J. G. Cottasche Buchhandlung Nachfolger, 1951), p. 372. "Voll Verdienst, doch dichterisch, wohnet der Mensch auf dieser Erde" ("Full of merit, yet poetically, dwells / Man on this earth").
47. See his *Vorträge und Aufsätze* (Pfullingen: Neske, 1954). The essay is available in English in the collection of his essays translated by Albert Hofstadter, *Poetry, Language, Thought* (New York: Harper and Row, 1971).
48. See his *Erläuterungen zu Hölderlins Dichtung* (Frankfurt-am-Main: Klostermann, 1944) and his *Holzwege* (Frankfurt-am-Main: Klostermann, 1950).
49. Pater, *Plato and Platonism*, p. 124.
50. See T. S. Eliot, "Tradition and the Individual Talent," in *Selected Essays: 1917–1932*, pp. 3–11.
51. W. H. Mallock, *The New Republic*, new ed. (New York: Scribner and Welford, 1878), p. 278.
52. Iain Fletcher, *Walter Pater* (London: Longmans, Green and Co., 1959), p. 41.
53. Wright, *The Life of Walter Pater*, 2:11.
54. A. C. Benson, *Walter Pater* (London: Macmillan Co., 1906), p. 54.
55. See Pater, "Wordsworth," in *Appreciations*, pp. 37–63.
56. *Letters of Walter Pater*, p. 34.
57. Benson, *Walter Pater*, p. 209.
58. Pater, *The Renaissance*, p. 186.
59. Pater over many years was unfailingly regular in his attendance at the Chapel of Brasenose College, being present for both the morning and evening services. And, outside Oxford, he sought out such centers of

Catholic liturgical life as St. Alban's, Holborn, and St. Austin's Priory,
Walworth. Mrs. Humphry Ward's story (in her book *A Writer's Recollec-
tions*, vol. 1 [New York: Harper and Bros., 1918], pp. 161–62) about his
having once scandalized at his dinner table the wife of a distinguished
Oxford professor by denying that any reasonable person could govern
his life by the opinions of a man (Jesus) who had died eighteen centuries
ago is sometimes cited as evidence of agnosticism. But such badinage is
not unknown even amongst professional theologians, particularly when
they may feel it appropriate to administer a shock to some kind of smug
and unthinking orthodoxy. And it would seem that, on the occasion re-
counted by Mrs. Ward, Pater felt that such a shock very much needed to
be served out. Mrs. Ward was present, and she says that he "had been
. . . pressed controversially beyond the point of wisdom. . . . The Professor and his wife . . . departed hurriedly, in agitation."

60. Amos N. Wilder, *The New Voice: Religion, Literature, Hermeneutics*
    (New York: Herder and Herder, 1969), p. 236.

61. Wallace Stevens, "An Ordinary Evening in New Haven," in *The Col-
    lected Poems of Wallace Stevens* (New York: Alfred A. Knopf, 1955), p.
    475.

62. Percy Lubbock, *The Craft of Fiction* (London: Jonathan Cape, 1926), p.
    195.

63. R. V. Osbourn, "*Marius the Epicurean*," in *Essays in Criticism*, vol. 1,
    no. 4 (October 1951): 387.

64. T. S. Eliot, "Arnold and Pater," in *Selected Essays*, p. 355.

65. Harold Bloom, *The Ringers in the Tower: Studies in Romantic Tradition*
    (Chicago: University of Chicago Press, 1971), p. 188.

66. Ibid., p. 192.

67. See Walter Pater, *Imaginary Portraits* (London: Macmillan Co., 1894)
    and *Gaston de Latour* (London: Macmillan Co., 1897).

68. Pater, *Marius the Epicurean*, 1:143.

69. "Diaphaneitè" [*sic*], in *Miscellaneous Studies*, p. 219.

70. Pater, *Marius the Epicurean*, 2:218.

71. W. H. Auden, "For the Time Being," in *The Collected Poetry of W. H.
    Auden* (New York: Random House, 1945), p. 412.

72. See Gerald Monsman, *Pater's Portraits* (Baltimore: The Johns Hopkins
    Press, 1967), pp. 71–74.

73. In his book *Hebrew and Hellene in Victorian England* (Austin: Univer-
    sity of Texas Press, 1969) David J. DeLaura says that "there can be little
    doubt" (p. 325) that Pater's insistent use of a *universal commonwealth*
    as an image for the Church "is a version of the 'great association of na-
    tions' . . . described by Newman" in the lecture on "Christianity and Let-
    ters" that belongs to the second half of the *Idea of a University*. And it
    may be that Mr. DeLaura is right in part, but I should think that anyone
    who knows Frederick Denison Maurice's *The Kingdom of Christ* (Lon-
    don: J. G. F. and J. Rivington, 1842) would find it difficult not to feel

that, in this matter, Pater is *far more* echoing Maurice's view of the Church as the universal family of man qua man.

74. Benson, *Walter Pater*, p. 111.
75. Ibid., p. 106.
76. Monsman, *Walter Pater*, p. 102.
77. Matthew Arnold, *God and the Bible* (New York: Macmillan Co., 1913), p. xi.
78. T. S. Eliot, "Little Gidding," in *Four Quartets* (New York: Harcourt, Brace and Co., 1943), p. 38.
79. Graham Hough, *The Last Romantics* (London: Gerald Duckworth and Co., 1949), p. 151.
80. Among the great men of the Oxford Movement, John Keble was, of course, notable in part for his strong and constant emphasis on "reserve," on the necessity of keeping Christian faith and practice pure of all ostentation and display and lust for immediate effect. Pater met Keble on only one occasion, in the period when he was a pupil at the King's School in Canterbury, probably at some point in 1855; and it would seem that each was profoundly impressed by the other. At this time one of Pater's closest friends was his schoolmate John Rainier McQueen, he and McQueen and one other boy, Henry Dombrain, being known at the King's School as "The Three Inseparables." And Thomas Wright reports (*The Life of Walter Pater*, 1:132) that a relation of the McQueen family, Mary Ann Virginia Gabriel, expected the young Pater to prove to be in time "a second Keble," an expectation supported in some measure perhaps by the verse of Pater's that survives from this period of his life and from his early days at Oxford and that suggests how much he was then under the influence of *The Christian Year*.
81. David Tracy, *The Analogical Imagination* (New York: Crossroad, 1981), p. 177. Chapters 3, 4, and 5 of this book present a suggestive interpretation of "the classic" and "the religious classic."

5/Santayana's Poetics of Belief

1. Horace Kallen, "The Laughing Philosopher," *The Journal of Philosophy*, vol. 61, no. 1 (2 January 1964): 19.

2. George Santayana, "Apologia Pro Mente Sua," in *The Philosophy of George Santayana*, ed. Paul Arthur Schilpp (Evanston: Northwestern University Press, 1940), p. 603.

3. The phrase is Charles Hartshorne's, but, though his term makes a convenient umbrella for much of the inconsistency with which Santayana has been taxed, the particular meanings with which it is freighted in Professor Hartshorne's use are not at issue in my appropriation of it. See his "Santayana's Defiant Eclecticism," *The Journal of Philosophy*, vol. 61, no. 1 (2 January 1964): 35–44.

4. Santayana, "Apologia Pro Mente Sua," pp. 504–5.

5. George Santayana, *Realms of Being* (New York: Charles Scribner's Sons, 1942), p. 206.

6. George Santayana, *Reason in Common Sense* (New York: Charles Scribner's Sons, 1905), p. 104.

7. George Santayana, *Scepticism and Animal Faith* (New York: Charles Scribner's Sons, 1923), chap. 7.

8. See Santayana, *Realms of Being*, pp. 155–57.

9. *The Journals and Papers of Gerard Manley Hopkins*, ed. Humphry House and Graham Storey (London: Oxford University Press, 1959), p. 127.

10. George Santayana, "A General Confession," in *The Philosophy of George Santayana*, ed. Paul Arthur Schilpp, pp. 28–29.

11. See Santayana, *Realms of Being*, p. 134.

12. Santayana, "A General Confession," p. 14.

13. See Santayana, *Scepticism and Animal Faith*, p. 179.

14. Santayana, *Realms of Being*, pp. 418–19.

15. Ibid., p. 249.

16. George Santayana, "Ultimate Religion," in *Obiter Scripta*, ed. Justus Buchler and Benjamin Schwartz (New York: Charles Scribner's Sons, 1936), p. 290.

17. Ibid., "Literal and Symbolic Knowledge," p. 128.

18. Ibid., p. 108.

19. George Santayana, *Soliloquies in England* (London: Constable, 1922), p. 142.

20. Blaise Pascal, *Pensées*, trans. William Finlayson Trotter, from the edition of the text prepared by Léon Brunschvicg (London: J. M. Dent, 1908), pp. 19–20.

21. Santayana, *Realms of Being*, p. 190.

22. Ibid., p. 191.

23. See Santayana, *Scepticism and Animal Faith*, chap. 26.

24. Santayana, *Realms of Being*, p. 15.

25. Ibid., p. 646.

26. Santayana, *Scepticism and Animal Faith*, p. 273.

27. Ibid., p. 274.

28. Santayana, *Realms of Being*, p. 350.

29. George Santayana, *Platonism and the Spiritual Life* (New York: Charles Scribner's Sons, 1927), p. 81.
30. George Santayana, *The Idea of Christ in the Gospels* (New York: Charles Scribner's Sons, 1946), p. 251.
31. Santayana, *Realms of Being*, p. 673.
32. Ibid., p. 708.
33. Ibid., p. 711.
34. Ibid., p. 719.
35. Ibid., p. 727.
36. John Herman Randall, Jr., "The Latent Idealism of a Materialist," *The Journal of Philosophy*, vol. 28, no. 24 (19 November 1931): 648.
37. Santayana, *Realms of Being*, pp. 218–19.
38. Santayana, *Scepticism and Animal Faith*, p. 177.
39. George Santayana, *The Life of Reason; or, The Phases of Human Progress* (New York: Charles Scribner's Sons, 1954), p. 490.
40. Ibid., p. 489.
41. George Santayana, *Interpretations of Poetry and Religion* (New York: Harper and Bros., 1957), p. 6.
42. Ibid., p. v.
43. See Matthew Arnold, "The Study of Poetry," in *Essays in Criticism*, 2d series (London: Macmillan and Co., 1896), p. 1: "Our religion has materialized itself in the fact, in the supposed fact; it has attached its emotion to the fact, and now the fact is failing it."
44. Santayana, *Realms of Being*, p. 398.
45. Ibid., p. xiii.
46. Henry David Aiken, *Reason and Conduct: New Bearings in Moral Philosophy* (New York: Alfred A. Knopf, 1962), p. 348.
47. Edward W. Said, *Beginnings: Intention and Method* (New York: Basic Books, 1975), p. 287.
48. Ernst Cassirer, *The Philosophy of Symbolic Forms*, vol. 1, trans. Ralph Manheim (New Haven: Yale University Press, 1953), p. 111.
49. Martin Heidegger, *On the Way to Language*, trans. Peter D. Hertz and Joan Stambaugh (New York: Harper and Row, 1971), p. 155.
50. Ibid.
51. Jacques Derrida, "Structure, Sign, and Play in the Discourse of the Human Sciences," in *The Languages of Criticism and the Sciences of Man: The Structuralist Controversy*, ed. Richard Macksey and Eugenio Donato (Baltimore: The Johns Hopkins Press, 1970), p. 250.
52. Roland Barthes, "Science versus Literature," in *Structuralism: A Reader*, ed. Michael Lane (London: Cape, 1970), p. 411.
53. Michel Foucault, *The Order of Things: An Archaeology of the Human Sciences*, an anonymous translation of *Les Mots et les choses* (New York: Vintage Books, 1973), p. 300.
54. Even the most bilious scold of the New Criticism and the most intrepid

defender of mimeticist theory, the late Ronald Crane, when he undertook in his Alexander Lectures at the University of Toronto (*The Languages of Criticism and the Structure of Poetry* [Toronto: University of Toronto Press, 1953]) to specify the nature of the object which the poem imitates, declared it to be something "internal and hence strictly 'poetic' in the sense that it exists only as the intelligible and moving pattern of incidents, states of feeling, or images which the poet has constructed in the sequence of his words by analogy with some pattern of human experience such as men have either known or believed possible, or at least thought of as something that ought to be" (p. 56). Which was in effect for Crane to forswear any merely "representationalist" view of literary art as an affair of copying or reproducing what is already *out there.*

55.   Murray Krieger, "After the New Criticism," *The Massachusetts Review,* vol. 4, no. 1 (Autumn 1962): 188.

56.   Murray Krieger, *The Tragic Vision* (Chicago: University of Chicago Press, Phoenix Books, 1960), p. 236.

57.   Leo Bersani, "From Bachelard to Barthes," in *Issues in Contemporary Literary Criticism,* ed. Gregory T. Polletta (Boston: Little, Brown, and Co., 1973), p. 92.

58.   Edward Said, "*Abecedarium Culturae*: Structuralism, Absence, Writing," in *Modern French Criticism: From Proust and Valéry to Structuralism,* ed. John K. Simon (Chicago: University of Chicago Press, 1972), p. 371.

59.   Geoffrey Hartman, *Beyond Formalism* (New Haven: Yale University Press, 1970), p. xi.

60.   Roland Barthes, *Essais critiques* (Paris: Seuil, 1964), p. 156.

61.   The term is Hayden White's. See his "The Absurdist Moment in Contemporary Literary Theory," in *Contemporary Literature,* vol. 17, no. 3 (Summer 1976): 401.

62.   Ibid., p. 402.

63.   Pierre Emmanuel, "Plus silencieux que le silence," in *Chansons du dé à coudre* (Paris: Egloff, 1947), p. 55.

64.   John Herman Randall, Jr., *The Making of the Modern Mind* (Boston: Houghton Mifflin Co., 1940), p. vii.

65.   Early in 1948 Thomas N. Munson, S.J., sent to Santayana the M.A. thesis he had done many years before on his thought. And in his letter of reply, in the course of trying to sort out the various confusions he felt Fr. Munson's essay reflected, he spoke of how deeply affected he was in his formative years by a passage in Plato's *Parmenides* "about 'ideas' of filth, rubbish, etc., which the moralistic young Socrates recoils from as not beautiful, making Parmenides smile. That smile of Parmenides," he said, "made me think." (See *The Letters of George Santayana,* ed. Daniel Cory [New York: Charles Scribner's Sons, 1955], p. 373.)

6/Stevens's Route— Transcendence Downward

1. *The Collected Poems of Wallace Stevens* (New York: Alfred A. Knopf, 1954), p. 464.
2. Wallace Stevens, *Opus Posthumous*, ed. Samuel French Morse (New York: Alfred A. Knopf, 1957), pp. 206, 207.
3. Julian Huxley, *Religion without Revelation* (London: Max Parrish, 1957), p. 58.
4. See Milton J. Bates, "Major Man and Overman: Wallace Stevens' Use of Nietzsche," *The Southern Review*, vol. 15, no. 4 (October 1979): 811–39.
5. S. T. Coleridge, *Biographia Literaria*, vol. 1, ed. J. Shawcross (London: Oxford University Press, 1907), chap. 13, p. 202.
6. Wallace Stevens, *The Necessary Angel: Essays on Reality and the Imagination* (New York: Alfred A. Knopf, 1951), p. 61.
7. This remark of Stevens appeared on the wrapper of *The Man with the Blue Guitar and Other Poems* (New York: Alfred A. Knopf, 1937).
8. Simone Weil, *Gravity and Grace*, trans. Arthur Wills (New York: G. P. Putnam's Sons, 1952), p. 78.
9. A. Alvarez, *The Shaping Spirit: Studies in Modern English and American Poets* (London: Chatto and Windus, 1958), p. 132.
10. Joseph N. Riddel, *The Clairvoyant Eye: The Poetry and Poetics of Wallace Stevens* (Baton Rouge: Louisiana State University Press, 1965), p. 168.
11. *Letters of Wallace Stevens*, selected and edited by Holly Stevens (New York: Alfred A. Knopf, 1970), pp. 426–27.
12. Lucy Beckett, *Wallace Stevens* (London: Cambridge University Press, 1974), p. 118.
13. *The Poems of Gerard Manley Hopkins*, ed. W. H. Gardner and N. H. Mackenzie, 4th ed. (London: Oxford University Press, 1967), p. 90.
14. Ibid., p. 70.
15. See Coleridge, *Biographia Literaria*, p. 202.
16. See Harold Bloom, *Wallace Stevens: The Poems of Our Climate* (Ithaca: Cornell University Press, 1977), pp. 204–8.
17. A. J. Ayer, *Language, Truth and Logic*, rev. ed. (London: Victor Gollancz, 1946), pp. 42–43.
18. *The Poems of Gerard Manley Hopkins*, p. 66.
19. Randall Jarrell, *Poetry and the Age* (New York: Alfred A. Knopf, 1953), p. 144.

20. Martin Heidegger, *Being and Time*, trans. John Macquarrie and Edward Robinson (New York: Harper and Row, 1962), p. 236.
21. See Martin Heidegger, *Basic Writings*, ed. David Farrell Krell (New York: Harper and Row, 1977), p. 221: "Man is not the lord of beings. Man is the shepherd of Being" ("Letter on Humanism").
22. H. D. Lewis, "Revelation and Art," in *Morals and Revelation* (London: Allen and Unwin, 1951), p. 212.
23. See Heidegger, *Basic Writings*, p. 210: " 'Being'—that is not God and not a cosmic ground."
24. *The Collected Poems of Dylan Thomas* (New York: New Directions, 1953), p. 10.
25. Teilhard de Chardin, *Hymn of the Universe*, trans. Simon Bartholomew (New York: Harper and Row, 1965), pp. 83, 28.
26. See Amos N. Wilder, *The New Voice: Religion, Literature, Hermeneutics* (New York: Herder and Herder, 1969), p. 236: "If we are to find grace it is to be found in the world and not overhead."
27. As he was looking toward the preparation of *The Collected Poems*, Stevens proposed in a letter to Alfred Knopf (27 April 1954) that the volume be entitled *The Whole of Harmonium* (L, 831). Mr. Knopf raised objections, however, and the formulation finally settled on was *The Collected Poems of Wallace Stevens*—"a machine-made title if there ever was one," said Stevens (L, 834).
28. Frank Kermode, "Dwelling Poetically in Connecticut," in *Wallace Stevens: A Celebration*, ed. Frank Doggett and Robert Buttel (Princeton: Princeton University Press, 1980), p. 268.

7/Epilogue– Heidegger's Vision of Poetry as Ontology

1. A. J. Ayer, *Language, Truth and Logic*, rev. ed. (London: Victor Gollancz, 1946), p. 42.
2. Martin Heidegger, "Brief über den Humanismus," in *Platons Lehre von der Wahrheit* (Bern: A. Francke, 1947), p. 76.

3. Martin Heidegger, *Being and Time*, trans. John Macquarrie and Edward Robinson (New York: Harper and Row, 1962), p. 236.

4. See Martin Heidegger, *Was ist Metaphysik?*, 5th ed. (Frankfurt-am-Main: Vittorio Klostermann, 1949). An English version of the lecture ("What Is Metaphysics?" trans. R. F. C. Hull and Alan Crick), together with the Postscript which Heidegger prepared in 1943, appears in *Existence and Being*, ed. Werner Brock (Chicago: Henry Regnery Co., 1949), pp. 355–92.

5. Martin Heidegger, "What Is Metaphysics?" in *Existence and Being*, p. 378.

6. See Martin Heidegger, Preface, in William J. Richardson, S.J., *Heidegger: Through Phenomenology to Thought* (The Hague: Martinus Nijhoff, 1963), pp. viii–xxiii.

7. Martin Heidegger, "Hölderlin and the Essence of Poetry," in *Existence and Being*, p. 313.

8. Heidegger's view of Nietzsche is set forth in his *Nietzsche*, 2 vols. (Pfullingen: Günther Neske, 1961).

9. The principal documents in the case are perhaps *Platons Lehre von der Wahrheit* (Bern: Francke, 1942); *Vom Wesen der Wahrheit* (Frankfurt-am-Main: Klostermann, 1943); and *Über den Humanismus* (Frankfurt-am-Main: Klostermann, 1949). To these may be added the later works in which the critique of Kant is set forth—*Der Satz vom Grund* (Pfullingen: Günther Neske, 1957); *Die Frage nach dem Ding* (Tübingen: Max Niemeyer, 1962); and *Kants These über das Sein* (Frankfurt-am-Main: Klostermann, 1963).

10. See Martin Heidegger, *Gelassenheit* (Pfullingen: Günther Neske, 1959). The English version, translated by John M. Anderson and E. Hans Freund, bears the title *Discourse on Thinking* (New York: Harper and Row, 1966).

11. Martin Heidegger, *Discourse on Thinking*, p. 88.

12. See Martin Heidegger, "On the Essence of Truth," in *Existence and Being*, pp. 319–51.

13. Heidegger, *Discourse on Thinking*, pp. 54–55.

14. Ibid., pp. 46–57.

15. Martin Heidegger, "Über den Humanismus," in *Platons Lehre von der Wahrheit*, p. 76.

16. Martin Heidegger, Postscript to "What Is Metaphysics?" in *Existence and Being*, p. 385.

17. See Martin Heidegger, *Einführung in die Metaphysik* (Tübingen: Max Niemeyer, 1953). The English version, translated by Ralph Manheim, bears the title *An Introduction to Metaphysics* (New Haven: Yale University Press, 1959).

18. See Martin Heidegger, *Kant und das Problem der Metaphysik* (Bonn: Cohen, 1929); 2d ed., Frankfurt-am-Main: Vittorio Klostermann, 1951.

The English version, translated by J. S. Churchill, bears the title *Kant and the Problem of Metaphysics* (Bloomington: Indiana University Press, 1962).

19. See Martin Heidegger, *Erläuterungen zu Hölderlins Dichtung* (Frankfurt-am-Main: Vittorio Klostermann, 1944).

20. See Martin Heidegger, *Was heisst Denken?* (Tübingen: Niemeyer, 1954). The English version, translated by Fred D. Wieck and J. Glenn Gray, is entitled *What Is Called Thinking?* (New York: Harper and Row, 1968).

21. See Martin Heidegger, *Der Satz vom Grund* (Pfullingen: Neske, 1957).

22. See Martin Heidegger, *Identität und Differenz* (Pfullingen: Neske, 1957). The English version, translated by Joan Stambaugh, is entitled *Identity and Difference* (New York: Harper and Row, 1969).

23. Marjorie Grene, *Martin Heidegger* (London: Bowes and Bowes, 1957), p. 111.

24. See Martin Heidegger, *Erläuterungen zu Hölderlins Dichtung*.

25. See Martin Heidegger, *Holzwege* (Frankfurt-am-Main: Vittorio Klostermann, 1950).

26. Ibid., p. 45.

27. Ibid., p. 61.

28. Ibid.

29. "Hölderlin and the Essence of Poetry," in *Existence and Being*, p. 312.

30. In his book *Earth and Gods: An Introduction to the Philosophy of Martin Heidegger* (The Hague: Martinus Nijhoff, 1961), Vincent Vycinas's interpretation of Heidegger's notion of "gods" soars off on a highly speculative flight, and I remain unconvinced of its cogency and of its having any clear relevance to what is actually being said in the Heideggerian texts—though my own "demythologization" of Heidegger's argument has been influenced in some degree by Vycinas's exegesis.

31. See *Erläuterungen zu Hölderlins Dichtung*, pp. 47–74.

32. Martin Buber, *I and Thou*, trans. Ronald Gregor Smith (Edinburgh: T. and T. Clark, 1937), p. 7.

33. *The Note-Books and Papers of Gerard Manley Hopkins*, ed. Humphry House (London-New York: Oxford University Press, 1937), p. 309.

34. "God's Grandeur," in *The Poems of Gerard Manley Hopkins*, p. 66.

35. Though Heidegger's metaphor about the "shepherding" of Being is adumbrated at many points in his writings, it figures most centrally in the *Brief über den Humanismus* (*Letter on Humanism*). And, though *man* is here said to bear this office, the *Letter* implies that it is a vocation whose ideal exemplifications are to be seen in two special types of man—in "the thinker" (*der Denker*) and "the poet" (*der Dichter*).

36. See *Erläuterungen zu Hölderlins Dichtung*, pp. 9–30, 75–143.

37. Ibid., p. 23.

38. Ibid., p. 138.

39. Irwin Edman, *Arts and the Man* (New York: W. W. Norton, 1939), p. 27.

Edman speaks of Crane's "somewhere" having a story of "three" ship-wrecked men adrift in a small boat—and actually misquotes the opening sentence which he gives as: "They did not see the color of the sky."

40. Ibid., p. 29.
41. See John Crowe Ransom, *The World's Body* (New York: Charles Scribner's Sons, 1938).
42. The phrase is Austin Farrer's: see his *The Glass of Vision* (Westminster: Dacre Press, 1948).
43. Robert Jordan, "Poetry and Philosophy: Two Modes of Revelation," *The Sewanee Review*, vol. 67, no. 1 (January–March, 1959): 13.
44. Trans. R. F. C. Hull and Alan Crick, *Existence and Being*, pp. 319–51.
45. Heidegger, *Discourse on Thinking*, p. 62.
46. Ibid., p. 68.
47. Heidegger, *Der Satz vom Grund*, p. 188.

Bibliographical Notes and Acknowledgments

The essay on Matthew Arnold originally appeared in *The Journal of Religion*, vol. 59, no. 3 (July 1979). A very considerably abbreviated version of the essay on Pater was issued in *New Literary History*, vol. 15, no. 1 (Autumn 1983). And the essay on Santayana first appeared in *Boundary 2*, vol. 7, no. 3, pt. 2 (Spring 1979). My thanks are herewith tendered to the editors of these journals for the permissions which they have kindly given for the reissuance of these materials. And I am grateful to the Yale University Press for permitting me to use portions of two books of mine which they published (*Negative Capability*, 1969; and *The Wild Prayer of Longing*, 1971) in the essay on Heidegger which forms the Epilogue of this volume. I am also indebted to Alfred A. Knopf, Inc., for permission to quote passages from Wallace Stevens's *Opus Posthumous*, *The Necessary Angel*, the *Letters of Wallace Stevens*, and *The Collected Poems of Wallace Stevens*.

Nor can I fail to speak of my gratitude for the willingness of various friends to read portions of this book and to share with me their responses—J. C. Levenson, Irvin Ehrenpreis, and Robert Langbaum of the University of Virginia; J. Robert Barth, S.J., of the University of Missouri; and Charlotte Crawford Watkins, professor *emeritus* of Howard University. Needless to say, as authors commonly declare in this connection, they bear no responsibility for such errors and misconstructions as are here to be found.

Index